LEADING
FROM
WITHIN

LEADING

FROM

WITHIN

MARTIAL ARTS SKILLS FOR DYNAMIC
BUSINESS AND MANAGEMENT

Robert Pater

Park Street Press
Rochester, Vermont

Park Street Press
One Park Street
Rochester, Vermont 05767
www.InnerTraditions.com

Park Street Press is a division of Inner Traditions International

Library of Congress Cataloging-in-Publication Data

Pater, Robert.
Leading from within : martial arts skills for dynamic business and management /
Robert Pater.
p.   cm.
Originally published: Rochester, Vt. : Destiny Books, c1988. With new introd.
Includes bibliographical references and index.
ISBN 0-89281-794-1 (alk. paper)
1. Management.   2. Executive ability.   3. Organizational change.   4. Martial arts.
I. Pater, Robert. Martial arts and the art of management.   II. Title.
HD38.P318   1999
658.4—dc21   99-24435
                                          CIP

Printed and bound in the United States

10 9 8 7 6 5 4 3 2 1

Text design and layout by Priscilla Baker
This book was typeset in Minion with Gill Sans as a display face

For Franz Pater
who taught me the power of gentleness

CONTENTS

ACKNOWLEDGMENTS

Thank you to the many who have helped this book come to be. To my colleagues Paul McClellan, Craig Lewis, Gordon Graaff, René Changsut, Charlie Braxton, Dan Lucas, Rob Russell, Kevin Myers, Larry Vance, John Chapman, Paul Vance, and John Glenn, skilled professionals who use their considerable abilities to change the world. Thanks to them for their support as my "training partners," both in- and outside of martial arts practice. To my martial arts instructors Chow Hung-Yuen and John Clodig—insightful and highly developed men who unselfishly have shared their knowledge with many; and to an early instructor, Walter Muryasz. To those martial arts masters and leadership theorists who have blazed the trail, especially to my mentors and friends Jack Gibb and Bob Crook. To my wife, Susan, for her love, tremendous ongoing support, and call for balance in our lives; my daughter, Kyra, and son, Brian, special souls who have enriched my life with their vitality and joy and "forward pressure"; my mother, Rita Pater, and sister, Debbie Hauptman, for their love and support; and to Carl and Lilian Greenberg for their faith and caring over my lifetime. To Ehud Sperling for his vision and to the memory of Don Cioeta, who was extremely helpful as my first editor. To people—leaders, line staff, supervisors, senior executives, everyone—with whom I have worked who are open-mindedly seeking better ways; to those who have successfully applied martial arts principles to their professional and personal lives; and to those who are actively making this world a better place to be.

INTRODUCTION

Have you ever wished that work were less of a struggle? Most people have. It's easy for most of us to feel overwhelmed by the mental and emotional turmoil of day-to-day living in these times of never-ending change. But most people also have experienced those times when all the gears seemed to be moving in synchronicity, when the world seemed calm and fluid. At such times we accomplish even more than we ever thought possible—and with little wasted effort and far less tension. If you are someone who would like to increase the frequency of these "good to be alive" days, but never thought there was anything you could do to achieve them, I have news for you. For centuries select martial arts have armed their advanced practitioners with strategies and techniques enabling them to *live* the principles of "effortless effort."

First you need to start by taking a hard look at what doesn't work for you. For instance, take this too-common situation: You try to institute a change in your organization that others have requested—a new procedure, new piece of equipment, different benefits—only to have these same individuals then resist the change. In this situation it's easy to become angry and frustrated—"What's the matter with them? I gave them exactly what they wanted!"—and to take things personally, or to give up and form lasting, negative perceptions of others. People clearly are nonlinear and not always logical in the way they think. But martial arts experts—and master leaders—know that there are underlying rules of human nature that, if incorporated in planning and execution, give us power. If ignored, these principles will overcome you. It is no different than trying to stop the current of a river with your fingers. There is no sense in wasting precious energy on needless resistance when there is so little extra to spare. Just as yanking on a tangled rope can harden a knot, resorting to blind force when confronting workplace snags can result in getting even more frustrated. A beginning student of the internal martial arts (those that emphasize boosting the ability to sense and direct changing forces) is similarly frustrated. Why, she wonders, doesn't my wing parry work like my instructor's? My arm is in the same position as his. But while the student and instructor's elbows might appear to be at similar angles, there are definite differences of force, direction, and feeling in them. And these make all the difference between controlling larger, faster, stronger opponents and being swept away by another's light brush of force. How you do something is often more important than what you do.

But for many people it's not realistic to first hunt down a truly capable instructor and then spend decades physically training in a martial art that will address their individual needs. So this book is aimed at helping you, both as a reader and leader, to learn how to better make extremely small changes that can have a dramatic impact on your decision-making process, self-image, and ability to perceive "hidden" yet important forces, and to feel more in control and in harmony with your work environment. Working with people from a wide array of cultures worldwide has made it plain to me that we all seek some kind of power, that we all long for control. By distilling and applying "secret" essentials from advanced martial arts, this book is designed to help you develop the most critical kind of power—power from within. It shows you how to apply this "software" to realize your desired results more easily and simply. By selecting and judiciously employing the right techniques, you can better bypass those everyday frustrations that are obstacles to reaching your goals, to inspiring others, to living a "big life."

The martial art of leadership is the art and science of making (the right) things happen. Of course, those in positions of corporate authority have an advantage. But we've also worked with people who were without title or authority and who were still powerful agents for change. Many times these catalysts have had more influence on what has happened in an organization than those with the official stamp of position. Consider the parallels between leadership and martial arts. Some qualities people associate with both master leaders and expert martial artists are:

a powerful presence, an ability to remain calm under pressure, maintaining personal control, the ability to respond fluidly to change, and to be in harmony with themselves. When expertly applied, both disciplines:

- are ultimately practical—they work!

- are science and art—while both have underlying principles based on research, a leader's higher level of effectiveness results only from good judgment, timing, and creative action

- use natural forces of human nature in working with others, rather than fighting their strength and resistance

- direct change to become an ally—their users must be ready for the unexpected

- make efficient use of power from the focused and calm use of technique

- are lived daily—not turned on and off—to achieve a consistency of behavior

- focus on personal development in which self-control is vital

The goals of black-belt leadership and of this book are to help you further develop:

- increased power and balance

- the ability to act practically and efficiently

- skills for taking advantage of changing circumstances

- realistic methods for reaching goals through people

- a mindset of continual improvement

- an approach for becoming "natural"—developing default habits and reactions that serve, rather than conflict with, your highest goals

- improved self-control

CHANGING THE WORLD

Two of the most famous martial arts masters in the past one hundred years did just that—change the world—both of them evolving from individuals with humble beginnings into men who were world-changing forces. Neither of these men were strong or powerful youths. In fact, as these tales go, Jigoro Kano and Gichin Funakoshi each watched their fathers being bullied by ruffians and internally vowed that things would be different for them. Thus they studied the martial arts, trained hard, and became experts, far transcending their initial desire for protection from intimidation. But they didn't stop there. After moving beyond their own fears, their focus shifted to helping others in similar positions and in so doing, helped transform their culture. Each adopted and refined a traditional martial art—practices that had become clandestine and inbred—into something useful for their society. Both Professor Kano, the Japanese founder of judo, and Gichin Funakoshi, Okinawan father of modern karate, have had a great impact not only on their own country, but on the world as well. Each of these men created huge organizations, which still exist today, fueled by loyal groups of practitioners who have in turn spread the message of self-devlopment.

The martial arts are said to have originated in China as an exercise system to fortify Buddhist monks. Over the centuries, techniques were tested and refined, taught and adapted, and amazing methods were developed that enabled adepts to defend against larger attackers, even against groups of would-be assaulters, and to break wood and stone with their bare hands and feet. The many martial arts have a common theme: utility is the proof in the pudding; the techniques have to do the job. The methods of martial arts are timeless.

Ultimately the martial arts are not about fighting. Like all leaders martial artists focus on developing the power of control, maintaining inner calmness under attack, and using concentration to attain goals. These powers also can be yours to apply to your work and to your life. The techniques in this book have already helped thousands of people and can help you cut through overwhelming problems at work, tap a reservoir of calmness during trying times, and shatter the obstacles to high performance.

THE STRATEGY

"The greatest warrior conquers himself first," is an ancient martial arts maxim, because true leadership comes from within. Martial arts practitioners learn in three stages. Students first focus on themselves, learning to control their own actions and reactions. You train to withstand pressure, not to freeze when you have to think fast and act strong. In this initial stage of learning, the best students pay primary attention to themselves to more accurately assess their own strengths and inefficiencies. In the second phase the focus is on developing understanding of others and the mechanisms that make them impressive allies, weak compatriots, or formidable enemies. In the third phase, budding martial arts experts study the interaction between themselves and others. When someone moves in a certain way, how do I respond? And how can that person counter my new movement? This stage is known as the field of continuous change.

My management and organizational consulting experience suggests that black-belt leaders develop in similar ways. Mario Bisio, a karate practitioner who owns a chain of upscale clothing stores, agrees: "You have to be disciplined with yourself before you can exercise good business discipline." The "Power and Control" techniques in the first part of this book will help you to increase your personal productivity, manage stress, harness the power of dedication, and leverage a small amount of effort into large returns. "Success," wrote karate master Gichin Funakoshi, "cannot be attained alone. Any person's time and power is limited. A wise leader enlists others in working toward organizational goals." The second section of this book highlights simple methods for harnessing rather than fighting people's natural reactions and emotions. It offers proven techniques for developing a strongly self-motivated staff, being effective without wielding a big stick, and using conflict to generate creativity. The third section, Mastering Change, provides strategies for reacting successfully to forces you cannot control, planning for organizational strength, and becoming an agent of productive change.

All the sections include the experiences and observations of leaders who have successfully applied martial arts principles in their organizations. Not all are martial arts practitioners, but they are all "black-belt leaders." This doesn't mean they are masters, just that they have learned how to apply the principles wisely. Several of our black-belt leaders appear in more than one chapter as they apply various martial arts concepts to organizational problems.

You can also apply these methods to developing other individuals into people who are independently decisive, yet team players, innovative and still stable, and people who have the judgment to leverage change toward long-range opportunity, while still getting the daily job done. This book shows you specific martial arts strategies that can boost creativity, control, and effectiveness. It will help you hone your skills and expand your power, while enjoying your work more. To reap full benefit of these strategies, focus on carrying them over to your personal life as well.

Far from being esoteric or philosophical, the martial arts strategies in this book are simple and practical. The same principles can be applied to excellent leadership. When Intel president Andrew Grove writes of using "leverage," organizational and motivational psychologist Kurt Lewin about "balancing forces" for productivity and change, author/consultant Tom Peters on "increasing power through proximity" (close to the customer), they are using martial arts principles. My colleagues and I have applied the strategies and techniques in this book to thousands of people—senior executives, middle managers, employee leaders, supervisors, and trainees—in a wide range of industries in Europe, Asia, the Middle East, and South and North America. And those who have used these techniques report that they work.

This is not a manual of Japanese management. Martial arts principles, while developed in the East, are available to all of us, old and young, female and male. The keys to mastering these principles are knowledge and practice.

I first began studying jujitsu and aikido in 1972. Since then I have practiced several martial arts—tae kwon do, kenjitsu, hapkido, and several others—and since 1993 I have been actively practicing wing chun kung fu. Once I had gotten past the magical image of being a martial arts "superman," I was immediately impressed by the beauty of the discipline. Its approach to self- and people-management reinforced much of what I already knew: it makes more sense to direct overwhelming forces than to try to stop them. Control yourself and you can more readily influence situations. I've met many martial arts–practicing leaders who concur. The martial arts are the basis of their most useful planning and implementation strategies.

Since 1973 I have incorporated martial arts methods into my own management style, and since 1976 into my organizational consulting. In 1985 I started a consulting organization that applies martial arts principles to worldwide workplace safety. The principles work within my own company, in presentations to hostile groups, and in finding ways to change highly resistant systems. But it doesn't matter what has worked for me or for anyone else, only what works for you.

Use this book wisely. If something doesn't make sense to you as you read, put it aside for now. You may find it useful at another time. You may already have had many experiences of effective leadership. As you move through this book, don't search only for new techniques, but also look for explanations of what you've experienced and for reminders of what you already know. You can make quick improvements when you understand what's behind your "lucky" accomplishments or when you apply one of your existing skills to a new area. Success is less a matter of knowing what to do than it is remembering to do what you know.

The ancient martial artists had a saying, "The best secrets keep themselves." There are no magical results without work. Inspiration, persistence, and patience open the door to powerful performance. An old martial arts tale tells of a shopkeeper in ancient Japan who was repeatedly robbed. (Bear in mind that in feudal Japan business people were at the bottom of the social order, beneath the nobility, the samurai warriors, artisans, even the peasants who provided food.) This one businessman became fed up with getting his wares stolen and so decided to train in the martial arts. After ten years of dedicated practice, he became quite accomplished.

One day as he was walking along the road with a friend, a snarling brigand brandishing a large knife sprang out of the bushes, threatening him and demanding his property. Without thought, the businessman sank to his knees and began to beg for his life. The friend looked on and, prodding the shopkeeper, barked, "You're not just a businessman, you're a martial artist!" "That's right!" replied the shopkeeper who promptly arose and, drawing upon his daily practice, disabled the attacker.

It is so easy during times of demand, stress, and change to forget who we are and what we can do, and to retreat to old, perhaps outdated, images of who we used to be and of what we can't do. But it is important to remember who you are and what you have accomplished and learned—often through painful experience. And if you see a friend who forgets who they are, wake them up and remind them of the skills they possess. Through practice, martial artists actually reprogram their reflexes, and while actual leadership expertise won't come from just reading a book, you *can* act and react with more focus and control and foster more dynamic and responsive organizations by applying these martial arts principles to your work and life. You, too, can become a black belt in the art of leadership.

I

MASTERING
YOURSELF

Don't fight with yourself. Then you have one less enemy. How can you control anyone else if you can't control yourself?
Chow Hung-Yuen, Sifu, Wing Chung Kung Fu

When a person can control himself, he can do amazing things.
John Clodig, master, Shidare Yanagi-ryu Aikijujitsu

The art of karate is a never ending quest for perfection . . . of developing the spirit and body to defeat your opponent . . . one's self.
Tak Kubota, The Art of Karate

Before the struggle, the victory is mine.
Mitsugi Saotome

I

HOW TO BECOME
A BLACK-BELT LEADER

Power has to come from the inside out, not the outside in.
Forget about the other person's power. First, learn to control your own
power. Second, learn to control your opponent's power.
Third, learn not to be controlled.
Chow Hung-Yuen, master, wing chun kung fu

The true path of the Way applies at any time and in any situation.
Miyamoto Musashi

Leadership is a potent combination of strategy and character.
But if you must be without one, be without the strategy.
General H. Norman Schwarzkopf

It didn't take me long to notice, first as a manager, and then later as a
consultant, how much energy is being squandered in most organizations. It was disturbing to see how easily people became sidetracked by
unimportant tasks and how shortsightedness endangered professional
and organizational survival.

From my outsider's perspective this didn't make any sense: Force
was poorly applied, people seemed to operate with little control, and
organizations were left, at best, hobbling toward their goals. This was

10

not the way my organizational-development studies said it should be, and it certainly wasn't in line with my desire for high-level results.

With all the available courses and books on leadership, people continued to employ many of the same self-defeating practices: aiming at lower-priority objectives, using negative motivation, and having a general loss of focus and control.

There was no solace to be found in strategies that only worked on paper. The strategies I most trusted were those of the martial arts (I had been studying for two years at the time), because they provided a system of principles and methods that were eminently effective in their own arena.

Sensing an important connection, I reflected on and read further about the martial arts view of the world, comparing it to the strategies of management experts who had proven results to show. I began applying martial arts principles to my work when and wherever they seemed to fit, using them to control myself during trying times, to manage conflicts, and to accomplish critical objectives and goals. And lo and behold, they worked.

With the martial arts as my inspiration, I developed physical metaphors for complex personal, interpersonal, and organizational events. I demonstrated these in seminars, and surprisingly, at first, received a great deal of positive response.

Since those early days, I've applied these principles to my work as a manager of our consulting company—we have clients in every continent—and as an agent of change in working with organizations such as Alcoa, American Airlines, Anheuser-Busch, Boeing, BP Amoco, Conoco, Detroit Edison, Exxon, General Motors, Intel, James River Corp, Johnson and Johnson, Kodak, Lenox China, Lockheed, McDonnell Douglas, Potlatch, Schlumberger, Scott's Co., Smithsonian Institution, Textron, United Airlines, United Parcel Service, and many, many others. As with most of the internal leaders of organizations with whom we work, I have minimal positional power in their companies or groups and can only lead by influence.

Usually, during our workshops and consultations those initial skeptics come around as they begin to understand just what martial arts methods can do for them.

The results can be most rewarding.

THE ART AND SCIENCE OF LEADERSHIP AND MARTIAL ARTS

Morehei Ueshiba was one of the greatest martial artists of the twentieth century. Although small in stature, he could easily overcome multiple attackers or even huge sumo wrestlers. He was reputedly never thrown by his opponents or struck unawares. Rather than allowing his physical skills to wane with advanced age, he became more powerful and adept.

Karen Schomburg, Steve Flynn, Ron Swingen, and Arthur Considine have lives very different from Morehei Ueshiba's, and yet they all have something in common. All four are black belts: Ueshiba in the martial arts, Schomburg, Flynn, Swingen, and Considine in the art of leadership. Like those of the master Ueshiba, the skills of these other special individuals have evolved from individual aptitude and years of dedicated practice.

- Karen Schomburg is a manager at Boeing. The area she works in builds airplane prototypes for research and testing. In this traditionally male-dominated industry, Karen, an average-sized woman with a warrior's spirit, uses her talents in recognizing potentially disruptive forces, for the calm planning and considered communications that help to boost morale, as well as to promote productivity and safety in her business unit.

- Steve Flynn, a senior manager for BP Amoco Exploration based in London, has worldwide responsibilities for maintaining smooth work flow and production. He enlists his sense of humor and considerable empathy to spearhead cultural changes in this well-managed company.

- Ron Swingen is a senior manager at Mentor Graphics, a leading technology company in computer aided engineering (CAE). Ron's career has been varied, moving from teaching high-school physics to developmental work with IBM to engineering management at several large corporations. Wherever Ron has worked, he has received rave reviews from bosses and subordinates. But that has not been enough. Ron is determined to fulfill his own vision of a workplace that balances the demand of high-tech creating with individual development and satisfaction.

- Arthur Considine is a manager at American Airlines. Impeccably dressed, with a considered air and a reputation for being sincere and concerned, Arthur has successfully spearheaded numerous projects for his worldwide company.

Although their arenas are on different battlegrounds than Master Ueshiba's, Karen, Steve, Ron, and Arthur—and many others like them—employ martial arts principles to multiply their business strength. Decades of formal martial arts training are *not* a prerequisite.

Black-belt leaders can be any age or size, female or male, and work in business, government, or nonprofit organizations. They practice their art at many levels, often with great subtlety, but they always share certain important characteristics with martial arts masters. They get the job done, have a powerful presence, are undeterred by threat, and remain calm under pressure. They use their own fears to help them accomplish their goals. They act efficiently and take advantage of changing conditions. About them others say that they "make things happen" and that "you can count on them." Most importantly, they control themselves first, and this internal focus gives a black-belt leader an unbreakable spirit.

Like the martial arts, leadership is both a science and art.

Early in their training martial artists study how to execute a spinning kick without losing their balance—place the feet just so, twist the upper body to gain momentum, and look where you will kick. That's the science of this maneuver. Practice this form, the masters say, until you develop a feeling for the entire movement—until you sense where the technique really works and develop truly effective timing. Now this is the art.

It's the same with leadership. Strong leaders apply principles, based on in-depth studies, that boost productivity and morale. These include such focus areas as worker motivation, effective meeting dynamics, or change-management studies that examine reducing employee resistance to new systems. That's the science.

But in real life people are not predictable. Have you ever hashed out a problem with a coworker, believing you have come to a meeting of the minds, only to find that the next day that same rapport no longer existed? People do not always pick up where they left off. We are changeable creatures who behave in complex ways.

But studies can only predict the past and can never predict what will happen in individual circumstances. Most studies are done in a vacuum, without the multiple and often challenging variables that exist in the everyday chaos of organizational life. "Guaranteed" solutions rarely produce the expected results and nothing works *every* time in *every* circumstance. The art of leadership involves understanding which scientific principles are in operation and how to best adjust them to the current situation so that you are not merely following a formula that worked the last time, but doesn't apply to the present circumstances. Real solutions must be artfully timed and adapted to different people and ever changing complex situations. Beginners study only the science of a technique, but experts in both leadership and martial arts devote more time to the finesse of the art.

Don't be lulled into complacency. Things are never as smooth as they seem in a book or on the practice mat; situations never replicate themselves. Both the martial artist and the strong leader always have to be ready to adapt.

Many people enthusiastically begin martial arts study only to find their interest quickly wanes. It may be that something else came up that needed their time and attention, but in many cases beginners are frustrated by an unrealistic quest for instant power. People seem to think they can go to a few classes and effortlessly become another Bruce Lee or Chuck Norris, or that by merely copying their instructors they will quickly eliminate fear and master grace.

But it's not that easy. Becoming a proficient martial artist takes years of dedicated practice. First you must focus on understanding the science, then you slowly gain a feeling for the art. Ultimately, as Dan Inosanto wrote in *The Filipino Martial Arts,* "Knowledge comes from your instructors, wisdom comes from within."

Leaders face the same temptation of looking to the outside for all their answers. Many books, consultants, and seminars push simple solutions, but business history is littered with the corpses of discarded managerial quick fixes.

Unfortunately—and understandably—many managers are still tempted to do so. After spending a great deal of money and time on yet another instant cure they usually find that nothing really has changed except that their confidence and credibility have been compromised. Instead of seeking a magical, painless solution, black-belt leaders, like martial artists, know they can best advance in their respective forms by studying their science and developing their art. A few guidelines for developing mature martial artists is an excellent place to begin.

EMPLOY NATURAL FORCES

The more advanced the black belt, the more they employ a practical understanding of physical laws. This is the martial arts "magic" that allows small-framed masters to effortlessly overcome younger, stronger, and faster opponents.

The results can be impressive. For example, it is said that Yip Man, the modern grandmaster of wing chun kung fu, was a slight and unassuming person who wasted little effort on looking impressive, a point illustrated by the time that Yip Man went to the Hong Kong police station to show them wing chun. He demonstrated part of the *siu lim tao*, "little idea form." This first form comes from a martial art that has few movements and that people rarely find impressive to watch—nary a high kick or screaming high-tension block in sight. The police watched Yip Man and then laughed at his display, saying, "That's not a martial art!" at which Yip Man sat down on a chair and asked various people to attack him, all failing in their assault. After this, the policemen listened and learned from Yip Man rather than scorning him.

Human nature is incredibly powerful. Telling people to follow a thick book of procedures is like asking them not to comply or to outright resist. Or requiring that people not discuss their salaries either dares them to compare or implies that an unfair compensation structure is at play (and you can imagine the reaction to that perception).

People like to have choices and almost always resist a no-option situation, no matter how good it really may be. Understanding this, several martial artists position themselves so that their opponents can make only limited types of attacks; others aim their on-guard hands slightly away from the opponent to invite an apparently easy attack (for which the martial artist is well prepared).

Good leaders, like strategic martial artists, know to offer "restricted" choices—all of which are acceptable and move positively toward organizational objectives. Many times we make our own enemies, actually instigating the resistance we say we least want. Fight human nature—your own or others'—and defeat is imminent. Find a way to enlist human nature and you can help create miraculous changes.

Working with human nature means being relaxed and able to move and react effectively in a spontaneous manner. Chow Hung-Yuen reminds students, "it's not how hard you do it, but how easy and natural you do it." There's a big difference between a forced smile and a natural smile.

Being relaxed doesn't mean giving in or not accomplishing goals. But staying relaxed under pressure is easy to say and difficult to do. Internal martial artists—those who focus on perception and control of subtle changes in force and energy rather than speed, strength, and quickness—learn that it's a challenge to control themselves, to learn to relax. But they also learn that they can't control someone else if they can't control themselves.

TEN PRINCIPLES FOR BECOMING A BLACK-BELT LEADER

Following are ten principles for becoming a black-belt leader. I will refer back to several of these principles later in this book. Each describes a fundamental way to successfully work with forces that underlie everyday interactions. And each one is an essential element of the "internal" martial arts that can be physically demonstrated. Here is an overview.

1. Proximity

The next time you watch martial arts experts who rely on throwing, rather than striking their opponent, notice how much more effective their techniques are the closer they move in to their opponent.

Closeness gives power in numerous ways. Physics' Gravitational Law tells us that the closer two objects are to one another, the greater the force they exert on each other. Similarly, studies show that the closer two offices are, the more communication occurs between them. And when making presentations, moving in closer to participants (within reason, of course) increases your power to hold their attention. Comparably, Tom Peters refers to Management-by-walking-around (MBWA) as having an impact on others through seeing and being seen, that is, by getting closer to the work and staff. And a University of Minnesota study cited a long list of factors as contributing to lower back pain; uppermost was the physical distance a person was from the load he was trying to lift or move. In other words, closer is basically safer.

Distance weakens, closeness strengthens. Standoffishness blocks, getting to the heart of matters succeeds.

Develop your leadership power by reducing distance wherever you can: close the space between yourself and the work tasks of others, bridge emotional barriers whenever possible, stand at as "comfortably close" a distance as you can when conversing with others (this will change between cultures and among individuals). Look for ways to make proximity work for you—physically, mentally, and emotionally.

2. Contact

The aim of internal martial arts is to control an opponent's senses and balance. But this is easier said than done, and more easily demonstrated with a cooperative partner than a highly skilled attacker.

Contact is the beginning of a successful encounter, not the final goal. After establishing good contact, martial artists and leadership experts can employ their additional skills to direct the other person to a desired place. Making and maintaining contact is essential in accurately reading and countering an attacker's changing forces. And as a leader, making contact with others allows you to assess both the ebbs and flows of their acceptance or resistance to what you are saying and to move more toward more effective persuasion.

One factor that contributes to the high level of effectiveness of Etta Mason, a human resources professional with New York State Electric and Gas, is her ability to make contact with and fully respect a wide range of people—her supervisor, senior managers, union leaders, and line staff. Even those with different points of view report she is a joy to work with. Her success comes from communicating as much information as she can to those she works with. She actively seeks out coworkers to help with shaping considered changes. She solicits their viewpoints on different topics and lets them know as early as possible of new programs available. She reaches out to them in every way she can. She doesn't wait for them to come to her.

Chapter 6 will provide strategies and methods for attaining and maintaining contact in conflict situations.

3. On and Off

There is a story that tells how one day a bird landed on the hand of *tai chi ch'uan* master Yang Lu Chan. But, later, as hard as it flapped its wings, the bird could not fly away. As the bird attempted to take off from his hand, Yang Lu Chan detected the movement and slightly yielded so the bird had nothing against which to push off.

So it goes with the martial arts and leadership. Mature martial artists know that they waste their energy when they attack an opponent's strength, but maximize their resources when they fill the space of the other's weakness. They time their responses, letting go in the face of great force and coming "on" with their own strength when there is a clear path.

Energy ebbs and flows. Chinese kung fu artists refer to this as yin and yang. The concept of on and off entails economizing on energy by switching to avenues of lower resistance when you exert force. For example, many people waste their energy by getting tense when they are listening to others—they get defensive, wonder where the conversation will flow or what the person really intends, and plan how they will respond. Not only is this poor listening, but being continuously on makes it more difficult to respond when the other person is done. Instead, take the time of listening as a time to let go inside, relax, and become receptive. This doesn't mean making yourself an unguarded victim, just using as little energy as possible when it's not time to be fully on. There will be an opportunity to respond with fuller force later, when it's your turn to speak.

Chow Hung-Yuen, master of wing chun kung fu, says,

> Chinese philosophy is based on harmony and balance. When you are positive, I am negative. When you become negative, I switch to positive. I don't mean that I think about it. If one hand is heavy and the other light, don't fight with the heavy hand. Attack with the light one instead. If there are two doors, one hard to push and one easy to push, why not go through the one that's easy to open? If you are fast, I am slow. If you are slow, I am fast. If you are hard, I am soft. If you are soft, I am hard.
>
> Remember that in the universe things always balance. When I punch, I'm "on." When you block my arm, I'm "off." But being off doesn't mean limp, it means I don't resist. Instead I redirect your oncoming force before turning back "on." This idea is hard to learn, but ultimately

very important. When you give, I take. When you take, I give. When you use force, I don't; when you don't, I do."

When he's not helping craft beer at Anheuser-Busch's flagship St. Louis Brewery, Steve Moreno is a peer trainer for the company. When not at work, Steve practices martial arts. As a result he is less reactive at work than he used to be, not letting things get to him, while still maintaining a firm stand and supporting his coworkers. Now he picks his battles more wisely, identifying the times when and the places where he can make the strongest impact.

Being off means being ready and waiting to respond at the appropriate time. It does not mean being passive. It is more akin to a computer in energy-conserving mode, which when needed can be turned on to full power without a moment's hesitation.

4. Secondary Pressure

What someone cannot feel, they cannot effectively resist. Expert martial artists don't give their opponents anything to counter. They don't struggle, but initiate movement from a secondary part of their bodies—their elbows, hips, or knees. This additionally provides them greater leverage and more power.

In leadership, this principle can be used in conflict situations. When giving a presentation, black-belt presenter Rob Russell doesn't let himself bristle in the face of an attacking comment. Breathing deeply, he calmly takes in what is being said, paraphrases the message in a way that strips the fangs from the original comment, and then responds to the entire group in a manner that solves the problem, rather than further escalates it. He doesn't get trapped into allowing himself to be put in a position of fighting back.

Chapter 5 gives more examples of applying secondary pressure in motivating others.

5. Centerline

Wing chun kung fu master Chow Hung-Yuen says,

> There's a center to my body and a line between our centers. I control this centerline no matter how the body is turned. I deflect oncoming energy by turning it away from my center.

> I push forward on center. When I push toward your center and there's nothing there, nothing in the way, I connect. When I push forward on the centerline and meet resistance, I redirect it. If you deflect my attacking arm I can still continue toward you with the rest of my body.
>
> The line between us is like a train track; there can be only one train on the track at a time.

By first determining the centerline between you and others or between two units, you can then exert force in the direction that helps the other move where you wish.

There's more on the Centerline principle in chapter 9, "Becoming an Agent of Change."

6. Structure/Letting Go

To be effective, people and organizations need structure. But when the structure isn't working, there is a time to let it go and allow it to change into something new. Among the biggest problems many would-be leaders have is a desire to set and hold onto a form, such as unbending policies and procedures or rigid adherence to organizational pyramid charts.

A good leader, like a developed martial artist, knows that there is a time to reexamine ways of doing things. When others push strongly and determinedly, it is time to redesign the control structure. I am not referring to the rounds of self-inflicted "restructuring" that organizations have undergone in past years, which was often merely a term for cutting workforces and raising workloads. Letting go is not abandonment. One can structure a new initiative and still let go of or modify any elements that are being strongly resisted.

Structure should change upon the valid pressure of outside forces of market conditions or internal staff concerns about why the old ways are no longer working. Restructuring haphazardly is advocating collapse without real control. The true test of the need for restructuring is this: does productivity, work quality, and morale rise when these changes are made or does staff feel increasingly adrift and insecure? Because no one can predict what will happen, it is best to first try a trial restructuring.

7. Sitting Back

According to martial arts instructor Dan Lucas, one of the seventeen "musts" of wing chun is, "Some of your strength must be kept in reserve."

In sparring, being overeager to attack leads to overcommitment. Similarly, being overenthusiastic about taking a new direction may cause others to become more suspicious and resistant—just as they would be of an overly eager salesman. Be interested and enthusiastic without leaping blindly and without reservation into a new approach. This will prove less stressful for you and others and less embarrassing if the project turns out to be problematic.

This doesn't mean you should be noncommittal or unexcited. Genuine enthusiasm can move organizations as long as it's balanced with good strategy.

8. Forward Pressure

Forward pressure means continuing to focus on your objectives, not getting distracted or sidetracked by being pushed and pulled in different directions. In certain martial arts, practitioners work to develop "spring pressure." Spring pressure means that, after making contact with an opponent, if she relaxes her guard, the martial artist's arms "spring" forward with no thought or extra action being required. Just a spontaneous reaction to the opening.

For leaders this means being consistent in letting others know you are dedicated and firmly fixed upon your objectives. Unlike many managers who just push, Vince Adorno, Alcoa plant manager, uses forward pressure intelligently. He calmly and persistently communicates his high expectations of himself and his staff, letting them know they can do their best to work as a team, productively, with focus. Wherever he has gone, morale, efficiency, quality, and safety are elevated. Vince is among the best plant managers I've had the fortune of meeting.

Quite often, using forward pressure can make the difference between those who succeed and those who give up almost within sight of their goals. But this martial art principle, when practiced with sensitivity and awareness of others' reactions, will give you an advantage over others who blindly push, pressure, or cajole. The principle of forward pressure entails being resilient and flexible while simultaneously moving ahead.

9. Not Tensing/Not Stopping

The movement of master martial artists, like that of expert leaders, is fluid and continuous. This doesn't mean being hyperactive, nor does it mean not taking a breath to relax. It means not letting self-doubt or tension immobilize you.

Chow Hung-Yuen tells beginning kung fu students, "Keep moving, like flowing water. If I stop, I give you the chance to use your strength against me. I redirect any strength you have by moving with it. Keep moving; take action. Don't stop to think about your next move; it may be too late." In other words, don't allow yourself to get stuck. Take action before the cement dries. When you're making an important presentation, never stop yourself to announce that you have lost your place, have forgotten something important, or are unsure what to do next. Remember, no one knows what you forgot to say or do. They only see and hear what you reveal.

If others are frozen into a resistant or apathetic mode, get them moving. Initially it's important to spark reaction, with the understanding that "a body at rest tends to remain at rest, a body in motion tends to remain in motion."

Of course, don't try to create anger, but select areas of change that people are already questioning or complaining about. Make this energy work for you. It's easier to turn an adamant staff member into an ally than it is to "motivate" someone who has given up.

Don't stop in the midst of "battle" or you'll surely get hit. Keep moving forward, focusing on your underlying objectives. There'll be plenty of time to critique yourself and plan for future improvements once the spotlight is off.

10. Redirecting, Not Push-Push

Matching strength with strength only works when you know you are more powerful. Even then, this kind of fighting can be exhausting and can be counterproductive in that it attempts to force others to do things your way. Instead, give in to get your way.

Internal martial artists talk about "borrowing four ounces to gain a thousand pounds." What this means is that it is smarter to use just a little of your own energy to get an overreaction from your opponent that you can then put to your advantage. Someone operating from a forceful, overpowering mind-set is ripe to overreact or to be manipulated, neither of which a good leader wants.

Again from Chow Hung-Yuen:

I may be stronger than you, but why bother? If you depend on power, remember that the dinosaurs were extinct a long time ago. Borrow the power, then return it with interest. I can easily knock over a speeding motorcycle by changing its angle only slightly.

You can use power to overcome an opponent. An opponent can also use your power against you. My opponent is looking to generate power, I'm looking for an opening. In other words, he tries to generate as much power as possible and send his punch out, no matter what is there or what it meets. I don't try to contend with his power but try to redirect it or go around it in search for an opening.

Focus on redirecting force to conserve your energy and to maximize your power—not to wake up others' resistance. Chapters 5 (motivation) and 6 (conflict) will illustrate specific techniques for redirecting force.

The Samurai Connection

Perhaps Miyamoto Musashi's guidelines for warriors can work for you as they have for business leaders throughout the world. In the late sixteenth century, Musashi wrote a slim treatise on swordsmanship entitled *A Book of Five Rings*. Although in recent years this book has been available to businesspeople, here we will expand on specific, proven methods for applying these guidelines to a useful leadership strategy.

As one story goes, a booking agent for a famous television talk program tried to procure Musashi for a guest spot. The agent was nonplussed to discover that his desired "hot celebrity" had been dead and buried for hundreds of years! Admittedly, Musashi was a great warrior, undefeated in all his fights, allowing him to live to a ripe age, but, alas, still not long enough to appear on that TV show. Deemed a Kensei (sword saint) by his people, Musashi also transferred some of his battlefield insight to painting and other arts. As a legacy he left not only his own legend, but a book on martial strategy as well.

In *A Book of Five Rings* Musashi lists nine guidelines for developing warriors, guidelines that are also appropriate for developing black-belt leader skills.

1. Do not think dishonestly.

2. The Way is in training.

3. Become acquainted with every art.

4. Know the ways of all professions.

5. Distinguish between gain and loss in worldly matters.

6. Develop intuitive judgment and understanding for everything.

7. Perceive those things that cannot be seen.

8. Pay attention even to trifles.

9. Do nothing which is of no use.

When you understand how to apply them, these esoteric principles for the martial arts can readily promote black-belt leadership.

1. Do Not Think Dishonestly

Walter Muryasz, a professional martial artist who specializes in training black belts in many disciplines, has strong feelings about self-honesty. In his book *Precepts of the Martial Artist* he writes, "The martial artist must always be on guard against self-delusion of any form. There is no room for it in the martial arts. Reality is the teacher and the test."

Miyamoto Musashi agreed. In *A Book of Five Rings* he described the Way of a warrior as "having no illusions in your heart, honing your wisdom and willpower, sharpening your intuitive sense and your powers of observation day and night; when the clouds of illusion have cleared away, this is to be understood as the true path."

Black-belt leaders are critically honest with themselves. They assess their strengths and limitations without excuse, and work to become *deeply* sure of themselves. Take John Kerson, for example, a senior manager at a wood products company. At one time he had a promising career. Hopping quickly through the ranks, from machine operator to supervisor, then from manager to plant manager, John made the leap into corporate headquarters.

He has painfully discovered, however, that he is a fish out of water, and doesn't feel he can do a good job in his corporate position. John knows his strength lies more in the realm of interpersonal leadership than data management. He doesn't have a natural feeling for what he's doing, and his career is dying on the vine. He could probably continue—he knows how to cover himself well enough—but John is a black belt in the art of leadership and being mediocre isn't good enough.

24

So he is making his move. He's given himself six months to find a more suitable job, either internally (in a position where he can still be effective) or with another company. This is not an easy decision, just a necessary one.

It's tempting to blame others for our difficulties in an effort to try to escape personal responsibility. ("This job was a setup from the beginning"; "Those others fell down on this task"; "The market turned out to be too soft.") But you can't hide from yourself and still be effective. Somewhere, down deep, you know the truth, and ultimately, so will others.

In my experience most people don't see themselves accurately. They exaggerate their strengths, and at the same time privately inflate their weaknesses. Too hard on themselves in one way, they're too soft in another. Both excesses are dangerous. To be effective, to continue to grow professionally, the leader has to know what he really can and cannot do.

Self-knowledge recognizes that every strength is a potential weakness and vice versa. A kick may be devastating if it lands as desired, but it can also weaken the kicker's balance. Leaders with strong "people skills" can turn a disjointed staff into a smoothly working unit; but sometimes a staff can become sidetracked or blind to problems because of their reverence for such a leader.

Of course, knowing those areas in which you excel and those in which you founder is easier said than done. But for the honest-thinking leader, it's essential to develop sources of external criticism that you can listen to without feeling threatened:

- Develop candor with colleagues and peers so that the norm is "to tell it like it is." Request feedback from them on your strengths, weaknesses, and skill areas.

- Develop similar relationships with friends and family who can point out behavior patterns that may also show up at work. ("You never listen to me once you've made up your mind to do something.")

- Self-assessment tests may provide insight into your hidden strengths and weaknesses.

- Solicit feedback in the form of statistical indicators of performance, attitude survey results, and others' responses to your actions.

- Pay attention to how you receive feedback. Do you react defensively and seek to make excuses? These are danger signs. Can you accept the feedback calmly—and consider how it can help you? Are you seeking approval or are you genuinely looking for ways to improve future performance?

- Maintain a *freshly informed* approach. Don't start from a conclusion. Remember you have limits. You don't have to know what to do in advance.

- Most importantly, listen to yourself. Pay attention to that inner voice that communicates mixed feelings.

Being honest with yourself means understanding that it is likely you have mixed feelings about everyone and everything. This is natural. Even the person you love most can sometimes drive you crazy. And when you say you enjoy your job, the truth is that you may partly love it and partly dislike it. In most positions, there are tasks you look forward to and other have-to-dos that you wish you could avoid.

So it's natural to have mixed feelings about your job or about any procedure or plan. In fact it is dangerous to ignore or rationalize mixed feelings away. Know they are there, listen to them, and make them your ally. Mixed feelings help you in three ways:

1. They help you to reconsider before you leap into action. Sometimes actions appear totally favorable when you want to be rescued from an uncomfortable situation. You may forget that there is always a price to pay for precipitous action. If you are attuned to your doubting side, you may avoid leaping onto dangerous ground.

2. They help you plan for contingencies. Seeing the possible downside will make your plans more realistic.

3. They help you to understand others who disagree with your position. When you understand dissenters, you'll have more influence with them.

And don't forget to watch your interactions with others. In *The Tao of Jeet Kune Do*, Bruce Lee wrote, "To know oneself is to study oneself in action with another person." Others, especially difficult people, are your allies. There's nothing like a slow-tracking employee to upset an impatient manager. When you see yourself overreacting, you should be thankful that your weakness has been brought to the surface. Now you have an opportunity to work on becoming more patient, more disciplined—in short, a stronger leader.

Also develop a realistic view of your organization's strengths and limitations. It's great to be working for the team, but not by blinding yourself to its weaknesses. If you can't see the weaknesses, you can't change them.

Finally, recognize that self-assessment is an ongoing activity. How many organizations—or people—have you known that have slipped from a position of strength because they rested on their laurels? Yearly self-assessments may provide historical perspective, but real strengthening comes from daily observation. Continue to honestly monitor yourself and your organization.

2. The Way Is in Training

Daily practice is the key to ongoing improvement. Resting on your laurels or past successes will only take you so far. It's more what you're doing than what you've done that matters. When asked to explain how he so quickly became skilled in yet another martial art style, Paul McClellan explained, "It's not the number of years you put in, it's the number of hours." Paul has applied that same training approach to develop into an acknowledged master organizational trainer and presenter.

You become good at whatever you practice. What you put into your training is what you'll later get back. René Changsut, an expert and instructor in the Chinese martial arts of si lum, wing chun, and tai chi, talks about "eating bitter," the need to build a strong base of techniques. "Everyone who begins training wants to be doing the high, flashy kicks and other fancy stuff right away. But if you rush it, you'll stifle your progress. You have to be willing to do the 'unexciting' practices, like setting firm footwork patterns, that will ultimately support the speed, power, and balance you'll need to really be able to excel."

Chow Hung-Yuen agrees. He tells his students,

> Some people learn a hundred forms, but it only takes one to save your
> life. Rather than practice a hundred forms one time, why not practice
> one movement a hundred times and perfect it? The higher you go, the

farther you can see. The only thing you can try to do is get better every day, keep improving, and be better than last time. Try to make your first response right, the way you've practiced. The second or third move you might slip back into your previous habits, but at least try to get the first one right. Keep practicing. You can't pull on a plant to make it grow faster.

The martial artist is dedicated to self-improvement through training. No one becomes a black belt without hours of weekly practice over several years. In his book *Karate-do: My Way of Life*, modern karate founder Gichin Funakoshi wrote, "Only through training will a person learn his own weaknesses. . . . He who is aware of his weaknesses will remain master of himself in any situation."

The same is true for all black-belt leaders I have met; their efforts toward self-improvement never end. The *Hagakure*, a respected martial arts source written by Nabeshima Naoshige, plainly states that once you begin to feel that you are a master, you are no longer making progress—self-development withers with self-satisfaction.

In training you can't avoid correcting and doing the little things correctly over and over again. As martial arts master Walter Muryasz writes,

> The martial artist is always training in one form or another. In the beginning, the artist must practice form, *kata* (stylized combat against set invisible opponents), and movement. These cannot be rushed or neglected. They are the building blocks and corner stones for efficiency later on in the art. It is the constant repetition of movements, form, and kata that will eventually affect a change in the artist's normal way of living. Years later, he will naturally move in a manner which makes his [martial] art a by-product of the way he moves. The art will not become a contrivance and he can then say, 'There is no difference between the way I lift my cup and the way I avoid a strike.'

Training does not take place in just the controlled, and therefore, artificial, environment of the dojo (training hall). Training is an ongoing process of attentively weaving the threads of book and classroom learning with real-life experience, adjusting when unsuccessful. In essence, training is a process of trial and self-correction, not mindless repetition, but the art and discipline of learning that requires the utmost attention. Make it a habit to practice applying to your work what you've read, seen, and heard. Watch the results, then readjust accordingly.

This takes effort, even for an expert leader. Things rarely go as smoothly as described in a book, seminar, or anecdote about another company. And though it may be frustrating, this kind of at-work leadership training eventually creates natural and effective action.

A-dec's Phil Westover gives excellent seminars on effective use of training. He believes training is a waste of time *unless* there are realistic goals for the training. For example, it's not reasonable to expect a new student to fend off black belts after only one lesson. Nor will a two-week karate course refashion someone's life.

Positive thinking is nice; some people enjoy following rituals, but, as Chow Hung-Yuen saltily reminds his students, "You have to keep training if you want to improve. It's a fair game. If you practice, you improve. You can't buy it."

It is important to accurately distinguish between training's specific performance goals and the goals of educational presentations (such as stress control or time management, etc.) that are developmental in nature. The latter may raise morale and improve productivity in the long run, but they rarely show immediate performance benefits.

Remember that for increased productivity, classroom training should be applied to the job gradually and continuously. Many people return from attending training seminars eager to make work improvements, but are quickly frustrated by change-resistant systems. (Of course, a participant's unrealistic expectations of a quick change may be partially responsible for his plan's "bombing out.")

Schlumberger, a leader in oilfield services, is a truly international company. Their senior managers talk about the organization as being a *training* company where their staff is continuously learning to stay ahead of the curve on new technology and customer service. Firmly believing that training gives them both a marketing and cost-control edge, their staff travels worldwide to attend internal sessions on health, safety and environment issues, technology, communications, marketing, and other management topics.

In the martial arts, it isn't true that "those who can, do, those who can't, teach." In fact, teaching is an essential element of mastery. Only when you really understand the skills can you transmit them to others. In *Zen in the Art of Archery*, Eugen Herrigel quotes an assistant kyudo (archery) instructor who said, "A great Master must also be a great teacher. With us the two things go hand in hand."

One of the accomplishments of judo founder Professor Jigoro Kano was his development of a cadre of highly skilled students. Similarly, black-belt leaders I have met relish training their staff, just as they enjoy continually advancing their own skills and knowledge. When correctly applied, training is a powerful weapon for strengthening performance and raising morale of those with whom you work.

3. Become Acquainted with Every Art

Every martial art system has weaknesses and strengths. For example, in martial arts fighting, there are three "circles" of defense: the outside circle of the leg reach (kicking distance), the middle circle of the extended arm (punching distance), and the inner circle of the body (throwing, tripping distance). A predominantly kicking art like tae kwon do focuses on the outer circle; so students often practice staying outside of their opponent's reach. Practitioners of this Korean art are not as accustomed to a proficient grappling form of attack. Judo artists, on the other hand, are more comfortable at moving in on their opponent and going for the throw. But they are less practiced in defending against a good kicking attack.

Not seeing your weaknesses makes you more vulnerable to the attacks you haven't prepared for. What's the answer? Before you find yourself in a tight situation, gain balance by exposing yourself to a complementary system, so that when you step onto the battlefield, you can anticipate more realistically. You can best defend yourself against the knife only after you have studied the weapon and its tactics because at that point you are no longer only fighting theoretically.

Aikijujitsu ("blending-forces style" jujitsu) master John Clodig, like many martial arts experts, holds black belts in more than one style. He believes advanced students need to practice different forms of martial arts to gain perspective and says, "You'll never understand your own system until you leave it." (Note that this advice is intended for mature practitioners, not beginners who would be easily confused by flitting between several styles.)

Just as there are different martial arts, there are also divergent leadership styles, and it is important not to cling exclusively to the one you have adopted. Whether it be *stratified* and *centralized* or *participative* and *decentralized*, each style has something worthwhile to offer, and each has its strength, as well as its limitations. Know them all, especially the range of those used within your organization. When you are well informed you're less likely to be blindsided by a style you don't fully understand. You'll also be less threatened and better able to weave together different approaches to achieve common organizational goals. And just as important is that exploring different approaches teaches you more about your own style. Keeping abreast of leadership methods in other organizations—especially your competitors'—is also a good idea. Their progress may teach you about your own organization's patterns, weaknesses, and strengths.

Textron is a worldwide multi-industry company. Seeking to further improve their safety performance, Textron (led by Jay Small and Skipper Kendrick) extensively benchmarked safety and productivity records with their competitors and peers, even going so far as to interview the senior leadership of their top rivals. From this process they were better able to see the strengths and limitations of their current approach and to then make plans for long-term improvements. And their safety performance improved dramatically.

Become adept at all parts of a project: planning, budgeting, timing of milestones, decision making, evaluation, writing, editing, marketing (internal or external), making presentations, and distribution. The more you really understand what is involved, the easier it is to maintain the leadership needed to delegate and monitor work or change direction quickly.

You can also improve your leadership by referring to what you've learned in other arts. Just as Musashi, after his retirement, transferred his martial skills to *sumi-e* brush paintings, you can apply any other art you truly understand (athletics, public speaking, playing music, gardening) toward making you a stronger leader.

4. Know the Ways of All Professions

For the battle to be won, the generals plot broad strategy, midlevel officers direct the fighting, and the soldiers are on the line. Many staff support the operation—the food-suppy crew, the medical team, the record keepers, and so on.

Similarly, in any successful business, professionals have to work together toward common aims. Each has an essential part in the functioning of the organization. You can help this along by taking a general's perspective. A general's perspective helps you understand the crucial role your department plays. Also, remember how much power you really have. Too often, though, bright, otherwise capable leaders have a narrow perspective and so don't realize their ability to positively influence the overall organization. Someone once said that a "professional" in an organization is someone who has a lot of power yet continually complains about how powerless he is.

This tongue-in-cheek description is often on the mark. I have heard all kinds of managers—in personnel, accounting, data processing, training, sales, safety, industrial engineering, etc.—grumble that they "have the answers, but no one listens." I also notice that a popular seminar topic in professional association conferences is "Getting Top Management Support."

Something's wrong. Yes, technical competence and interpersonal relations can make you adequate in your position, but they are not enough. If you wish to influence the *entire* organization, learn the ways of all the different parts of that organization, and those of other professions as well.

Many of us believe our professional expertise is the missing element that will solve organizational problems. But remember, organizational professionals—including yourself—are often stereotyped by others. Marketing staff are said to shoot from the hip, sales personnel to promise customers anything to close a sale, and accounting professionals to be tightly controlled, conservative, and detail conscious.

While there may be *some* truth in these descriptions, don't allow yourself to be pigeonholed. If you aspire to influence others or become upper-level management, think globally. Start by seeing the limitations of your own training. Most training systems claim they have no weaknesses and that they fully prepare trainees to handle any and all situations, but, in fact, all systems have shortcomings. So whatever your background, broaden it. Become a comprehensive thinker while simultaneously developing specific areas of expertise.

- Seek exposure to professions far afield from your own. Take particular note of those you don't really comprehend, then fill these holes in your understanding. If you're a data processing manager, take classes or read books on salesmanship. A marketing specialist? Try human resource development.

- Also meet with other professionals. Take breaks with them, have lunch together, and attend their professional meetings. This immersion approach, while helping you understand other systems, also breaks down stereotypes (yours of them—and theirs of you).

- When speaking to other professionals, use *their* language. All professions have a jargon; it's a short-cut in conversation, as well as a way of recognizing others in the same field. Be able to speak of "cost-benefits" to an accountant, of "loss control" to safety specialists, and of "gains in learning transfer" to a management development specialist. With language flexibility you will be able to speak to different audiences more fluently.

- Begin to look at your own profession as if you were an outsider. Objectively assess the strengths and weaknesses of your training. Develop an understanding for different approaches (both radical and conservative) within your field; look for the value and weaknesses of each.

- Rotate responsibilities or jobs. Some organizations internally trade supervisors. This keeps the organization fresh and the staff alive, and provides perspective. Of course these switches are not made haphazardly. First supervisors are solicited for input, after which they work together closely for a smooth transition and orientation, advising those with whom they are rotating about problems that may arise.

- Most importantly, search for similarities between your profession and others. If you look past the terminology you'll probably discover underlying principles that you can also apply to your tasks.

With a widened perspective and a generalist's point of view, you'll recognize the interrelationships within your company. You can boost organizational flexibility and strength by blending seemingly disparate professional approaches.

5. *Distinguish between Gain and Loss in Worldly Matters*

In order to make the correct adjustments, the martial artist has to be able to see both when she is winning and when the tide is turning against her. This isn't as straightforward as it sounds. Too often people become sidetracked and lose sight of their ultimate goal.

It's crucial in the heat of battle that the martial artist not forget his true goals. If you are fighting for your life, remember what is truly important. If your true purpose is to win the battle, protect others, or build a dynasty, seeking revenge or trying to pump up your image may be useless diversions.

It is currently fashionable to criticize management for short-term profits. Books and consultants admonish managers to take a long-term perspective, and managers nod, yes, in principle, but in their hearts they know that management theoreticians don't deal with the complex pressures that they as managers feel. The same managers who read the latest books or attend in-vogue seminars continue to be misled by visions of immediate success.

There are endless examples of how an expedient decision to cut losses or reduce overhead has turned out to be costly after a short time. In one high-tech company, quarterly sales fell far below worst-case predictions. One division manager hoping to save costs had almost one hundred "unnecessary" telephone extension lines removed. Within seven months the short-term crisis had evened out and the lines had to be reinstalled at great additional cost. Unfortunately the disruption to customer service and project management had even longer-lasting effects than the added cost of installation.

If your own responsibilities aren't clear to you, how can you assess your own performance? Solicit direction from your supervisor. If you can't get a clear signal from above, consult with trusted peers, read company literature, follow the CEO's lead. Don't let yourself become lost. Stay on track and remember what it is you should be doing. Andrew Grove, Chairman of Intel, admonished readers of his *High Output Management* that "activity is not output." In other words, like the developing martial artist, leaders do best when they focus on results, not on how many hours they've worked or how many meetings they've attended.

Once you know what is really expected of you, look at matters with both short-term and long-term vision. Remember that an immediate loss may be turned into a large longer-term gain; and, conversely, a short-term gain may lead to a major long-term deficit.

This gain-and-loss maxim can be applied to the practice in many companies of charge-back accounting, a framework in which administrative departments are responsible for justifying their services. ("Yes, we can write you this software but we will charge the costs to your budget.") To departments accustomed to having captive markets within their own organization, this approach is often threatening at first. After all, under this scheme the data processing department must compete with outside vendors for work in the warehouse. But properly implemented, charging back can improve service and organizational morale. The ensuing competition can enliven an organization and sharpen productivity. It can also clearly demonstrate whether a department is pulling its own weight. So a charge-back system can help differentiate between internal profits and losses.

When you have losses in business, don't just accept them. Instead, find ways of converting them into gains. "Breakdowns are not necessarily bad," contends black-belt information manager Mary Devlin. "It depends on what you do with them. If you're going to make things happen, you are also going to encounter more and more breakdowns. I try to remember to see these as signs of organizational movement, indicators of areas needing refinement, or opportunities to clean up previously unsurfaced issues. And exposing people to this perspective can help them stay calmer and perform better."

Paul McClellan is an excellent martial artist who has successfully applied martial arts principles in his work as an international organizational change agent. To advance to further levels, Paul suggests the dedicated practitioner consider "investing in loss." In wing chun kung fu, this entails training to become comfortable in being apparently— but only momentarily—vulnerable. By "welcoming" the attack into his personal space, rather than automatically stiffening to fight the incoming force, an adept can easily surprise and control a much stronger opponent. Similarly, in yanagi jujitsu, the appearance of vulnerability can lead an attacker into overcommitting and losing his balance.

Investing in loss is a process of coldly examining and then letting go of the wooden reaction of directly pushing back against incoming energy. This is an advanced and amazingly effective approach that is best practiced under the guidance of an expert instructor.

6. Develop Intuitive Judgment and Understanding for Everything

Many martial arts emphasize developing greater sensitivity and more reliance on intuitive feeling. Chow Hung-Yuen teaches that "inside your mind you respond with what you feel, not what you think. Even when you're in the right position but apply pressure in the wrong direction, I take advantage of it. This is not for display or for competition. A bystander can't see this pressure, but you and I can feel it. That's why we can practice blindfolded or in the dark, because it's something you have to feel and not see. With your eyes open and in bright daylight, practice as though blindfolded and depend on what you feel rather than what you see."

So, if you practice the right way, learn all the techniques you can, work on them, be watchful, and keep in mind that you don't know all the answers in advance, then, perhaps, intuitive feelings will come and you will begin to understand.

The thought process is too slow. Analysis can't defend you against attacks. When a glass falls off the table edge, there is no time to think about grabbing for it. Think and it breaks, notice and respond intuitively and you'll catch it, moving faster than you even believed possible.

Thought is predictable, out of tune with the motion of change. Too much thinking can make you vulnerable. In *Precepts of the Martial Artist*, his technical treatise for advanced martial artists, Walter Muryasz warns against overthinking: "The more the conscious part of the opponent's mind is occupied, the easier it is to control. That is, the more thinking going on, the more openings occur. The more conditioned and unaware the mind is, the more easily it can be controlled. Thus, the martial artist's mind must become clear, aware, and open so as not to leave a place for his opponent to enter [and control it]."

When you use all of your resources—intellectual and intuitive— you'll have knowledge of *what* is going on combined with the feeling for *how* things are proceeding. A master of any art operates mostly on "scientific intuition." Knowledge plus real-life experience serves as the input, and the feeling for "what's right to do here" is the end product.

In all organizations, moments of opportunity or crisis can pop up at any time:

- A valued employee informs you that she has been offered another job; should you simply let her leave or should you try to convince her to stay?

- An important customer is lukewarm about your new product idea; should you abandon this line or develop it further?

- There has been a reported rise in employee stress; should you investigate why this is happening or should you avoid opening a can of worms?

What do you do? If there is time to think, do so. But sometimes there isn't. Here's where you let intuitive feeling guide your actions. *If you are calm*, use your intuition and go with your impulse. If you have prepared yourself in advance for moments such as these, disciplined your mind, and learned from your experiences, your intuitive reactions will be your best ones.

Real life is complex. It is impossible to capture the whole picture through analysis. Just when you think you've got everything understood, it changes. Nothing sits still. People are unpredictable, changing from moment to moment. The market rises and falls in peaks and valleys; no one knows what the economy will do or how seemingly distant events may affect an organization. The past hints at the future, but it is never actually repeated.

So what can you do?

- Develop your intuition in balance with your intellect. Pay attention to your internal messaging system.

- Orient your view to an organization's entire system. Perceive it as a living, breathing organism.

- Look beyond the rules. New martial arts students are taught that if an opponent punches straight out at them, they step back, always to the opponent's outside where it is safer. This gives beginners the security of accomplishing an effective movement. But the sidestep move doesn't always work. What if sidestepping carried you over a precipice? Or if you are too close to the attacker to be able to get to his outside? The beginner needs the rules, but the master *knows* the right timing and *feels* when to forget the rules. He doesn't let rules or forms trap him. He knows when they don't apply, when to go beyond them, and when to let them go.

Martial arts rules are guidelines for typical situations; but remember that real life rarely duplicates textbook examples. Look beyond forms and examples to find the underlying principles. With this concept in mind Bruce Lee described the martial art he developed, jeet kune do, as "the formless form."

Which is more important, keeping up an image or actually being effective? If you chose the latter, remember that thoughts alone can serve as an initial guide, but too much thinking without feeling and action can cause paralysis. Actions speak louder and prove more effective than any words. The adept lets feelings guide his actions.

- Keep things as simple as possible. One general manager I know loves theoretical models. During the middle of a meeting or in a one-on-one discussion, he usually rises abruptly to put up yet another graphic that "illustrates the problem." Don't make this mistake of falling in love with models for their own sake. Overdoing analysis removes you from reality. You've got the correct picture of the world, of the market, only as long as it stays exactly that way. Some managers will disregard any glitch, data, or feedback that doesn't fit their favorite model or analysis. Clearly, this is dangerous.

- Stay connected. Don't lead from mental castles in the sky. Keep your feet on the ground, know your product and service and market preferences, and sense organizational mood shifts.

7. Perceive Those Things That Cannot Be Seen

As part of a teaching demonstration, wing chun sifu Chow Hung-Yuen has been known, when visiting other martial arts schools, to put on a blindfold and invite students to attack him from the front. He calmly makes contact and is able to easily control their full-speed attacks. He then removes his blindfold, smiles, and says, "You feel the force, you don't see it. When you see it, it's too late."

To develop sensitivity to "unseen" changes of forces, wing chun practitioners practice *chi sao* (sticking hands). In real fighting, just as in real life, forces change rapidly and continuously. Although these forces may be difficult to visually notice, an expert can "touch hands" with another and redirect slight changes in the level and direction of an opponent's strength. Exercise in chi sao helps develop an expert's ability to prevail—even when a skilled and stronger opponent feints or quickly changes his attack.

A black-belt leader can develop sensitivity to others' patterned reactions of dealing with challenges, change, and conflict. Chow Hung-Yuen said, "Three rolls [in sticking hands] and I know your life history."

During one of his travels to Mongolia, it is recorded that aikido founder Morihei Ueshiba was threatened by an attacker who was ready to fire a gun at him from six feet away. Master Ueshiba disarmed the attacker. When asked how he was able to do this, he replied, "A very long time elapses between the moment a man decides to pull the trigger and the moment he actually does so." Clearly Ueshiba had developed the ability to anticipate an enemy's thoughts and actions.

Walter Muryasz has methods by which martial artists develop an ability to sense attack. He asks one blindfolded student to face a partner who is not wearing a blindfold and who stands just out of reaching distance. Muryasz instructs the blindfolded martial artist to relax, extend her perceptions, and tap her uniform when she senses her partner beginning to throw a punch or kick. Advanced students consistently sense an attack almost before it is launched.

You can also extend your perceptions by developing leadership antennae. Be on the lookout for the "invisible" factors that determine organizational reality:

- climate (atmosphere, mood)
- hidden agenda (notice which stories and tasks others keep returning to)
- intentions
- conflicts
- in what areas change is most resisted
- in what areas change is most welcomed

- what tasks or jobs don't get done

- who gets promoted and who doesn't

- what the competition is doing (study your competition's strengths and weaknesses; don't go into "battle" without adequate intelligence)

- clients' reactions (solicit feedback from customers who don't offer it on their own)

- environmental factors that affect productivity and morale—color, sound, use of space, lighting, temperature

- proximity of offices

- community perceptions of your business

These unseen factors form an early warning system that indicates organizational success or failure. The sum of these factors is often called the company's *culture*. Other staff will see the organizational webs woven from these strands, so it's best that you recognize them as well.

Often productivity trends aren't immediately indicated by statistical data. Renowned statistician and quality guru W. Edwards Deming warned managers to not overly rely upon statistics—this from a statistician! Clearly a black-belt leader.

If you extend your antennae and stay in touch with the elements of your organization's culture, you may be able to sense loss of momentum, incipient customer dissatisfaction, or when is the right time to act. By responding early, you'll save valuable time and address problems before they take firm hold. You'll also be able to seize opportunities as they appear.

It is just as critical to fine-tune your internal perceptions. When you are otherwise bored or overstressed, do the following self-checks:

- Feet—do I feel a connection to the ground? Are my shoelaces too tight?

- Knees—are they relaxed?

- Breathing—is it smooth?

- Posture—collapsed or too rigid?

- Arms—filled with unnecessary tension?
- Eyes—calm rather than squinted or darting?
- Stomach—relaxed?
- Jaw—relaxed? Not slack, but not clenching?
- Face—relaxed expression or frozen?

You can assume greater control only after you can accurately determine what is going on—both inside of you and within your organization.

8. Pay Attention Even to Trifles

In several of the martial arts I've practiced, slight changes in hand and foot position can make the difference between effortlessly deflecting force and struggling for control. A beginner or casual observer might not notice these subtle differences, but mastering martial arts involves a process of exploring and adjusting to ever more "trifling" changes that make large differences.

"From one comes many" goes an ancient samurai saying, meaning that little things add up until they spell victory or defeat. During the battle, will the sun be in our eyes or facing our opponent? What effect will the wind have on the contestants? Which small issues are indicators of an impending period of low morale? The trifles of today may become the troubles of tomorrow. Head them off while they're still small. Timing is the key to "trifle management."

In most organizations, communication travels in an inverted pyramid. Grassroots rumors start at lower levels of an organization. So pay close attention to the morale and performance of entry-level personnel. Intermittently go to lunch or have coffee with new staff. They'll see the organization with fresh eyes. Nurture clerical and hourly staff—they are important. People in these relatively low-paid, low-status positions probably have more contact with your customers than any other employees.

Pay attention to the effects of small things, like vacation schedules or when to call staff meetings. Learn to feel and use the natural forces in an organization—competition, attractions, jealousies, desire for or resistance to change—toward increasing company strength.

9. Do Nothing Which Is of No Use

Martial artists learn that efficient movements are strong and fast. The same is true in leadership. Don't waste energy. Running around looking busy, attending meetings, spending time on the phone, are not the issue. Getting the job done is.

- Don't squander energy in needless worry or tension. Being relaxed means using only as much energy as is needed to do the job. The world-class sprinter needs to be relaxed in the midst of the race, but tension is not necessarily his enemy. After all, he needs enough muscle tension to make the legs pump, to swing his arms for momentum, and to keep his upper body balanced over his hips. Misplaced tension, however, helps no one. Clenching jaw muscles during the race—or a task—only diverts energy away from finishing as quickly as possible.

  Make relaxation your ally. It releases otherwise bound energy, and helps you to feel more powerful. Relaxation is a skill that is developed with practice. A relaxed leader who can stay calm, even when everything is in upheaval, is more efficient. In dire circumstances, she is able to see opportunities unfolding. She believes in herself and, consequently, so does her staff.

- Know what efforts further organizational goals. There is no sense in working against the direction in which your organization is moving.

- Make only those decisions that need to be made. The only thing we have in this world is time; this is your most precious resource, so invest it wisely. Don't waste it on meaningless tasks.

  In *Zen in the Martial Arts*, Joe Hyams suggests that we must "conquer haste." Avoid pressuring yourself into making unnecessary or hasty decisions. Yes, there are deadlines that have to be met, but you can still control yourself and your time. Don't let yourself be *internally* hurried, even as you progress rapidly through your tasks.

- When under attack, there is a time to do nothing—if you are calm and alert. This attribute distinguishes an expert martial artist from a beginner. The new student, unlike the master, is prone to overreact to any movement. There is a time to do nothing, when waiting and watching is the proper course of action. Move off the line of attack (on a straight punch, this may just be a few inches to the side), then counterpunch or throw. The results can be disastrous if you try to do too much, grab that oncoming fist, cock back for a devastating hit, or try to force a throw. This will leave you vulnerable to even an unskilled counterattack.

Overactivity can harm a project just as surely as overwatering kills a plant. Being caught up in a frantic need for activity wastes energy and power, and depletes resources you will need when it is time to act decisively.

Ultimately, total positive action is the bottom line. A positive attitude is a good start, but is not enough by itself, because an attitude only determines how you initially approach something.

Work doesn't have to diminish your quality of life. The opposite is true. Personal growth can be easily accomplished through your life's work. If you control yourself, use leverage to increase your organizational power, and act courageously, you can become a black-belt leader.

Action Strategies: How to Become a Black-Belt Leader

- Focus on the art and the science of leadership. Start by studying the science. Become an expert at it.

- Dedicate yourself to training. Look for opportunities to sharpen your leadership skills. Practice what you have read, heard, and seen until new techniques become a part of you.

- Practice self-honesty. Know your true limitations (you don't necessarily have to admit these to others).

- Trust your feelings. Listen to and consider your inner voices.

- Develop your ability to train others. Through teaching, you can see what you truly know and in what areas you are unsure.

- Rotate jobs. Look for projects that will broaden your base of experience and provide an opportunity to test what you know.

- Broaden your perspective. Be a generalist. Practice thinking like professionals with training different from yours.

- Develop your supervisory antennae. Learn to detect an organization's climate from the moment you enter the building.

- Don't wait for things to break. Intervene before they fail.

- Do nothing which is of no use. Don't squander energy.

- Focus on results. Help others do the same.

- Remember that everything you do and don't do sets a precedent, as well as others' expectations. Be aware what messages you are really conveying to yourself and to those people who are affected by you—both directly and indirectly.

2

COURAGE: MOVING FROM FEAR TO HIGH PERFORMANCE

If you rely on strength, there's a limit to strength.
As you get older your strength naturally declines.
But there's no limit to how much control you can develop.

Chow Hung-Yuen

When we study the martial arts today, it is sometimes easy to forget that they grew out of violence and bloodshed. Martial arts masters were warriors, fighters who lived by the spear and sword. Death and combat were part of their everyday reality.

It is said that in Japan, those elite warriors who came to Zen monasteries to learn to overcome their fear of death became far more skillful warriors as a consequence. Although traditions and cultures have changed, I imagine that the taste of fear in men and women remains the same. Fear—in all its many forms—is still a component of daily life, and very much so in business "combat." It is often one of the biggest obstacles to high performance.

MASTERING FEAR

Tai chi chu'an master Andrew Lum says that fear comes from anticipation. In *Diary of the Way*, Mr. Lum is quoted as saying, "When you are in a dangerous situation you must never anticipate anything. What if

45

this happens? What if that happens? Nothing has started and you are getting all prepared—for nothing! You must have a calm mind. Anticipation creates fear."

> Mark out a path twelve inches wide on the floor and walk across it. No problem. Now lift this path two hundred feet in the air and walk across it. Your anticipation of falling may indeed make you fall. It is the same if two persons come to attack me. I do not say, "I have two persons in front of me; each one has two arms and two legs." In this way I have created eight problems. I have anticipated, and am drawing a negative conclusion that I have more of a chance of being hit. Here is a typical situation. A person walks up to me with a mad face and automatically I assume he is mad at me. Maybe he is mad at someone else and maybe he is not mad at all. Perhaps this is his natural expression, and with his tone of voice he is an entirely different person. If, before he says anything, I react to his mad face, I have already worsened the situation. I have met him negatively and with a bad attitude. This is the point: if you anticipate an attacker will hit with his right hand, you are not alert to his kick. Never assume. Your must be constantly aware.
> The fear caused by anticipation creates doubt and lessens judgment. But fear is not necessarily bad. In some ways fear can be looked upon as a good thing. If there is a little fear, one may be guided to the point of not doing. If you cannot walk a tightrope, fear guides you to the point of not trying it. Fear is part of a message to give a little fair warning. Even fear has positive value.

Does fear ever get in the way of performance? Without a doubt, but with the right attitude and training, you can make it an ally. Skilled leaders are those individuals who can harness the powers of heart and mind and find the courage to move toward the mission of their organization, particularly during trying times.

The martial artist must think, decide, and act under pressure. Walter Muryasz demonstrates how he defends himself in a frightening situation against four onrushing attackers. After one such demonstration, an onlooker approached Walter and asked why he wasn't afraid. "But I do feel fear," he replied. "I just don't let it paralyze me. In fact, the rush of feelings helps me move quickly." So he doesn't think of it as fear, but as energy that can be channeled into strong movement.

Leaders can use this same method when confronted by decision-making stress. There may be many things to fear—budget shortfalls or cuts, unpredictable markets, negative reactions by others to change, or the exposure of past mistakes. But don't allow fears of what might happen stop you in your tracks.

Sometimes fear comes from having to act and not knowing the right thing to do. Like Mr. Muryasz, instead of panicking, use your fear. It can motivate you to work harder and to prepare better. But also listen to it. The fear of negative consequences can encourage you to rethink or avoid making hasty decisions. In either case, the effect of fear can be positive, not negative and paralyzing.

THE POWER OF SELF-CONTROL

Imagine this: a much larger person strongly grasps you by both wrists. Are you trapped? Not if you think like an internal-style martial artist. You'll know that no one can trap you but yourself. Your fingers are free, you can still wriggle them. You can move your shoulders up and down. You can shift your feet and bend your knees. Only your wrists are trapped—not you. In fact, if you can train yourself simply to relax your wrists, not to resist from where you are held, you can bring your fingertips up to your head, just as if you were brushing your hair, while the attacker holds on helplessly. Either you control yourself or you give up control. But no one has the power to trap you without your allowing it. In fact, certain martial arts styles use this principle, in turn, to trap an opponent's hands. By crossing the attacker's wrists and adding the right force in a direction that makes her opponent instinctively resist, a martial arts expert can seemingly "lock" both opponent's hands with one of her own.

Martial arts adepts know they have to take charge of their own selves first because all power springs from self-control. They monitor when they are feeling out of control. At those times, they actively let go of the impulse to control others. A strong tactic is to unbalance your opponent. A jujitsu expert knows he has to be close to the opponent's center of gravity. He typically can't execute an effective throw at arm's length. The closer two bodies are, the greater the force they can exert on each other—it's the Gravitational Law.

In business, the closer you are *emotionally* to the "target" person or group, the greater your influence. A stranger may give me feedback about my style and, of course, I will listen. But although he stands a few feet away, he probably won't have as much influence with me as an old friend would, even if she resides three thousand miles away.

Emotional proximity equals power. And who is the person you are closest to, the person you can influence most easily? Yourself. That's why martial artists and expert managers focus first on controlling themselves. A little effort here is most useful.

Perhaps you know someone who doesn't focus on controlling himself. Nothing ever seems to go right for him. He's always complaining—employees won't do what they are told, upper-level management just doesn't understand. And he is too cynical to solicit managerial help. ("What do they know?" or "That's easy for them to say, they don't have to deal with all the jokers I work with.") He believes you have to force people to work and change. And in one way, he's right; employees don't work as productively for him as they would for other managers. The sad part is that he doesn't realize he is contributing to his own problems. To a certain extent, he is out of control.

Everyone has a need for control. When people feel out of control themselves, they attempt to force others, often in minor ways such as setting unnecessary dress codes, not allowing staff to place personal objects on desks, or insisting on rigid agenda-setting policies that prevent spontaneous meetings.

In trying to make others change outside one's sphere of influence—competitors, peers, customers, politicians, supervisors, employees, spouses, children—most people are ineffective and expend lots of effort without commensurate gain. And they feel helpless as a result. As psychologist Al Siebert said, the victim's theme song is "Wouldn't the world be a nicer place if everyone else would change?"

We all wish that everyone would change for our convenience, but they won't—at least not at our command. Even if we could succeed in changing others, it would not ultimately help us to be in control of ourselves. Controlling others wastes energy because it generates increased resistance.

So what can you do to *influence* others? First develop greater emotional closeness with them. This doesn't mean you have to see them socially or be their friend. A work relationship is fine if it is one in which you see and make an effort to understand their point of view. Make real contact and your ability to exert influence will soar.

When you are working outside your sphere of influence or feel overextended, momentarily retreat and watch calmly because another moment of opportunity will surely present itself.

But if you feel the desire to control others, watch out! It may be that you feel out of control of yourself. Be honest with yourself. Sure, there are times when we're filled with apprehension and must still project a self-assured image. But don't lie to yourself. Know your own real worries and fears.

The biggest problem of the stressed manager is the failure to acknowledge stress. Acknowledge your fears. And always admit what is obvious to others. People know when we are hesitant, so why bother denying it? ("No problem, everything is under control.") If you project mixed messages you run the risk of losing credibility. Instead, turn your fears into strengths. Before being confronted, calmly admit your concerns ("Yes, I am concerned about the staffing on this project") and consider how to best address it. This sets the stage for low-threat problem solving.

Most important of all, self-control protects you from ill-advised acts and words that once spoken can never be withdrawn. It's like getting kicked—the damage can last a long time. You may think the injury is forgotten, but those who suffer the impact of angry words may feel wounded for years.

A participant in a seminar told how she made this point to her son, after he had said something regrettable. First she asked him to pick up a claw hammer and nail and meet her in the backyard. "Please drive the nail into that tree," she said. He did it. "Now, turn the hammer around and pull the nail out of the tree." He did it. "Now, take the hole out of the tree."

You can fill the hole with wood putty, but the tree will never be the same. Similarly, apologies may soothe the sting of strong, angry words, but the relationship will probably be scarred. Haven't we all driven our share of holes into others' psyches and had holes—of various sizes— pounded into ours? If you would prefer not to keep changing companies and hometowns to survive, control yourself before anger gets the better of you. Stop yourself before you say or do something you can't take back.

HOW TO BECOME A WARRIOR, NOT A WORRIER

In an ancient martial arts story, a student admitted to his teacher that he was frequently beset by worries and fears. "You may not be able to stop the birds from flying over your head," the master told him, "but you surely can prevent them from building a nest in your hair."

Maybe you can't prevent worries or fears from surfacing, but don't feed them by dwelling on them. When fears do not spur you to positive action, let them go and they'll die a natural death. Exhaling slowly and deeply is a good way to set those cumbersome "birds" free.

Would-be leaders become tentative and less effective when they allow worry to consume them. They often become rigid, unable to take risks, and incapable of profiting from opportunity. Others will notice their self-doubt and question their leadership.

Rather than letting our worries back us into corners we should channel them into a spur for action. As physician Ken Paltrow tells people, "Be a warrior, not a worrier." First attack those tasks you fear. For instance, instead of being frozen by worrying about something like lack of job security, do something positive. Read a chapter from a professional career planning book or begin by writing out the pros and cons of a career change. Make an appointment with your boss to clarify your place in the organization or speak to a confidant to help you get your fear off your chest and get perspective.

Everyday leadership decisions may be as hard to face as major crises. But decisions must be made and actions taken, without any guarantee that they will be the correct ones. Does "decision fear" sometimes grip you? Here are a few ways around it:

- Consider whether the decision really needs to be made immediately. If not, wait.

- Analyze facts, then listen to your instincts. You can best pay attention to your instincts when relaxed, so use a favorite stress management technique to clear your mind and relax your body before making an important decision.

- When you have mixed feelings about a strategy, bring out these feelings for consideration. If you sense you have conflicting thoughts, but you can't bring them to the surface, take a walk and have a conversation with yourself to draw the feelings out. Carry a small tape recorder and use it to talk out the decision. Sometimes just speaking aloud can clarify your thoughts—it may not even be necessary to listen to your recordings.

- Remember that you may not have to make this decision totally on your own. Invite others to contribute. If you're stuck, consult a trusted mentor, supervisor, colleague, or consultant, and use them as a sounding board.

- Write out all sides of the issue. Then assign a weighted value to each advantage and disadvantage: Total the score of each side. You don't have to be bound by this device, but notice if your weighted decision corresponds to your overall feelings and thoughts.

- Bring two chairs face to face. Sit in one chair and argue for one side of the decision. Then switch chairs and argue for the other side. Continue until one side clearly dominates.

- Assign one side of the decision "heads," the other "tails." Flip a coin. Before looking at the coin, notice which side you hoped would come up. (It's not necessary to check the coin.)

Once you've made a decision, don't waste time and energy worrying about its result. Your decisions—and those of the greatest, wisest leaders—are sometimes wrong because of changing conditions, incomplete facts, or emotional involvement. Focus on making a high percentage of good decisions.

ATTITUDE CONTROL FOR A COURAGEOUS MIND

The right attitude is the foundation for a courageous mind. In 1981 I attended a martial arts retreat led by aikido master Mitsugi Saotome. After a dazzling display of self-defense tactics, Mr. Saotome laughingly dismissed his martial expertise. A winning attitude is really the key, he said. *"Before* the struggle, the victory is mine."

Ask any martial artist. Attitude makes the difference between whether a black belt's force "goes out" and breaks the brick or "pulls in" and damages the hand that delivers the blow.

Leaders frequently talk about attitude—how important a good one is. Superstars in a range of fields from sales to sports often credit their attitude as the reason for their success. But just what is attitude? Basically it is your initial approach to something. And a person's first position is crucial. Henry Ford probably said it best: "If you think you can or if you think you can't, you're probably right."

Aviation provides a useful analogy. A positive attitude means the nose of a plane is pointed up and it gains altitude; a negative one means the nose is pointed down. With a neutral attitude, the plane flies parallel to the ground, neither gaining nor losing height.

Frequently in the middle of a sports competition one team appears to become stronger, more coordinated and focused. People refer to this as "gaining momentum," which is nothing more than a change in attitude.

Your attitude doesn't do anything by itself; it simply determines the direction in which your effort is put. If you believe that you can't teach an old dog new tricks, then you probably won't see the value in spending the time to learn something new. (Just so you know, animal trainers disagree with this adage.) Fortunately, many people refuse to believe the "old dog" maxim. Take Grandma Moses as an example, a woman who became an accomplished and successful artist at an age when most people would hang up their brushes.

Ultimately everything starts as one sort of attitude or another. This book, for instance, was originally only a thought in the mind of the author. Studies show that attitudes are important in everything from health to performance to the ability to learn and adapt to change. But the next time you think of telling others they should change their attitudes, STOP. Think about how you can be more specific—*how* should they change their attitude? Also make sure you're providing a proper model. Are you able to change your own attitude?

Managers set their organization's tone because they're in the center of their department or company. Just as a pebble dropped in the middle of a lake spreads ripples throughout the water, a manager's attitude radiates directly to staff, and eventually through them to customers and the public. If you want good relations with clients and the public, you should treat your staff accordingly. In other words, managers determine the attitude that employees convey to customers.

Numerous studies reveal that the CEO's attitude is a prime determinant of employee morale. A manager participating in one of my seminars emphasized, "The leader must set the tone for the organization. If he is not enthusiastic about the goal, not honest on the job, and not positive, he will drag his staff down." In his excellent book *High Output Management*, Intel president Andrew Grove wrote of a depressed manager who, by trudging around the company with head hanging, spread depression throughout his department.

The ripple effect of attitude is like the child's game "pass it on." I hit Peter and Peter hits Sara and Sara hits William and so on. Not only that, but Peter hits Sara harder than he got hit and Sara hits William harder than she got hit. Without knowing it, many adults still play this game, only now stress and conflict are their punches. We feel pressured by our manager and then pass that pressure on to those we supervise. After bearing the brunt of a customer's ire, we often unload that same anger onto our coworkers.

Not only is there a ripple effect at work, but in our real lives the ripple also passes between work and home. Personal conflicts almost inevitably intrude on work. People beset with personal problems may not be completely disabled from doing their jobs, but they probably won't work in their top range of performance. Hopefully this lower range is still adequate. A leader who has unresolved personal problems will have an adverse effect on his staff, even though the underlying problems are in his personal life. Needless to say, this process also moves in the reverse direction—work problems can also intrude in our private lives. So be aware.

Fortunately, though, positive attitudes are just as contagious as negative ones. Remember to control your own attitude before others influence you negatively. In fact, a positive attitude can offset a generally negative environment. A forward-looking leader can help staff members overcome the depression caused by a poor industry-wide economy. Rather than accentuating the problem, the leader can both create and stimulate solutions. ("How might we use these times to our advantage?") A calm and confident attitude can influence others' willingness to change. Once we learn how to control our own attitudes, we can better help our colleagues and coworkers to do the same.

TECHNIQUES FOR ATTITUDE CONTROL

Attitude control, even for martial artists, requires effort. But this effort can pay large returns. Martial arts are a discipline. But discipline need not be grueling; it means *to learn*, not *to punish*. Discipline is an organized method, through self-control, for solving problems. We can achieve self-discipline by improving our self-control a little bit at a time. Soon these moments of control will lengthen, and as it does our power and effectiveness will grow.

A good place to start is with practicing single-mindedness. Martial arts training emphasizes not splitting our attention. Have you ever seen Japanese sword-fighting movies where one man single-handedly defeats scores of opponents? This is not just movie magic. In reality, even when several people attempt to launch a simultaneous attack, it is almost impossible for them to reach their target at precisely the same moment. From the martial arts expert's viewpoint, the attacks occur one at a time, albeit very quickly. The defender neutralized the attacker, then in the same flow (without pausing) moved to deal with the next threat.

Many people frequently experience the "attack" of multiple problems. It is important not to try and solve all problems at once. Deal with the most pressing of them first, find the best solution available, then move on to the next. If a solution is not at hand, move on and return to it later. Psychologist Kurt Lewin's studies have shown that people tend to remember tasks that have not been completed. Worrying about these wastes time and energy, so find a way to finish tasks—or set them aside.

The key to this approach is to be in the present, without distraction. Single-mindedness is critical in the martial arts. When sparring, there is only one thing in the universe—a fist, foot, or person coming at you. If your thoughts wander to anything else, you will surely get hit.

When in a position of leadership, focus totally on the activity in which you're engaged at that moment. Try not to let yourself be distracted by irrelevant thoughts and worries. Don't waste effort denying them or blocking them out. Just let them go for the moment.

If, for example, you're delivering an important presentation when you suddenly remember something you should have done earlier, remind yourself that there is nothing you can do about it during your talk. Right now all eyes are on you. This is an opportunity to influence many people and you need to put aside all irrelevant concerns. If you can develop this skill, you'll be able to give your all during crucial times.

In preparation for such a presentation, directly before the event take time to think about what might happen. Perhaps you have seen martial arts movies in which the protagonist mentally prepares himself the evening before the battle, readying himself to live courageously or to die with honor, but honestly facing all possibilities.

Martial artists also practice forms of exercises that are for mental and physical rehearsal. Going through the motions of fighting imaginary opponents helps to prepare them for the real thing, without the extra pressure that makes learning new methods more stressful. These forms also allow them to practice being in powerful positions. They enlist their imagination to program desired self-defense responses. They ask themselves, "What would happen if, as I walk to the corner, a large man leaped out of the shadows and tried to hit me on the head? What would I do? Sidestep to the outside, use this briefcase I am carrying to block at the elbow . . . ?"

In the same way, we as leaders can profitably rehearse our tasks. Before making a presentation or taking an interview, or anytime we have to perform under pressure, we can perform a kata to prepare ourselves. First rehearse the speech in your mind. Visualize yourself making that presentation, decisively handling the difficult questions calmly and confidently.

Most of us have adopted at least a few negative attitudes and thought patterns during our youths: I'm selfish, I can't draw a straight line, I'm small and afraid, I never could understand technical things, or I have two left feet. Even if once true, these judgments are now out of date—it is likely that you're much more experienced and more capable now. Allow your conscious mind to undo negative fears and thoughts residing in your subconscious.

Here is a powerful attitude-change technique used by martial artists to take command of themselves. They also use the period before sleep, when the subconscious is coming to the foreground, to focus on attitude control. During the day, the conscious mind is dominant over the subconscious; this position reverses during sleep. Just before going to sleep, look into your own eyes in a mirror. Don't stare or focus on how your hair has grayed or thinned, or how your skin has aged. Just look deeply into your own eyes as you would a friend's. If this becomes uncomfortable and you nervously look away, you are probably uncomfortable with yourself at that moment. Don't give in to fear and discomfort! Take a deep breath and look into your eyes again. If you need to, it is okay to look away, but return to eye contact as soon as possible.

Next, say aloud a self-programming message: I am becoming more confident with the new system; I am finding ways to use those changes beyond my control to my advantage; I am letting go of fear and job insecurity. Be sure your tone of voice has the qualities that reinforce your message—strength, relaxation, and calmness. Then go to sleep. In a matter of a few weeks, your attitude will gradually but steadily grow more positive. This works—but only if you practice it.

Reflection is another useful tool in adjusting attitude. Even in the midst of an attack, skilled martial artists take time, in the calm recesses of their minds, to reflect. *What is the nature of the attack? Who is the most dangerous opponent? Where are the safe places to position myself?*

Similarly, successful leaders take time, even when things are rapidly changing, to step back. Many spend a few minutes of each workday positively setting their attitude and mentally preparing for daily organizational concerns or ongoing work problems. Upon arriving at work, they go over what they are to accomplish that day and review their long-term goals.

Whenever you feel in need of a mental boost, it helps to breathe and silently talk to yourself. As you inhale, silently say to yourself in a calm tone of voice the first part of your suggestion—*I am becoming . . .*; finish the message while you exhale—*. . . more and more in control of myself each day.* A few repetitions work best. Your eyes may be either open or closed.

The power of this technique comes from combining breath and self-programming. It's also quite portable. You can use it to claim otherwise wasted moments whenever you are waiting, on hold, standing in line, stopped at a traffic signal, in the shower, or even when driving to or from work.

Successful martial artists have to learn to shift their attitudes. When in a strong grasp by an adversary, the best escape may be to yield flexibly to the point of attack. On the other hand, when the opponent is off balance, it's best to penetrate before he recovers, and get in that kick or throw.

Try this martial arts demonstration with someone. Stand to your partner's side. Ask her to stick her arm straight out in front, thumb up, and to take the "attitude" that her arm is made of string. Slowly and gently bend her arm. (One of your hands presses down on her elbow, the other up on her wrist.) Her arm will bend easily. Look at her expression and notice the demeanor.

Then ask her to shift attitudes and think of her arm as being made of wood. Her tension and facial expression will markedly change. Again, slowly bend her arm, *gradually and gently,* adding more force as needed. Wood is a material that resists, but will "break," suddenly bend in two, in resistance to a superior force.

Last, ask your partner to think of her arm as being made of steel. To help her form a properly steel-like attitude, remind her that, in the building trades, this metal is called an *elastic* material, its strength coming from its ability to give a little under force, not being too rigid. Again, attempt to bend your partner's arm. If she can sustain a "steel-like" attitude, her arm will become almost unbendable. Make sure to watch her face. Other people can readily see the change in someone's facial expression with each shift of mental state.

We are better able to shift our attitudes than we often realize. When the need arises, we can become string, steel, or wood. If we are trying to indicate to a superior that we really are giving in and will do it her way we become string. If we want to show a recalcitrant employee that we mean business, that the line stops here, we become wood. If we need to be friendly yet firm during important negotiations, we can become steel. People see our attitudes in our faces and treat us accordingly. Assuming the right attitude will reinforce what we want to communicate.

COURAGE TO RISK FAILURE

Martial artists emphasize that living courageously comes in part from conquering the fear of death. The *Hagakure*, a guide to warriorhood written in 1716 by Nabeshima Naoshige, says it clearly:

> If a samurai practices introspection and self-criticism all the time and
> if, in addition, he is disposed to give his life where and when the need
> arises, he will be perfect in all the martial arts and lead an exemplary
> life.

The true spirit of the Way can be summarized as follows: it is fitting always to protect life as long as life is appropriate. Through understanding the detachment of death, one can most fully appreciate the value of life.

So the samurai stressed that warriors must look death squarely in the eye. The only way to be truly alive and to live a full life is to accept the temporary nature of things—live honestly and without fear.

Believing in life after death, the samurai thought a good death would result in a good rebirth—as a warrior again. A "good" death came from being true to your values so that your death counted for something. The samurai felt that one who chose life inappropriately, out of fear, became spiritually dead.

This definitely applies to leadership. How? Some managers hang on at any cost—for a pension, biding time until retirement, or staying with an organization whose new direction is directly at odds with personal values. By doing so they are choosing life inappropriately; self-respect decreases when fear rules, and people who live in feaful desperation usually appear pitiful and weak to others and to themselves. They don't help the organization or themselves, and are no longer professionally alive.

But courageous leaders are willing to give up their organizational security at any time in order to say what needs to be considered, even if it might be unpopular. They will not be intimidated. They're not even afraid to recommend that their own positions be cut during a restructuring.

Clearly this is easier said than done. But courageous leaders know there is no job security in the conventional sense. The only real job security comes from knowing inside yourself that you can get another position and will survive.

Like samurai, deeply confident leaders are often blessed by good rebirths. Carol Maga is a true warrior and a black-belt leader. Her company asked her to head an organizational restructuring task force. She was the first to recommend that her position be eliminated. And it was.

People are impressed with this kind of courage, so I wasn't surprised that Carol was soon offered a more responsible managerial position within the same organization. In other cases, managers are reborn at new companies and find themselves stronger for the experience. At times a voluntary demotion also works out for the best. But accepting any demotion takes courage.

Samurai were told that if they wanted to come back from battle unharmed, they should give up thoughts of returning. The point is that the fear of death hinders the crucial survival skill of acting decisively. When you can no longer live with what you see to be the truth, be willing to let your job "die." Don't throw away your career; just give up the fear of job loss and do what you have to do. Ironically, you may end up being more respected for your courage.

This is not to say that leaving your position is necessarily the answer, but just know that you have the option to do so. Many upper-level managers privately admit that they believe they could not procure an equally good position were their job to evaporate. This kind of insecurity can lead to increased political "rear-covering" and lowered creativity.

Karen Nish is a divisional operations manager for the brokerage firm Smith Barney Shearson. She believes courage separates the up-and-comers from the pack. "I supervise several managers who have the potential to do a higher level divisional job. But some are so afraid of failing, of getting out of their little comfort zone. What's going to happen if they take the job and it doesn't work out? How would they be able to go backwards? If they are successful, will they feel pressure to continue to rise? When I was promoted to divisional manager I had the same concerns. I asked myself, 'Am I ready to change career paths and get out of the business if I fail?'"

Wise leaders know there will be a price to be paid when they enter a new situation. Whether that price lies in taking on increased responsibility, giving up the comfort of being immediately effective, having to learn new duties, renegotiating relationships with former peers or supervisors, or just plain risking failure, courage means knowing the dangers before entering the new battlefield. It means living with awareness, despite the risks.

Like the children's game "warmer-colder" ("You're getting warmer—now you're hot—you've found it"), seeming failures can be the means for homing in on the winning answers. IBM purportedly has a saying, "The faster you fail, the quicker you will succeed." Similarly, the best-seller *In Search of Excellence* exhorted managers to "Ready-Fire-Aim." In other words, sometimes you just have to try something and adjust until you're on target.

Just as we can feel generally healthy even when we have a sore throat, we can also continue to feel confident even in the face of outer "failure." Remember that today's failure may actually be the groundwork for tomorrow's success. If we try to learn to ski we'll see that all beginners fall frequently. It's embarrassing and perhaps painful. But learning to ski—or mastering anything new—means getting through this initial phase of discomfort. ("Am I making the right decisions?" "Do I look foolish?" "Should I have accepted this position?")

In 1980 I attended a week-long martial arts seminar at which the instructors were excellent. I had been a teaching black belt for years and was puffed up with youthful pride. But I was chagrined to discover that not only was I unable to do what the instructor was demonstrating—I had expected that—but I could not even understand his technique well enough to work on it. I was depressed for two days. A part of me tried to deny my discomfort. I told myself that this is different, that the instructors at the seminar were trained to attack differently. But the truth was that I wasn't progressing and I knew it.

It took me a few days to admit that I was uncomfortable, my pride shaken; I was a beginner again. But this was all right, I told myself. I could accept that fact and be comfortable inside, even though outwardly I was struggling and uncomfortable. Becoming comfortable with discomfort improved my outlook. More importantly, I spent the remaining four days of the conference soaking up knowledge and techniques that I have been able to build on to this day.

THE COURAGE TO BE INVISIBLE

There is a practical reason martial arts masters don't brag about their skills. If you don't broadcast ("I can break three boards with one kick"), the opponent is not forewarned. "Invisible" actions are difficult to counter or resist.

In this same way, invisible leaders can accomplish more. This means not giving in to the craving for recognition. Most people have this need, but much too often it gets in the way.

Craig Lewis is a long-term martial artist. As a consultant to international companies, Craig often finds himself mediating between strongly opposing camps—union and management, supervisors and staff, different departments. Relaxed, making strong contact with others, firmly grounded in his objectives, Craig is adept at listening for common concerns and then crafting mutually beneficial solutions. Neither Craig's words nor actions trumpet that he is a graduate of Harvard Law School, which might otherwise put undue attention on him and freeze others into a more formal conflict position. This is ethical, of course, in that Craig is not working as an attorney in these circumstances.

At times Shearson's Karen Nish is called upon to change procedures with branch managers she doesn't supervise. Karen's approach in such instances is to present a new operations picture in a way the branch manager can accept. Sometimes she will later hear the manager talking about the wonderful procedure *he* instituted. Part of Karen wants to say, "Wait a minute, this was my idea." But she doesn't, because she has found that by controlling her desire for recognition, she preserves rapport with her colleagues and, thus, ensures effectiveness for the future.

Ironically, not trying to gain recognition means we often win the greater prestige of being seen as a doer. Seeking approval usually doesn't pay off anyway because trying too hard to impress others makes us look desperate or weak; it can also divert us from taking difficult—and necessary—actions. Just as important, a "look-what-I-just-did" posture can be detrimental to team spirit. Instead, if you don't constantly have to call attention to your own accomplishments, you gain more actual respect with a group.

In *Further Up the Organization*, Robert Townsend quotes Lao-tzu:

As for the best leaders, the people do not notice their existence. The next best, the people honor and praise. The next, the people fear; and the next, the people hate. When the best leader's work is done, the people say, "We did this ourselves."

According to Steve Christie, Executive Director of the International Communications Association, managing a large association is a "back-of-the-scenes kind of job. The directors and officers are the outward face of the association. . . . The director is really the guiding force behind it and tries to make sure that the volunteers, board members, and staff proceed on the right course, are at the right place at the right time, saying the right thing."

In Chinese *beon tung soi* means "a half-full bucket," and refers to someone who knows a little about a subject but acts like an expert. A half-full bucket makes the most noise, Chow Hung-Yuen reminds his students.

Sharing the credit and the responsibility will eventually pay off in a more vigorous organization. Christie further says, "If people really sense the job they're doing is needed and their efforts are crucial to an activity, you get much more response and activity from them than if you just assign some silly nonsensical type of job."

Jim Guseman is a training specialist at Burlington Northern Santa Fe Railroad. Even as a unionized representative, Jim has been able to catalyze system-wide change at his company. In tandem with several managers, he has piloted programs at his division that have subsequently spread throughout the larger corporation. Although he has relatively little positional power, Jim has transformed his enthusiasm to try new things, tenacity, and reputation for results into corporate-wide influence and change.

THE COURAGE TO GIVE IT AWAY

Black-belt leaders are confident enough of their abilities to "give away their power." But while dividing up and allocating tasks would seem one of the easier jobs managers must perform, it rarely works out that way.

Even managers with good intentions often do more grumbling than delegating. They mean to spread the workload among subordinates, but typically wind up doing most of it themselves. And it is not that they don't do good work. It's just that any one of us is limited in what we can accomplish; It's hard for nondelegators to get everything done. They often wind up with employee morale problems as well.

Delegation is an issue of fear. First it can be the fear of things not being done "the right way," or more correctly, "their way." When we delegate a task, people rarely do it the way we would. They may do it better, they may do it worse, but undoubtedly they will do it differently. Underlying an "if-you-want-it-done-right-do-it-yourself" attitude can be discomfort with change or a mistrust of staff, or often insecurity in ourselves.

Concern with being shown up can be another underlying fear. What if I give you this project and you do it better than I could? You may become more acclaimed than I am, or you'll find that I don't know all the answers.

A third delegation fear has to do with issues of personal security. If I give up what I do best, what will I do then? Probably something new and uncomfortable (that may force me to change, adapt, and grow).

If we have problems delegating, it's essential to be honest about our own motivations. Look beyond surface mistrusts and discomfort to the deeper internal fears that flourish best in the dark. Confront them and weed them out if they're depriving you of the ability to delegate. Here are some tips for developing the courage to delegate:

- Choose the way of power, not the way of fear. When deciding between delegating a familiar task and one you don't know well, delegate what you know. By delegating the familiar, you can give subordinates expert advice, monitor their work, and learn new skills yourself. If you delegate unfamiliar tasks, it becomes the blind leading the blind.

- Think of delegating as helping people to grow—both those you're leading and yourself. Expert leaders usually report that helping their people to develop into accomplished, confident workers is a major personal benefit. If you don't have enough confidence in your staff to delegate, consider not managing them at all. In these competitive times, managing when you feel this way is like leading an uncertain army into battle. You're asking for disaster. Change something. Strengthen your staff or replace them. Or change jobs yourself.

• Give up the desire to be indispensable. No one truly is. Extra work and lowered staff morale are the price of seeming irreplaceable. It's not a good payoff.

THE COURAGE TO CREATE

Creating is forged by understanding both the underlying patterns and the uniqueness of every situation, and that it is all right to put forth ideas that are less than sterling. Being creative usually means freely coming up with many ideas, only a portion of which might be usable.

In *The Zen Way to the Martial Arts,* Taisen Deshimaru writes, "Life's problems are different for each of us and each of us needs a different way of solving them. Therefore, each of us has to create his own method. If you imitate, you'll be wrong. You have to create yourself."

Beginning martial artists generally don't create. Rather they are more than happy to mimic their instructor's moves. They practice defensive reactions to specific attacks from set angles—a straight thrust to the stomach, a round kick to the ear, a cross-hand grab. But this is not yet true martial artistry. In real life, situations are uncontrolled and attacks do not follow classic models. The straight stomach punch may veer into a hook, the round kick can slip down to the neck, or the grab can be combined with an elbow strike. High-level skill entails developing new movements as called for by the nature of the attack and the layout of the room, actually changing the defense in midair to something that may never have been done before.

Almost all managers say creativity is important, but in my experience few practice it. They allow fear to block them. Obviously, in the middle of an attack or crisis, it can be frightening to create a technique or to try something new that may not work. We could lose life or limb. But in reality we may encounter an attack for which we know no defense. Pretending this attack is similar to one we've experienced may not protect us. But if we can't create a solution, we will die just the same.

Creating means finding a different way to do something. One software development manager described his role of developing technology as "creating reality." You have to be unwilling to settle too quickly, to get too comfortable, or always to agree with the status quo. This can be risky, especially if you're not independent by nature. But keep in mind what one wise person said: "If two people in the same organization always agree, one of them is unnecessary." If you don't create, you may be the one to go.

Creativity, of course, is not an excuse for blind rebelliousness, just as honesty is not a rationale for insensitivity. Someone who disagrees for disagreement's sake is not being creative. This kind of reflexive response usually cloaks the fear of not being heard, or of being seen as weak or passive.

Mentor Graphics senior manager Ron Swingen says, "I think creativity comes once I've chosen to do something different. The rebel aspect might get me on the course. But once I'm there, now what am I going to do? I've pushed off or I've opted out, but that was only a beginning. Now, from here on, I have to do something—I've got to be able to swim—or learn fast."

The courage to create means being willing to risk ostracism or rejection; it means not accepting any problem as unsolvable and never being satisfied with mediocre results.

A second fear that kills creativity is the concern of looking foolish. Ask anyone who creates for a living—artist, software developer, or organizational designer—they'll tell you, "I do have many good ideas. But what you don't see are the countless terrible ones I throw away."

Creating means being willing to fail. Ultimately, volume is the key to developing a few good ideas: come up with many ideas, sort through them, then focus on those with promise. Quite often initially mediocre ideas are the stepping-stones to great ones.

Don't be waylaid by the temptation to find an easy answer, one that has been successful for others and will seemingly involve no risk. ("General Electric does it this way—you should too." "Have a difficult employee? Just send him to our seminar; we'll straighten him out." "Everyone needs to read this book and manage exactly like the authors say.") But these solutions are unlikely to help unless they are creatively adapted to your situation.

Just as with self-defense skills, the courage to create ultimately comes from practice. But creating without a strong understanding of the fundamentals usually leads to impractical plans that don't work in real-life situations. It takes time and experience to learn how to realistically test new techniques. Change is possible, but rarely easy. A leader may markedly increase her effectiveness—but not effortlessly, not entirely smoothly, and only with persistence.

So you need to observe critically, listen to what others have to say, and actively search for new ideas. Then ask yourself which approach would work best in your situation. Will participative management techniques really apply to your organizational culture? Can you adapt them into some different but workable form?

People may rebel if we try to implement the Japanese practice of starting the workday by formally reciting the company motto. But we can adapt its underlying principle by assembling our staff in the morning for a few minutes to discuss the purpose of this day's work or to positively set their attitude and plan of action. For example, United Parcel Service drivers meet for a few minutes at the beginning of each shift to discuss potential safety hazards and other concerns. These meetings have helped to greatly reduce accidents. Another option is to offer prework physical stretching exercises for those who are interested.

It is important to have the courage to discover your own solutions. Here are some tips for creativity:

- Think of yourself as an artist creating your own organization and career as though it were a sculpture. Where should your organization be reshaped? What tools do you have to do this? Ask what limitations for your organizational culture go with working in this medium.

- Practice simple relaxation techniques each day. Letting go stimulates creativity.

- Develop brainstorming muscles. Create first, and evaluate second. List—without criticizing—possible solutions to problems, both by yourself and in groups. Practice turning off critical thinking while brainstorming.

- Write down six qualities unique to your organization, characteristics differentiating it from other companies in your field. (For example, the fact that you have many long-term employees; or that your staff is highly family-oriented or enthusiastic about sports; or that you have many new managers.) Then think of ways that employee programs can address these.

- Meditate as martial artists do to tune in to your intuition. Before making any big decision, STOP! Take some time alone, relax, and listen to your inner voice. Do you have any inclinations toward or against the pending decision? Whether you choose to follow your inner hunch or disregard it, take note of the results of the decision. How accurate are your inner feelings? How well do you listen to yourself? At first this voice will speak faintly. Listening is a skill you can learn.

- Read a practical book on creativity. (See Roger von Oech's *A Whack on the Side of the Head* or George Prince's *The Practice of Creativity*.) Select one technique out of those suggested and practice it three times each week.

- Using outside hobbies or skills as metaphors, think of other ways to develop your art of leadership and creativity. How can gardening principles be applied to helping *people* grow? Can you use skiing methods to help you stay on balance as you move through organizational "moguls"? Can golf concentration techniques help you perform when you are about to close a deal?

The martial arts teach that true power can only spring from within. We need to inspect ourselves as we would a weapon and assess our flaws and virtues. Ultimately only we can correct our weaknesses and polish our strengths. We have the greatest effect when we move within our sphere of influence, harnessing the energy of a positive attitude and the energy from our commitment to advance our professional strengths and that of our organizations.

Developing Courage: Techniques for Action

- Practice something out of your range of comfort. Take note of your discomfort, but don't give up. This new activity can be as simple as playing a sport with your opposite hand or changing the order in which you dress—or something more complex—learning to program a computer, or to speak before a large group.

- Take reasonable risks. Be willing to stand by your opinions, but be equally able to admit when you have steered far off course. Have the courage to look awkward in public. Try new things and smile at yourself if you feel slightly foolish. Be willing to say, "I don't understand."

- Monitor your behavior closely when you are afraid, threatened, or angry. Catch yourself before you lose control of what you say or do.

- Mentally consider giving up job security; don't allow the fear of losing your job to ruin your ability to take reasonable risks.

- Practice attitude control every day, even when things are going smoothly.

- Spread recognition to staff members. Silently congratulate yourself on the job you are doing, even when others get credit. Notice if this approach results in more vigorous staff commitment and efforts.

- Think differently and try something new. Apply the unknown to what you know. Think critically and act creatively.

3

USING LEVERAGE TO BOOST YOUR STRENGTH

Don Angier, master of shidare yanagi-ryu, performs an impressive demonstration. He asks a black belt to rush him and although he is a man of small stature, Angier easily repels the much larger attacker with one small, easy punch. There's no wind-up, and he apparently exerts no effort. How does he do this?

Angier explains, "You don't need to pull back your fist to punch forward. And don't tense up unnecessarily. Just relax and let your power flow into your opponent." This is the principle of leverage: using minimal force for maximum gain. A jujitsu practitioner does not have to be big to get the job done. He knows that a small focused force can produce impressive results. Leaders can also employ this principle.

Leaders should use both mental and physical leverage. The first step in this is establishing a presence. Rightly or not, others judge our confidence and competence by how balanced, relaxed, and calm we appear. The majority of leaders have a strong presence or charisma. They exude confidence, move with power and grace. Rarely flustered, they seem perpetually calm and balanced.

How we deal with the physical world is a test. If we don't know how to use our bodies efficiently to lift a chair or open a heavy door, how can we expect to move an organization? Size or physical strength is not the issue. It's knowing how to use our energy—mentally and physically—that gives us a strong demeanor. There are tangible martial arts methods to help us develop a strong presence.

DEVELOPING PHYSICAL LEVERAGE

Martial arts adepts know that a strong body engenders a clear mind. Like beginning martial artists, we have to learn how to control our balance, posture, and breathing.

Moving with Balance

Balance is an interesting word, refering both a mental and physical state. A weak person may be said to be a pushover, easily swayed, or unstable. Think of the implications of "mentally unbalanced."

In a martial arts demonstration of the center of balance, one person lies on his back and an *obi* (sash) is slipped underneath him just below the navel. Two people take each end of the belt and lift him by it. He balances, perfectly suspended. When the obi is positioned a little off center, he no longer balances. Extra strength is needed to control his weight.

A small shift at the center of gravity can also have a major effect on our balance. This is an important principle for physical well-being. Without physical balance, it is difficult to achieve relaxation or to maintain energy reserves. The less balanced we are, the more muscle tension we need to keep from falling over. Conversely, being balanced takes less energy, employing natural posture to keep you upright against the force of gravity. So the more balanced we are, the lower our baseline tension level and the more energy we'll have to direct toward our work. Martial artists call this life energy *ki* (Japanese and Korean) or *chi* (Chinese), as in the *ki* in hapkido or aikido, or the *chi* in tai chi ch'uan.

The easiest way to develop good balance is through the *hara*, our center of gravity. Located inside our lower abdomens, the hara literally means "life center." Find the hara by mentally relaxing your lower abdomen, your inner core. When you sit or stand, feel the pull of gravity, the weight of your upper body falling through your lower abdomen, down through your legs and into the ground. When angry or upset, let your weight settle through the hara. Feel the hara open as if empty. Don't tighten up your lower abdomen; this will make you feel uptight. Instead, let it relax.

Also, feel your weight open hara as you perform normal tasks. Let this feeling remain in the background, in the same way that you can speak in a meeting and still read others' reactions without being distracted from your talk.

Motion generated from the center of gravity is always balanced and powerful. Feel any movement—walking, shaking hands, writing—as generated from the hara, in the same way a motor drives a machine's extensor arms and legs. When you point your fingers, feel them being lifted by the hips, like a winch smoothly hoisting a bar. This economy of motion will leave you with more available energy. In addition, you will feel and appear much calmer. Or as Michel Random wrote in *The Martial Arts*, "Concentration on the hara creates a stable and serene strength."

Posture Power

All martial arts emphasize taking appropriate stances and postures. Our posture has many effects on our ability to control ourselves and apply our physical and mental powers to the world around us. One mature martial artist put it this way: "Whenever one of those guys sizes me up, thinking he can intimidate me, I *move*. I don't know quite how to say it, but I can control the situation, pretty much get what I want, by how I stand."

Leverage means "realizing a sizeable return from expending a small amount of effort." By controlling our posture we direct our power more efficiently, and so have greater mastery over ourselves.

Try not to think of posture as a static position. In fact, posture is an ever changing state, a sort of frame-by-frame motion picture that's more than just sitting upright or standing straight. Strong posture has many wide-ranging effects.

- *Mental alertness.* Try this. Exaggerate a slumped position. (It doesn't matter if you collapse back into a chair, slump over a desk, or stand with shoulders overly rounded.) Notice how alert you are. Are you more or less prone to daydream? Most people report they become far less alert when slumping. Breathing is shallower because the weight of the upper body collapses onto the diaphragm, the muscle responsible for deep breathing. You can feel this tension in the diaphragm by placing your hands just below the rib cage as you slump. Shallow breathing reduces the oxygen supply to the cells and the first organ affected by oxygen deprivation is the brain. So if you slump while trying to make an important decision or working out the nuances of a vital business relationship, your brain may be working at only half power. As a result, your mind can drift and you aren't as able to concentrate.

When you want to feel more alert or you need your full mental power before making important decisions, align your posture and take a few deep breaths into your center. This clears the mind and often allows you to consider other options that you couldn't previously see with your brain in an oxygen-deprived state.

- *Energy/vitality level.* Try slumping again, but this time notice your level of physical energy. Is it higher, lower, or the same as a few moments ago? Cells create energy through a process called oxidation; less oxygen means less energy created. Posture control is a relatively simple method of raising your energy level.

- *Efficiency.* Posture control means moving efficiently, in balance and with a minimum of wasted motion. This not only conserves your energy, but helps prevent strains and pulled muscles that result from overuse or overextension. Properly positioning yourself, with good posture, near your work and telephone will eliminate overextending that can gradually wear you down.

- *Communication.* Your posture communicates nonverbal cues to other people and to yourself. For example, we picture depressed or unconfident people as slumped, and rigid or anxious people as being stiff.

What posture do you associate with a powerful martial artist? His back is probably straight and strong without being rigid. Think of the posture of the most powerful people you know. How many of them are slumped or overly tight? Most I've met convey a sense of presence. They seem relaxed, strong, and in control. How much of their demeanor do we read from their posture? Posture control enhances our presence, so that we actually seem bigger and more powerful.

Besides communicating to others, our posture also affects how we feel. If we feel hopeless or trapped with no way out, we may be slumping, which makes us less alert mentally, and less able to do something to rescue ourselves. Adopting the right posture puts us in an action mode that can lead to effective performance. Brainstorming and decision making will improve markedly when we adopt an alert posture.

Hindrances to Good Posture

With all these benefits—mental alertness, increased energy, greater physical efficiency, and the ability to communicate a positive presence—why don't all people adopt strong, effective posture? They may have problems that prevent good posture:

- Poor self-image shows itself in weak, collapsed posture.

- Poor physical conditioning may be reflected by stiffness or rounded shoulders.

- Poor movement habits, such as bending with locked knees, or standing at an uncomfortable distance when moving objects, can make people physically awkward—and injury prone.

- Past injuries, such as a broken or sprained back, may make a relaxed, strong posture difficult to maintain.

- Clothing can shift a person's weight or restrict natural, relaxed movement. Examples are high heels and tight waistbands, jackets, skirts, or pants.

Elements of Posture

For the first two years I studied *kenjitsu*, my sword instructor had me do only one movement. He tested my postural strength with small pushes from different directions and observed closely. He insisted that the correct posture should be a building block to more advanced, powerful movements. As boring as this study was, he was right. My sense of power increased until it spilled over into my other movements in the unarmed arts.

Posture can be broken down into eight elements that describe how the joints align and force is transferred within the body. The body is a system in which each affects all the others.

1. Ankles and feet. Weight should fall through the arches, not over the heels or toes. Walking on the heels, as many people do, reduces physical balance and usable strength. This can lead to feelings of being weak, intimidated, and easily controlled. Check the wear patterns on your shoes. Do the corners of the heels wear faster than the mid-sole? If so consider a small adjustment. Lean forward slightly until your weight falls through the arches. Standing more upright may feel like falling forward, by comparison to your old posture. If you do feel you're falling, ask a friend to press you forward *lightly*. If your posture is right, you will know it—your balance will be strong.

Here's a good way to properly place your weight over your arches. Lift your heels off the ground by standing on your toes and the balls of your feet. Then, bending the knees, let your feet come down flat. Bring your weight straight down; make sure not to drift back to your heels. This exercise usually places weight correctly.

You can even balance over the arches when wearing high heels. With these shoes you are, in effect, perpetually walking on a downhill slope. You can be balanced going downhill, but not by walking in the same way as you would on level ground. Adjust your balance accordingly, until your weight falls over the arches. Don't allow your shoes to undermine your balance.

On the other hand, if you walk by falling onto your toes, correct your balance by "sitting back" on the arches. Again, check shoe wear to tell if you walk on your toes. Does the front of the sole wear faster than the heels? Those who walk on their toes usually find themselves stumbling frequently.

2. Knees. Knees are physiological shock absorbers. Locking your knees reduces their springlike effectiveness, making it more likely that force will be transferred to the upper body. If someone walks or jumps with locked knees, the impact moves to the head and neck. Knees are also important to body balance. Standing or walking with locked knees is like being on stilts.

Moreover, tension in the knees, as in any joint, spreads upward. So locked knees often result in lower back tension. Try standing and placing your hands on your lower back muscles. As you slowly lock your knees, you'll feel the lower back tighten.

For best balance, control, and relaxation, put a little spring in your knees, and avoid standing or walking with knees locked. When waiting in line, practice unlocking by rhythmically, slowly, and imperceptibly shifting your weight from foot to foot, with your knees slightly flexed.

3. Hips. Too much hip cant (being swayback) adds to lower back tension. While standing, tuck the hips slightly under you, as if you were just beginning to sit down.

4. Spine. The shape of the spine affects your body balance. Perhaps more importantly, it strongly influences your emotional state.

There are three basic spinal shapes—C-shaped (slumped), I-shaped (rigid), and S-shaped (natural). If you have ever looked at a skeleton or an anatomy chart, you can probably visualize the natural, slightly flattened S-curve of the spine.

As mentioned above, a slumping, C-shaped spine reduces oxygen intake, thus lowering mental alertness and physical energy. Slumping is not, as some people believe, a relaxed posture, but creates a level of tension in the upper back and neck to which many people become accustomed. To check this, place your hands on the muscles along the neck, then gradually slump in your chair, and notice how muscular tension in the neck increases.

But expert martial artists believe anything can be turned to their advantage. There is even a time when slumping is useful. When your mind is racing and you can't shut it off—*What am I going to do about that contract? Will the merger go through? Should I start looking for another position?*—slumping slows things down temporarily. You'll only need a little such collapsing to decrease mental alertness and slow thought, so be careful not to go overboard. Action is the bottom line. Slow things down only to the point that they are manageable. Then, adopt an S-shaped posture, so that you are better able to make a plan that will change things for the better. Sit up naturally. Lean forward, move your hips back so they are supported by the chair. Take a deep breath and relax, without collapsing. You'll be more alert and ready for crucial decisions.

With I-shaped posture, weight falls over the heels, and deep breathing is difficult. A rigid, inflexible body loses the ability to absorb the impact of walking and other normal movements—and results in increased tension, especially in the neck and shoulders. In the same way that a heavy plank standing on end can be easily toppled, such rigidity makes you a pushover for outside forces.

In general, a natural S-shaped posture is the most relaxed and the best for body balance; it also promotes clear thinking and strong inter-personal communication. To bring yourself to S-shaped posture while sitting, reach behind your chair and grasp one wrist with the opposite hand. You can't easily slump in this position. This technique is suitable for staff meetings. Not only can you breathe deeply, you will convey confidence as well.

If you become fatigued when sitting for long periods, support your lower back in a nonslumped position with a small throw pillow. Not only will the pillow reduce back pain and fatigue, it will also help you deepen your breathing and maintain an emotionally and mentally pow-erful position.

5. Neck and head. The neck is a column that supports the head (it weighs about the same as a bowling ball). Head position has great influence on our balance and power.

In martial combat, grabbing the front of an opponent's hair may pull some out, as well as anger him, but won't efficiently affect his balance. Pulling the hair on the back of the skull has a similar result. But you can easily take him off balance by lightly grabbing his hair at the crown.

For maximum balance and strength, as well as minimum neck ten-sion, the crown should be the highest part of the head. This works both in walking and sitting. To get this feeling, pull your hair up at the crown. (If you don't have enough hair on the crown, pretend you do.) Place your hands on the neck muscles while you slowly move your head up and down. Most people find the crown-high position causes the least ten-sion. Relax while keeping this crown-high position. In other words, stand proud and tall. Walk with your head held high, but don't put your nose in the air.

6. Shoulders. Keep the shoulders relaxed and down. Don't hold them up. Carrying the shoulders high has several negative effects. It makes deep breathing very difficult. (Try raising your shoulders and notice what happens to your breathing.) It increases neck/head tension. It raises your center of gravity and tends to make the knees lock. (Try it.

Raise your shoulders while standing. Watch what happens to your knees.)

When people get angry, their shoulders often rise, which, in turn, makes them feel and appear out of control. They appear "uptight." Anger can be a powerful tool when it signals others that we are serious and expect immediate action. But don't let anger make you lose control. When we are angry, we can still remain relaxed by letting our shoulders stay down. Just exhale and roll them back and down if they begin to inch up.

7. Elbows. When our arms hang to our sides they have a natural bow. It's unnatural to lock them. When we overstraighten our elbows our arms become a lever against ourselves, slightly raising the shoulders. The elbow is also more vulnerable to injury in the hyperextended position. Typically, people lock their elbows when they overreach.

8. Hands. How we use our fingers makes a big difference in our strength and physical balance. A jujitsu grasp emphasizes the strength in the thumb and last two fingers (the ring and little fingers). These fingers are connected to long, strong muscles that, in turn, indirectly connect to the center of gravity in the hips. Use your entire hand, but when you want increased strength and control, grab and hold by emphasizing these fingers.

Controlling these eight postural elements may seem like a tall order, but because everything is connected, a small effort at shaping the spine will improve our control over all the other elements.

Breathing: Stoking the Inner Fire

Breathing ignites our chi or energy level and is the gateway to subconscious mastery. Because every martial art focuses on developing both the body and the mind, breath control is an important part of martial arts training.

Breathing is the only essential bodily function that can be controlled both consciously and unconsciously. When our attention is not on our breathing, we keep breathing just the same. Focus on it consciously, and we can adjust our breath.

In order to strengthen your power, practice one of these breath-control techniques.

• *Take natural, full breaths.* Always inhale through the nose. First fill your hips, then let the rib cage expand, and finally fill into the chest below the shoulders, so the collarbone rises.

Exhale in the reverse order. As air leaves, let the shoulders lower, the rib cage deflate, and finally the abdomen contract. If you are breathing naturally, your shoulders will actually rise and fall slightly. This is a good exercise to do before sleep; eventually it becomes part of your normal unconscious breathing pattern.

• *Exhale fully when you feel disheartened or intimidated.* Have you ever seen samurai movies in which two swordsmen duel? Both wait and watch. Suddenly, there is a flurry of powerful action; only the victor walks away. In fighting of this sort, skilled swordsmen watch their opponent's breathing. They know that actions taken while inhaling are weaker and less positive. When they see the opponent inhale, they attack. So to limit their vulnerability, they practice a "fighting breath"— long exhalations with imperceptibly quick, yet full inhalations.

During crucial times, when you feel under the gun, control your breathing and focus on exhaling. Make your exhalations long and even. Breathe in normally. Naturally, if you exhale fully, a partial vacuum is formed in your torso that makes it easier to inhale fully. Breathing this way will help you to overcome fear and to act with all your strength.

• *Use sound to monitor your breath.* When you exhale, make a "huuuh" sound from deep in your abdomen (not shallowly forced from your throat). Monitor the sound you make—is it short and choppy? Practice making the sound of your breathing long, smooth, and even.

• *Raise your energy level with* misogi *(deep cleansing breath).* When you exhale, make sure to expel all the air out from your diaphragm, ribs, and between your shoulders. On inhaling, fill your entire body cavity, especially the hara, ribs, and shoulders.

• *Breathe to reduce physical or emotional pain.* Tae kwon do practitioners learn to do this when they receive a solid blow during sparring. Place the tip of your tongue on the roof of your mouth, at the front of the palate. Exhale sharply from the abdomen. As the pain subsides, gradually slow down your breathing and continue to let it emanate from the lower abdomen.

Maximizing Physical Leverage

If you wish to increase your understanding of leverage, use your body during the day to explore the principle. Practice how to open a heavy door with minimal effort. Discover precisely where to push and how to get maximum strength from your body. (Hints: Touch the door with the outside edge of your hands and sidestep to push, rather than falling into it.)

Some other ways to increase physical leverage are these:

- *Keep your head, shoulders, and knees pointed in the same direction.* Martial artists know this is generally the strongest body position when you are delivering a blow or executing a throw.

  If you want your presence to be strongly felt, don't swivel your head to talk. Instead, turn completely. You can even move your chair around to face the other person. This may seem like some effort, but you will feel and be seen as stronger and more capable. Conversely, if you purposely wish to weaken your impact (to appear less threatening or more distant from the other person), don't turn completely to converse—point your knees away.

- *Let your eyes lead.* When a martial artist throws his opponent, his eyes look in the direction of the throw. Looking back while moving forward considerably weakens the movement. This works mentally as well. When you're going to execute any strong action or introduce a new program, look ahead. Don't allow yourself to dwell on past movements or mistakes.

- *Use counter motions.* As you walk, notice which arm swings forward with which leg. In balanced walking the arms and legs are in opposition: the left arm naturally moves with the right foot and the right arm with the left foot. These counter motions keep you balanced from side to side.

- *Avoid static postures.* Holding rigid poses loads extra forces on your body. Moreover, others may see you as inflexible (or change-resistant).

- *Break up repetition.* Machines are designed for repetition, but people thrive on variation. For instance, if you do a lot of phone work, intersperse personal meetings and paperwork into your day.

MENTAL LEVERAGE

In *Zen in the Art of Archery,* kyudo master Awa told student Eugen Herrigel, "To shoot well, you must forget your physical strength and shoot only with your strength of mind." Of course, martial artists first train their bodies, but they know that a strong mind is the key to high-level accomplishment under pressure.

"Act as if the goal was [sic] infinity," Awa also taught. "A good bowman shoots farther with a bow of medium power than a soulless bowman with the most powerful bow. The result is not due to the bow but to the presence of mind, to the vitality and the state of alertness with which you shoot."

In the martial arts there is an expression that describes levels of expertise: "Big circle, little circle, no circle." The beginner makes large inefficient motions, "big circles." He broadly copies an effective image and toils laboriously, but with poor results.

The advanced student moves in "little circles." She has learned to trim away unnecessary actions; her movements are crisp, focused, and effective.

Oh, but the Master! He moves in "no circles." Barely seeming to shift, he seems always to be in the best position, at the right time, effortlessly. Although he is older and less energetic than the novice, the Master easily dominates the encounter.

Effectiveness is a product of energy (time and effort expended) and efficiency. As the martial artist ages, he loses—as we all do—the edge of energy and naturally becomes slower. But the expert more than makes up for this by moving in smaller circles. Rather than jumping two feet away from an oncoming punch, he "slips" it by two centimeters. Many martial artists have reported that they began to better understand their art only when they could no longer rely on youthful speed and strength.

Small motions are faster, concentrating rather than wasting power. Bruce Lee, a relatively small man, developed a "One Inch Punch" that, without wind-up, could send much larger opponents reeling.

Like the martial arts expert, we, too, can use natural laws, physics, and human forces to increase our power and effectiveness as leaders.

High- and Low-Leverage Activities

Most of us have seen a karate expert break bricks, wood, or ice as part of a martial arts demonstration. All of his body weight is focused on a small area. If well controlled, this concentration of force is sufficient to shatter hard materials without causing harm to the martial artist.

In much the same way, concentration of our energy and force is useful in resolving problems at work. It's easy to become sidetracked in the daily press of meetings, reports, and contacts. We may be deluded into thinking that our job is defined by these activities. But as Intel chairman Andrew Grove contends, "activity is not output."

Managers who believe their role is only to hold meetings, supervise staff, discipline, hire, and fire—in short, to fulfill all the traditional organizational responsibilities—are missing the point. The true job of any leader is to make sure his unit produces the necessary product or service that moves the organization toward its mission; it is not merely his daily activities or what he *personally* does. This applies to a multinational corporation, a division, or simply to a small group of people he supervises.

In *High Output Management*, Grove notes three ways to elicit the most productivity from what you do.

- *Influence one person over a long period of time.* Examples include teaching a technique to someone *when they really need it,* giving motivating performance appraisals, promoting, or delegating wisely.

- *Influence many people simultaneously.* Hold carefully prepared meetings or training sessions. Communicate via memo, videotape, or e-mail. Enlist the natural grapevine to spread information and deputize people to become strong committee members or peer trainers.

- *Influence many people over a long period of time.* Nipping problems in the bud, doing necessary research and strategic planning, hiring, making timely decisions, assigning a new supervisor—all qualify.

Don't take any of these ordinary activities lightly. Each can increase the returns on your efforts. But using inappropriate leverage can also have negative effects. It is possible to:

- *Create negative conflict.* By punishing or dominating others in front of their peers, you can create long-term enemies or a group of detractors.

- *De-motivate someone.* Name-calling, perfunctory performance reviews, giving new employees sink-or-swim orientations, meddling, bailing someone out of a needed learning opportunity, failing to recognize extra effort, and insincerely delegating tasks can demoralize someone or significantly reduce motivation.

- *Squander people's time.* By being unprepared for meetings or arranging useless training you run the risk of alienating those with whom you work.

- *Adversely affect many people for a long time.* This may be the result of spreading a negative attitude, planning poorly, conducting inadequate market research, avoiding decisions, or any other action that seriously jeopardizes organizational survival.

To become a more effective leader, concentrate on positive, high-leverage activities that use measured force, at the critical moment, and in the precise location, to move toward the desired direction.

Measured force. People often apply far more force than is required—they use cannons to kill flies. The master knows not to hard-block an incoming punch two feet away; deflecting it a safe two inches away is enough. Using too much force not only wastes effort, it is also dangerous. A trained opponent can counteract an overly forceful block by spinning around the contact point to deliver a devastating kick or strike.

Similarly, too much force in managing may provoke resistance or counterattack.

William Burroughs's essay, "The Discipline of D. E." (in his book, *The Exterminator*), is based upon the principle of measured force. His main character discovered D.E., Do Easy. "D.E. simply means doing everything you do in the easiest and most relaxed manner you can achieve at the time you do it. You can start right now, moving books, sorting papers. Consider the weight of an object. Consider its shape and texture and function and exactly where it belongs. Use the amount of force necessary to get the object from here to there. Don't fumble, jerk, or grab an object."

Burroughs has suggestions for training yourself in the art of D.E.: "Now someone will say . . . 'But if I have to *think* about every move I make' . . . You only have to think and break down movement into a series of still pictures to be studied and corrected because you have not found the easy way. Once you find the easy way, you don't have to think about it. It will almost do itself." Burroughs is right: Practice changes default habits.

D.E. is the way chosen by internal martial artists and also has strong leadership applications. Remember Lao-tzu's recommendations for leading "invisibly." Direct as lightly as you possibly can, not with a heavy hand. You don't have to and can't do everything yourself. Although it's easy to become overwhelmed trying. So instead of taking everything on yourself, encourage your people to generate creative solutions. If their ideas are not helpful now, they may be later. Enthusiastic, bright people can adapt inappropriate ideas into useful ones.

Using of measured force has many benefits: you become a model for those you lead in how to apply effort wisely, you guard against wasting energy and learn to keep something in reserve for the unexpected, and you reduce the likelihood of conflicts caused by "pushing too hard."

At the critical moment. In the martial arts, as in leadership, timing is crucial. One strike when an opponent's guard is down is much more effective than repeated attempts at a well-guarded person. For the leader, this means early intervention is usually the most effective. Unfortunately, some managers I know don't seem to understand the principle of "the critical moment."

A hospital administrator, newly appointed to his position, assigned forty-five department managers to various task forces. These ad hoc groups were asked to make specific recommendations that would help the hospital survive in a highly competitive environment.

Each of the nine task forces worked hard for four months, then presented their reports. After this there was a vacuum in which the administrator neither acknowledged nor reacted to the recommendations. Finally after seven months he issued a general "thank-you-for-your-work-on-the-committee" memorandum. This was too little, too late. By this time, the managers' morale was low. They already felt that it wasn't worth putting time into this administrator's project since he appeared to disregard their efforts. As a result, the administrator's credibility plummeted.

The best thanks come when people are receptive and interested, not when they are disenchanted or their guard is up.

In the precise location. Martial artists aim for precision, knowing that "close" may not be enough. So they study pressure points to probe and specific target areas where they can aim the attack.

Similarly, when A-dec's Phil Westover was looking for ways to institute a new process, he looked for areas where it would do the most good. After extensive study, Phil was convinced that motion analysis techniques could boost productivity in dental chair assembly. (Phil previously employed this same method at a Western Electric Plant to improve assemblers' efficiency from 100 percent of the "company efficient standard" to 300 percent!) But motion analysis has been traditionally resisted by employees—except those paid on a piece-work basis. Employees often resent having their work closely observed and measured, and then being told to change their methods, so Phil knew that grassroots acceptance was needed for the motion analysis to take hold. But could he sell this to employees?

First, Phil approached the natural leaders to see if they would volunteer to be videotaped doing their jobs. Most of these staff members felt honored to be asked. Each volunteer performed the same task three different ways, nonevaluatively labeled X, Y, and Z.

Then Phil approached a carefully selected sampling of those work groups who were most likely to be receptive to change. Group volunteers viewed the tapes with Phil and together they recorded the times required for the task. Each group assessed the strengths and weaknesses of the X, Y, and Z approaches.

For the groups who requested it, Phil taught the motion analysis principle involved, that is, how they could work more efficiently. Soon productivity zoomed.

Phil was effective here where others might not have been. By pinpointing a location where change was needed, and by approaching the most influential individuals (using willing volunteers) and selecting receptive work groups, Phil turned a small experiment into widespread company productivity gains—an excellent demonstration of leverage use.

Toward the desired direction. Judo practitioners have to know how to position an attacker so he will fall, no matter how large he may be. Besides knowing opponents' *kuzushi* (balance points), judo students quickly learn that a strong push won't necessarily bring an adversary to the ground. A lateral force pushes a balanced attacker back, not down. It may sound simple, but students spend years in practice learning that they have to aim their force down to get the opponent to fall.

Everything we do should move us a step closer to our goals. As in bicycling, using leverage here means making a small push that puts us many strides closer to our destination. "Doing Easy" means eliminating unnecessary tasks and ones that cannot be completed; these only distract us and drain our energy. By concentrating on high-leverage activities, we can make the most of our creative energy.

Through martial arts leverage methods, we can magnify our power to accomplish what we previously believed was beyond us.

Using Leverage: Techniques for Action

- Observe those who have a strong influence on others. Watch how they carry themselves and move. Compare this to your own movements. Consider getting videotaped as you go through any task; critically review the tape, and watch your posture and movements.

- Concentrate on your center (hara) to increase your calmness and balance during challenging times.

- Select one breathing technique and practice it daily. Note the immediate and longer-term effects.

• Control your posture. Note how adopting different postures affects you and others.

• When doing anything—writing or listening, etc.—practice moving as compactly as is comfortable while still being effective. Incorporate this into hobbies and other activities. Check to see if you are doing things as "easy" as you can. Practice opening doors and moving objects as effortlessly as possible.

• Focus on output, not activity. Allocate time to high-leverage activities. Periodically monitor yourself to check if you are expending minimal effort toward your goals. If not, consider switching methods or goals.

II

MANAGING PEOPLE

When a person enters upon an undertaking, he prays fervently that he will achive success in it. Further, he knows that he needs the help of others; success is not to be attained alone.
Gichin Funakoshi, Karate-do: My Way of Life

4

KEYS TO DEVELOPING COMMITMENT

The power of commitment is wondrous
and can transcend all other forces.
Karate Shihan (Master) Tak Kubota, The Art of Karate

The Chinese curse, "May you live in interesting times," seems increasingly relevant today. In organizations around the world, people seem to focus more on their own objectives, needs, and image, and less on group and organizational goals. Yet at the same time the explosion of information and technology means that people have to rely more upon each other to achieve significant results.

A strong twenty-first-century leader has to be able to harness the commitment of self-focused individuals to a unifying objective. How can this be done?

Martial artists derive strength from their *Do* (pronounced "doh"), which means their "Way of Life." Several styles of martial arts have "Do" in their names: judo, the Way of yielding; kendo, the Way of the sword; tae kwon do, the foot-fist Way; hapkido, the Way of harmonious forces.

In *The Martial Arts,* Michel Random writes about Do, "It is much more accurate to use the word 'Way' rather than 'law.' Traditionally the Way is what absorbs man's whole being. The law is a judicial system which one obeys either voluntarily or under constraint. The Way, moreover, gives the idea of a constant but unending attempt at one's own perfection."

For many, the martial arts are a spiritual path that emphasize connection to nature and to God. The credo of the International Karate Association states: "The power of karate comes from the God within." Aikido founder Morihei Ueshiba said, "True budo [martial arts] is at one with the universe, which means being united with the center of the universe. True budo is a labor of love. It involves giving life to all that exists and not killing or opposing one another. We progress in life with this strength of spirit and we strive to maintain a global view of the world."

Powerful dedication to the Do can be felt by others. Master Tak Kubota wrote, "There is a level of purpose in karate that manifests itself as an 'aura' which cannot be seen or touched—it is sensed. . . . No one would dare attack." This is not mystical double-talk. Many martial arts anecdotes attest to masters who were "unattackable" because of their highly developed *wa* (internal harmony). I have seen aikido master Mitsugi Saotome call forth a black-belt student to rush and attack him. But Saotome does not move out of the way. He calmly smiles and placidly offers his hand. The attacker actually forgets his original intent and shakes the Master's hand. He feels extremely foolish when he realizes he has been so easily diverted from his charge. When you encounter someone who seems totally confident and calm, there is no point in attacking. You know you can't win.

The Way of the samurai is the way of power. It is also the way of protection and concern. Discipline is continuous, not hit or miss. Commitment to mission helps the warrior stick to her path, not letting her attention stray too far. So what do martial artists do when they feel disconnected and at odds with the world? Train, spar, practice kata (fighting form), and meditate.

In practicing martial methods, student's bodies are used and often abused. They endure twisted wrists, pulled hair, punches, and kicks. As one martial arts student quipped, "In the martial arts you let your friends beat you up so that other people can't." Understandably, there are times when martial artists ask themselves why they put in so much time and endure such discomfort.

A sense of commitment helps overcome these feelings of pain or adversity. It puts discomfort into perspective as the price of reaching a higher goal. Just when it appears their resources are depleted, martial artists call on their secret weapon—their strength of purpose. Commitment to a higher purpose unleashes a power that bolsters strength and provides needed perspective.

Martial artists are value-driven, whether their mission is to protect themselves, others, heighten their harmony with nature, increase self-understanding, or master fear. This sense of mission and purpose is equally useful on the battlefield, in the boardroom, or at the plant.

As a leader your mission, should you decide to accept it, is to harness commitment, first your own and then that of others, to create a vital organization. Enlist ideals in your worklife. Develop your own Do, your own Way of leadership.

In recent years many organizations have gone through the motion of creating a "mission statement" that, in reality, became just another document to be filed and forgotten. As in all trends, the benefits of these mission statements didn't seem to last. Insincere, unlived mission statements usually backfire. Everyone in the organization begins to watch out for inconsistencies and "do as I say, not as I do" actions. I have seen such poorly executed mission statements anger staff and lower morale.

But we shouldn't throw out the baby with the bathwater. Truly and honestly tapping the commitment of everyone in your organization can have miraculous results.

THE POWER OF HARMONY

Have you ever noticed how martial arts quotes and stories are filled with nature metaphors? For example, Tak Kubota writes, "The way of karate is as solid as the mountain and as empty as the sky." And legend has it that the Shaolin monks developed several fighting styles after observing animals attack and defend. In one famous story, a monk was inspired by the life-and-death attack and defense dance of a shrike and a viper. As the bird struck, the snake recoiled; as the serpent struck, the shrike moved out of range.

Internal martial artists value harmony with life and with nature (that is, the natural laws of physics). In *Precepts of the Martial Artist*, Walter Muryasz writes, "The martial artist completes the function of his art, which is to act in harmony with the changing nature of violence and conflict. The body and mind must harmonize with the laws that govern their mechanics."

If a large attacker is even slightly unbalanced and you apply downward force toward his kuzushi (point of imbalance), he will fall. Movements in accord with the natural design of the body are always stronger and easier. It is easier to bend someone's arm the way it is designed to go. Going against the joint will not only take more effort; it will be more strongly resisted.

Many martial artists advocate using "the path of least resistance," which in Western culture is usually misinterpreted to mean taking the easy way out. But in the martial arts the path of least resistance means getting to your goal without wasting a lot of energy, in other words, by working efficiently and in harmony with nature.

This is the path taken by water. In *The Art of Karate,* master Tak Kubota writes, "The essence of water and the power of the self are one and the same." And later he writes, "Movements of the *kata* [practice fighting form] should be as effortless as the tides." Likewise, in order to master kenjitsu (swordsmanship), the artist must develop a state described as "the reflection of the moon in the water"—in other words, a state that is calm, harmonious, and aware, merely reflecting the opponent's intent at the moment of attack.

THE WAY OF BUSINESS

A martial arts feat, such as breaking a brick, requires unwavering commitment. Those who demonstrate brick-breaking agree on the importance of belief. You're not just shattering materials; you're demonstrating—mostly to yourself—your inner power, which can get through things, even hard objects you once feared might hurt you. The martial artist has to transcend doubt and focus all her power on the "break." If she lets her focus drift, even for an instant, force will not be correctly transmitted and her hand can easily be damaged.

Have you ever known individuals who worked long hours on a groundbreaking project, or who gave time to a cause about which they felt passionately, people who extended themselves without complaining of feeling "stressed"? It's as if they tapped a special kind of power that springs from their commitment.

But some people trudge through life in another way—feeling as though they are only going through the motions, marking time, and not accomplishing anything worthwhile. They wake up thinking about the meaninglessness of their jobs, as if the week were too long, or that a Monday lasted many more hours than a Friday. I sometimes poll executives at seminars about their personal concerns and surprisingly often they select, "Not sure if my work has real meaning" as a major issue.

Privately many leaders report feeling alienated, depressed, powerless, and without direction. Loss of motivation is not the benchmark of only the mediocre; successful, intelligent executives suffer from it as well. For these leaders, work has become either a necessary grind or solely an individual crusade. How much can I attain? How far can I go? What personal recognition can I accrue? This "how-much" motivation can be difficult to sustain.

If you want to avoid a depressing rut such as this, or if you, like martial arts experts, want to elevate your work from average toward something exceptional, you can develop focus by recommitting to a set of values in which you believe.

For example, many managers and line staff for the U.S. Postal Service report that the organization has often been marked by low morale. But come the Christmas season, employee morale improves impressively, even though the workload multiplies. Why? Because, as one employee explains, "This is the time we live for. We have a real mission—to carry the holiday spirit."

Never underestimate the power of dedication to a mission, but like all forces it has a dark side as well. Terrorists, for example, draw their power from such dedication. Fanatical commitment enables a small number of individuals to hold sway over a much larger group. And while they may be extreme and misguided, there is something to learn from terrorists' determination. With a balanced instead of blind determination, we can tap the power of commitment in a more healthy manner—for ourselves and those we influence. You can help develop it, hone it, and direct it.

Lao-tzu's *Tao Te Ching* (Book of the Way) is an ancient treatise on effective leadership (*Tao* is the Chinese for *Do*). Business can be a Do, a Way of life, dedicated to improving the quality of living. As with their martial arts counterparts, black-belt leaders are also commitment-driven. Both groups of individuals know that true commitment generates power and makes life worth living.

Karate master Tak Kubota writes, "To each his viewpoint of his experience, to all the common path of their goal." A unifying mission can help align people toward the organizational goal, and a common purpose makes an organization more than simply a mass of people going in many different directions, performing overlapping or disconnected tasks.

Government manager Bill Thomas concurs. Like most martial artists, Bill, an extremely bright man who is a skilled communicator and a voracious reader, enlists commitment, determined to make his state agency a service organization on a par with the business world's elite. He says,

> It's absolutely essential in any organization for the top management to create a mission, for all employees to know where they're going. It's probably more pervasive and influential than anything else top management can do. Each of our "missioned" employees can turn the wheel to steer the organization where it's going. So you don't have to turn it by yourself or wrestle it away from them. They do the work too.

A mission is like looking through a telescope; it tells you where you're going. It can also be a mirror. By looking at a mission, you can tell whether your actions are consistently strengthening the organization's well-being.

Like the martial artist, we can start by formulating a personal values statement. An articulated belief system can provide perspective to the countless minor struggles of life. An important contract has suddenly been canceled? Tax code changes are cutting into profitability? The company is being merged or acquired? Competition is mounting? We can take solace in our values. Remind yourself of your purpose and do not allow pressure-produced tunnel vision to stall your productivity or destroy your motivation.

One leader I know has made a professional commitment to "Helping [his] staff grow." My current personal mission is "To serve as a force for positive change in the world—helping people and organizations to become safer, stronger, and more in control."

Black-belt leaders regularly reaffirm their commitment. They might place a few reminding words on their desk or wall to turn to during trying times. Some repeat their commitment to themselves each morning—twice on days when they wonder why they are bothering to show up to work at all. I remind myself of my mission before every seminar I present.

Balance is vital for effectiveness both in the martial arts and leadership. An idealistic visionary may be able to look into the future with long-range perspective, but his weakness is in dealing with details and completing the daily job.

Then there are those individuals without a higher purpose. People who study martial arts only to dominate others usually don't progress far. A recent study employed a standardized test, the Minnesota Multiphasic Personality Inventory (MMPI), to measure levels of anger in martial arts students. The MMPI revealed that beginning martial artists who were taught martial arts philosophy along with physical movements had markedly lower levels of anger after six months of study than those who only learned how to stand, kick, and punch. In addition, those who had elevated personal values remained martial arts students longer than those who didn't have such a philosophy.

Similarly, when people in the workplace are bereft of vision, they often see no purpose in their job beyond reacting from one day to the next. Their narrow perspective prevents them from reaching beyond the details of daily problems, thus limiting what they can accomplish.

Don't allow yourself to become fixed at either of these extremes. Remember your Do and practice the details of your art every day. Try to keep yourself balanced and looking ahead. Develop a set of values for yourself that you can apply in real life, values that not only help you to accomplish your daily tasks but that help you to grow and become someone better.

AN EFFECTIVE COMMITMENT STATEMENT

By design, commitment statements are idealistic and general. They point to a destination for the organization; they aren't designed to provide exact coordinates. Aikido founder Morihei Ueshiba stated his art's mission very simply: "Aikido is the realization of love."

On a black-belt exam, a martial artist is often evaluated by two criteria—his spirit and his technique. Techniques, like objectives, are easier to assess: Is he balanced? Does he exhibit control? Are his movements efficient and effective?

The *jing* (spirit), which many masters consider more important, is much more difficult to see. One does not gauge it in the same way as *waza* (technique). Does the artist exude purpose, dedication? Is he calm under attack, showing a winning spirit? Or is he overproud of his power and prone to use excessive force?

Similarly, statements of commitment are a matter of the spirit and should not include goals or objectives that are measurable and specific. Goals generally have one- to five-year plans and focus on behavioral output. Objectives are specific actions that bring you closer to your goals. These are important to formulate, but don't confuse these with values; your values should drive your goals and objectives.

For example, profitability can be either a goal or an objective (a vehicle of ensuring that the mission continues to be fulfilled). So getting a 15 percent return on investment or increasing market share may be important goals, but if your organization does not make an adequate profit, it may not be able to remain in business to fulfill its mission of improving the quality of life in your community. Very few people are driven to accomplish purely monetary goals.

The most effective declarations of commitment are well defined, inspirational, easily understood on an emotional level, well communicated to employees and to the public, and consistently applied. If the statement is meant to arouse staff spirit it has to become part of their thinking. And this won't happen if it's not easily understood, or if it uses language that distances people from desired actions.

For example, declarations such as "To provide needed services to clients, disseminate information, propagate a climate of trust and cooperation among employees, and be a responsible community member" are too long to remember, too uninspirational, and generally don't help motivate people. And believe it or not I've seen a lot worse.

Be practical: think like a martial artist. In the martial arts, short, focused punches are generally the most effective. Similarly, the punch of a commitment statement lies in its brevity. Keep it short and simple. All members of your organization will be more likely to embrace it that way.

Aim for internal consistency. If your mission as a hospital is "to improve health and well-being in our community and in the world," it is crucial that you also improve the health and well-being of your employees and their families. If this doesn't happen, both the company's credibility and worker morale will plummet.

Crafting a Living Credo: The Johnson and Johnson Way

Real values statements have a purpose beyond simply making an organization appear politically correct or serving as catchy marketing vehicles. They can become living guidelines for your company that structure support and commitment toward positive action.

Johnson & Johnson is frequently among the leaders of most-admired companies, as well as historically having been a highly profitable one. Johnson & Johnson's founder, Robert Wood Johnson, who transformed the company from a small family-owned operation into a worldwide corporation, had a strong belief in the importance of commitment and values at work.

In 1935 he published a pamphlet, *Try Reality,* that urged other corporations to develop "a new industrial philosophy," which focused on responsibility to customers first, then to employees, community, and lastly stockholders.

In 1943 Johnson wrote and published the "Johnson and Johnson Credo," a one-page statement that addressed these values in greater detail. Johnson simultaneously promulgated the credo throughout the company and emphasized that Johnson and Johnson management was expected to apply it to their daily business actions. Johnson believed that commitment to strong values would aid business profitability.

To this day Johnson and Johnson executives meet yearly to review and update their credo, which is available from the firm or on their Website (www.jnj.com/home.html), which lists their credo in thirty-six languages. The executives search for examples of where the credo is not being followed and then "corrective action is promptly taken."

Following are a few samples from their credo at the time of the writing of this book:

- We believe our first responsibility is to the doctors, nurses, and patients, to mothers and fathers and all others who use our products and services.

- We are responsible to our employees. . . . Everyone must be considered an individual. We must respect their dignity and recognize their merit. . . . We must be mindful of ways to help our employees fulfill their family responsibilities.

- Employees must be free to make suggestions and complaints. . . . We must provide competent management, and their actions must be just and ethical.

- We are responsible to the communities in which we live and work and to the world community as well.

- We must be good citizens—support good works and charities. . . . We must encourage civic improvements and better health and education.

- We must experiment with new ideas.

- Research must be carried on, innovative programs developed, and mistakes paid for.

Further, their website states, "At Johnson and Johnson, improving the health and welfare of children around the world is an integral part of our business."

In 1982 and in 1986 the company went through what it refers to as "The Tylenol Crises." During these years, a pain relief product it manufactures was tainted with cyanide and as a result several people died. Company executives met in emergency sessions and, using the credo as a guide, took responsibility for the problem—even though many observers believed the tainting of the product was beyond Johnson and Johnson's control. With Johnson and Johnson's good name and reputation at stake, company managers and employees made countless decisions inspired by the philosophy embodied in the credo.

By the manner in which they responded, Johnson and Johnson turned what could have become a disaster for the company into a public relations victory. Today this case is often studied in business schools as an example of excellent management.

Johnson and Johnson further describes the credo as being a living and useful statement: "Its principles have become a constant goal, as well as a source of inspiration, for all who are part of the Johnson and Johnson Family of Companies."

About fifty years after it was first introduced, the credo continues to guide the destiny of the world's largest and most diversified health care company.

Values and Profit: The A-dec Do

Values pervade the martial arts. Judo master Henry Seishiro Okazaki wrote, in an unpublished paper, "Every student of Judo should realize that honesty is the foundation of all virtues. Kindness is the secret of business prosperity. Amiability is the essence of success. Working pleasantly is the mother of health. Strenuous effort and diligence conquer adverse circumstances. Simplicity and fortitude are the keys to joy and gladness; and service to humanity is the fountain of mutual existence and common prosperity."

Like Johnson & Johnson, the A-dec company has found that managing by values can be profitable. Ken and Joanne Austin, owners of A-dec, the largest manufacturer of dental equipment in the United States, started out modestly; now they own A-dec's industrial park—all one hundred acres of it.

Because of its richness, clarity, and proven effectiveness as a management tool, their values statement, "The A-dec Way," is summarized here.

> "Striving for Excellence": At A-dec our working philosophy is a commitment to strive for excellence in all we do. Recognizing the need to maintain control of our future, we looked inside A-dec to define the secret of our past success and as a result developed the "A-dec Way." The A-dec Way is a written expression of the operating philosophy which governs all aspects of our company.
>
> Fifteen "principles of concern" and six "questions of test" make up The A-dec Way:
>
> Principles:
> 1. Demonstrate concern for people
> 2. Provide for opportunity and assist in self-development
> 3. Provide an atmosphere encouraging self-satisfaction and pride
> 4. Encourage team effort
> 5. Maintain complete fairness, honesty, and integrity

6. Maintain open, consistent, and regular communication
7. Encourage public service
8. Encourage creativity
9. Commit ourselves to productivity and quality
10. Maintain consistency
11. Dedication to improvement
12. Keep things simple and basic
13. Build on a basis of "need"
14. Give attention to detail
15. Conserve resources

Questions:
1. Is there a need?
2. Is this the simplest and best way to do it?
3. Am I using time and material effectively?
4. Am I helping make A-dec better for everyone?
5. Can I be proud of what we are doing?
6. Have I communicated?

This statement reads a lot like Musashi's nine guidelines (see p. 23). Having worked with A-dec over six years, I've seen that, while the organization is not problem-free, it does follow the A-dec Way. The company is down-to-earth as well as successful. I have spoken to many A-dec employees, past and present, who all described A-dec as a special place. Most former workers regret having left.

The importance A-dec places on values is evident in the company's treatment of its staff: Employees are paid well and are expected to perform accordingly; a premium is placed on flexibly adjusting to an employee's individual needs; A-dec provides free coffee to its staff; its plant is exceptionally clean and the cafeteria and grounds are beautifully maintained. Job-relevant education and training are provided; promotion from within is encouraged; and courses on personal development are offered.

Consistent with their values, A-dec incorporated group technology into one pilot area of their manufacturing process. Traditional assembly-line jobs in which one employee drilled holes and another bolted together dental chair components were replaced by a team approach. In their new arrangement, a team of employees is responsible for producing a prescribed number of chairs, and employees in that unit are trained in all assembly functions. In keeping with the A-dec philosophy, the first group-technology "family" was composed completely of volunteers.

What began as an experiment at A-dec has turned into a rousing success. Not only did productivity skyrocket, but other employees have pressed to have their jobs reformatted into groups. And the timetable for converting them has been shortened by years.

Tours for visiting executives interested in A-dec's black-belt leadership style are regularly provided. I once asked the personnel manager why he took valuable time to do this. What was in it for A-dec? I asked. He said there were two benefits. One, Ken and Joanne had made a commitment to spreading effective leadership to businesses and people everywhere and the tours helped meet that goal. Two, employees took pride in their company being a model for others. They knew that their hard work maintained this status, thus it helped to motivate them.

DEVELOPING COMMITMENT THROUGH VALUES

For a values statement to generate power, it has to be personalized and wholeheartedly accepted, whether by a martial artist, a leader, or a staff member. This means that inconsistencies within the statement must be resolved. Walter Muryasz writes, "The martial arts may be the path [that one] has chosen to self-understanding, but he must never lose sight of the fact that his art, its use and original purpose, was born in the reality of violence. For the martial artist, to lose sight of this fact is to lose the foundation which gives the art its life, vitality, and its purpose for being. The reality may have been born in violence, but the purpose is harmony and the end of conflict. Somewhere between the two points, the artist is himself changed—reborn—the flower of the art."

For a leader, the act of formulating a values statement can be both difficult and enlightening. People often have an array of thoughts and feelings, some of which may be in conflict. Mixed feelings can split our energies in many directions so that we are unable to accomplish much that is meaningful. The martial artist's power of focus arises only when he can uncover his true purpose and use it to set his course.

Frequently when an organization takes the time to articulate its values, it becomes clear that staff members have conflicting ideas of what the organization is about, where it should be going, and what it should be doing. And this can be uncomfortable. But just as the martial artist must train to go beyond discomfort, confronting conflicts in values is crucial to resolving the problem of employees working at cross-purposes.

Remember, as the martial artist does, that true motivation and change come from within. If the values statement is meant to serve as a vehicle for boosting commitment and internal motivation, it is best to include as many people as possible in formulating it, soliciting comments from all staff on the first draft.

The way we go about getting input makes a statement in itself. Attempting to force or pressure people into participating—which I've seen numerous times—will be wryly or angrily received as inconsistent with the values statement and most often will backfire. Instead make yourself available to staff for response to the statement. You should present your request for feedback as if you were driving a train. You are moving a focused, powerful machine toward its destination. You can take one of several parallel tracks, but no one person can derail the train. Make it clear in advance who was involved in drafting the statement and what points of view were considered. Explain that you are looking for adjustments, not a whole-scale reformatting, and welcome staff feedback with the promise that everything expressed or requested will be considered, although some suggestions may not end up in the final version of the statement.

Helping Commitment Come Alive

Martial expertise combines a living philosophy with the development of natural reactions such as moving without thought to avoid an unexpected kick. This kind of skill takes time to develop and refine. Similarly, implementing a strong values statement is not an easy task. Too often a leadership team spends hundreds of hours developing a statement, files or posts it, only to then forget it exists.

To inspire and align staff, the values statement has to become part of daily work activity. Studies show the spirit and attitude of leaders are extremely influential in affecting an organization's morale. So it's best to begin implementing the values statement by ensuring that all leaders in your organization—both on the management and employee sides—wholeheartedly support it. If top managers do not really believe in the mission, then midmanagers won't either; if union leadership disagrees or feels that their input is not considered, line staff will not come aboard.

Strong, clear values can become an internal guidance system that reminds us of our priorities during chaotic or crises periods. Making decisions during stressful times can be dangerous; such plans may only reflect concerns that arise during the most extreme moments, not those of normal day-to-day operations. These policies are the result of what many call "knee-jerk leadership," "managing by crisis," or "being in a reactive mode."

Before making crucial and long-term plans consider your values. In this way your decisions are more likely to be in line with your desired direction. You'll retain your perspective, reduce decision-making stress, and stay on target.

- *Frequently use the commitment statement.* The best way to persuade your employees to use the commitment statement is to frequently use it yourself.

- *Remind yourself of your values.* Use the mission to allocate time among competing activities. Ask yourself, "Does this activity help us get closer to fulfilling our values?" If not, give it a lower priority and less of your time than more compatible activities.

- *Resolve conflicts by referring to your values.* Look for a common ground that is greater than any issue in dispute.

- *Remind staff what their commitment to service helps accomplish.* An organization realizes its global mission by turning values into action. Receptionists are not merely greeting people, and computer staff are not just processing data. Every staff member plays a vital role in helping the organization fulfill its values.

  It is important that the staff sees the positive effects of the organization's values—the woman whose life was saved because of the fire extinguisher your company manufactures or the distant family reunited by your airline. Because many internal staff members are too far-removed from the customer to see first-hand these positive results, it is imperative that others in the organization be their eyes and ears, bringing to them these inspiring anecdotes.

Be sure to make public any customer letters that pertain to your values, such as those thanking employees or letters reflecting about how your company's goods and services have helped them. Also ask staff members with direct customer contact (sales, customer service, repair) to pass along stories of satisfied customers or examples of how your organization's values are at work in the world. After internally publicizing one of these success stories, thank all staff for their efforts. This not only gives credit where it is due, it also inspires the staff to commit more deeply to the organization's values. When telling of the boy who was healed at your hospital, don't just thank the medical staff, also acknowledge the clerical staff who did the necessary scheduling, those who facilitated the required insurance clearances, and the employees who supported family members during the procedure. Remember that everyone in the organization helps get the job done.

It is also good practice to encourage others to develop their own values statements, which help them to have greater success and sustain them during hard times. When difficult periods arrive and morale tails off, remind staff members of their part in the organization's mission.

Using the values statement is also an excellent way to encourage your staff to grow. When employees are faced with a trying problem, refer them to the values statement (one Johnson and Johnson manager asks staff, "What would our credo suggest here?"). Most workers have some leadership qualities that can be developed. By encouraging them to apply organizational values to their work, you can help develop them into more committed and more consistent and powerful leaders.

- *Publicize it.* In an interview with the *New York Times,* then IBM CEO John Akers stated, "IBM will be permitted to grow and prosper only where people and governments understand that we are indeed helping to solve society's problems."

A values statement can attract suitable prospective employees, as well as value-driven investors. A good statement can be included in advertising, as Ralston-Purina's has done with "Helping pets live longer."

Incorporating values into your company logo and corporate graphics can also serve an organization well. For example, a food processing company might display pictures of a family at a holiday dinner or healthy children eating, thus further associating the idea of health and happiness with their products. Some organizations have even commissioned company songs that espouse their values.

Developing and applying organizational values can nurture strong commitment and supply the focus that helps decrease employee inertia, dissension, and uncertainty.

Action Strategies: Harnessing the Power of Do

- Ask strong leaders about the values that guide them.

- Develop a personal values statement and share it with a trusted friend. Remind yourself to think of your set of values daily. Make sure that you are living what you deeply believe in and applying your values as a guide in professional and personal activities.

- As a martial artist does before a critical fight, note in what areas you are afraid or disillusioned. Then remind yourself of your values commitment. Internal power flows stronger through a committed, focused person.

- Remember the martial relationship between having a strong purpose and being "unattackable." When you feel besieged, ask yourself, "Is this happening because my 'level of purpose' is weak?"

- Tour an organization whose values are well-defined. Ask its leaders the hard questions: How did you get to this point? What problems do you have with the values? What should we watch for in our own company? Be a general to your staff and help them to develop a set of values for your organization, department, or group. Refrain from imposing your personal values on them. Instead, help draw their values out. When you have developed a values statement, look for opportunities in your organization where you can apply this.

- Check your business code of ethics for consistency with the organization's values.

- Bring inconsistencies to the surface. Make them fair game for staff discussion. Seek an honest resolution of inconsistencies.

- See everyone in your organization as a potential leader.

- Train line staff as peer instructors.

- Remind yourself of times you have broken through fearsome barriers. Assess what gave you the power. Remember such strength is inside you, awaiting your call.

5

THE ART OF MOTIVATION

My martial art isn't a hard or soft style, it's both. I don't resist force,
or meet force with force and so it's a soft style. But when there's an
opening I use all the force I have, and so it's a hard style, too.
Chow Hung-Yuen, wing chun master

Karate is like flower . . . sometimes soft, sometimes fierce.
From the creed of the International Karate Association

When you watch martial arts masters throw larger opponents to the
ground, you do not see an exhibition of blind force. They *don't* fight the
opponent's momentum or block his strength. Against a stronger or
faster opponent, they could be quickly overpowered, so instead they
control themselves, staying calm and ready for the right opportunity to
move their opponent to the ground. Expert martial artists know that
how and when they move themselves will directly affect their opponent's
reaction. The same holds true for master leaders, and the same martial
arts principles, applied in a controlled manner, can be used to inspire an
employee or colleague—in other words, used to "move them."

Most managers I've met sincerely want to motivate their employees
to do their jobs creatively and enthusiastically. They strive for higher
productivity, stronger customer relations, and improved morale. Yet we

106

often see articles such as this one from *The Wall Street Journal:* "Loyalty Ebbs at Many Companies as Employees Grow Disillusioned," or "More Honesty Tests Used to Gauge Workers' Morale." Why are people not motivated? Many managers ask, What do I have to do to reach them?

Here are several martial arts strategies for creating movement that you can apply to staff motivation:

- know what doesn't work: don't create resistance

- balance softness and hardness

- create and steer movement by the soft power of invitation

- adjust the work climate for better movement

- strengthen your team

KNOW WHAT DOESN'T WORK: HOW NOT TO CREATE RESISTANCE

For centuries the martial disciplines have critically observed how people react. In *Precepts of the Martial Artist,* Walter Muryasz, a master of physical movement, writes, "The way of movement not only deals with the movement of the body, but also the movement of the mind. To know the movement of the opponent's mind, study the movement of your own mind. Know how the conscious mind reacts and deals with the thoughts and feelings that the unconscious mind throws up to it, and how it dictates your physical responses."

Begin by observing yourself. Notice how you resist excessive force directed at you. Watch others. It doesn't matter who they are or where they work, craftspeople or clerical staff, in offices or in the field. People resist when they are pushed too hard.

Martial artists deal with forces. In a practical sense, they understand Newton's Third Law of Dynamics: For every action, there is an equal and opposite reaction. Simply put, force creates resistance; this is an unconscious reaction.

As an experiment, face a partner and place your hands together palm-to-palm. Without warning, let one of you push hard. Notice the reaction. When one pushes, the other pushes back. Sometimes he responds with more force.

While we may not physically push against others or get pushed in return, a lot of this does go on at work, mentally and emotionally. Even when the pushing is not physical, the response is the same. Motivating by pushing increases resistance and escalates conflict.

Many organizations are mired in productivity-draining resistance caused by overly aggressive managers and supervisors. Kurt Lewin, a behavioral scientist who applies physical principles (he calls it "Field Theory") to industrial management, labeled managers who exert coercive influence "superchargers." These supervisors, Lewin found, are indeed able to make their employees work. *But only when the employees feel the direct presence of the boss.* Naturally, the supervisor can only be in one place at a time. Employees stop working whenever the boss is somewhere else, whether it's just around the corner, on vacation, or merely not checking their work. Also, coercing one or two employees is one thing, but pushing a group to perform is an overwhelming task.

How can this approach work with more than a handful of people to supervise? To be effective, this style of motivation may require a large number of watchdog supervisors. The trend, however, in many organizations is the reverse—toward reducing the number of supervisors; therefore supercharging won't be feasible.

Under the too watchful eye of a boss, coerced employees often do only the bare minimum. They don't take risks or try to be creative. This is a classic maneuver of resistance, so effective that it is often used, especially in Europe, as an alternative to strike action. It is called "work to rule," which means following the rules to the letter. Similarly, you may hear an employee say, "I'm sorry, that's not in my job description," which is just another form of resistance.

As with most traditional motivational strategies, the supercharger approach puts employees under more stress. Breathe down their necks, drill it into them until they get it, and make them give you a full day's work for their pay. Is it any wonder employees resist being motivated this way? In a modified supercharger approach, some managers use heavy-handed threats and modest rewards to make people work. If you use the carrot and stick, employees will match your expectations. They'll be as creative and enthusiastic as donkeys.

Technology has updated supercharger methods. Computers can measure each keystroke an operator enters; electronic eavesdropping on employees' conversations or e-mail or Web usage can check their performance. Microprocessors can monitor drivers' mile-by-mile behavior. It's no secret when this is done. Predictably, employees rebel. They solicit militant unionization for protection, file more grievances or workers' compensation claims, or come down with stress-related illnesses. Morale plummets, which drags down the quality of service too.

There's nothing wrong with monitoring work—in fact, it's important to do—but if you use it as a threat or if you give employees reason to believe you don't trust them, they'll act accordingly. Admittedly, it's easier to overpower some employees more than others—the meek and those with strong needs for approval. But don't expect these same people to be creative. It just isn't *their* style. The more creative you want your staff to be, the less supercharging makes sense. If you want staff members to develop better, more cost-effective ways to do the job, to adapt to unpredictable situations, or to respond successfully to clients with different needs, then reduce coercion—and avoid supercharging.

BALANCING SOFTNESS AND HARDNESS FOR MOTIVATIONAL POWER

The Power of Softness

Martial arts masters agree that softness is not weakness, but derives from control. Softness is really sensitivity to changing forces, allowing the expert to read and then fluidly redirect the force of a stronger attacker. Softness also means being watchfully relaxed, which allows the martial artist quicker response times. In *Aikido and the Harmony of Nature,* Mitsugi Saotome wrote that students can only attain expertise through balancing hardness with softness:

> In making a fine sword, the iron is continually stressed. Forged in flames, it is softened by the heat of aggression so that shaping and refinement may take place. It is beaten, pounded, folded back upon itself, heated, pounded until all the impurities are driven away. Plunged into water, the temper is set, the fires controlled, and wisdom prepares to sharpen its edge. The process is very complicated and no part can be omitted. Its hidden layers number more than a million. But

the finished product is simple and pure of line. It is strong, yet flexible, and its surface reflects all which is around it.

The study [of martial arts], too, is built up layer upon layer. Hard and soft training must both be experienced. If you are always training hard, consumed by fire, you will lose your sensitivity to your partner's reaction, you will begin to ignore the all-important thread of communication between you. If you are always training softly, immersed in water, you will never be stressed enough to discover your strength. You will lose reality, you will lose the fire, and you will lose the Way.

Most people who first meet René Changsut are taken with his unassuming calmness; clearly they have never sparred with him. René, an instructor of three Chinese internal arts, is one of the most potent martial artists from whom I have had the pleasure of learning. But René doesn't waste his energy trying to impress others. He is focused within. He doesn't seem to mind that others might underestimate him if it came down to a conflict. He fully respects the power of surprise.

Similarly, I have seen John Clodig, a master of aikijujitsu, *effortlessly* throw strapping, highly trained attackers coming at him full speed, as well as those cautiously trying to break through his defense; but when introduced to new acquaintances John couldn't be more low-key and friendly.

Master martial artists generally don't make a big thing about their strengths, their "hard" core that gives them their power. They move like everyone else, without stomping, glaring, puffing up, or otherwise signaling "look how strong I am."

Managers who only know how to rant and rave and pressure their staff to perform are weakened by their limited style. Superficial hardness induces resistance in others and stress in everyone, including the manager. This kind of brittle approach is especially unsuitable to managing creative staff who are the cornerstone of many organizations.

Kenjitsu adepts know that a sword left unsheathed loses its edge. Similarly, a perpetually confrontational management style is blunted by automatic resistance or indifference. People get accustomed to the rages of the always blustering manager and learn to ignore them. By comparison, a "soft" style makes chosen movements of confrontation even stronger. Mary Devlin, an information manager for a large public utility, says, "Of course there are times I stand up on my hind legs and say, 'This is it!' But I try to do that only when it counts. When I do say, 'No!' people pay attention, because I don't say it that often."

Softness is flexible and unthreatening. Think of steel sheathed in velvet. It's gentle and inviting outside, firm yet not brittle within. You can change your nonverbal demeanor by visualizing yourself as being "covered steel." If you're uncomfortable thinking of yourself as "soft," call it something else. Perhaps you prefer "flexible." "Subtle management" is what Omark Industries' training manager Janet Lewis says allows work groups to act as self-determinedly as possible.

One wise leader I know looks for "soft power" when promoting. "We go through an extraordinary process when we promote someone from nonmanager to the managerial ranks. We look for the courage to be soft, for people who aren't into heavy power. We want managers who have the confidence to make decisions but with the courage to consult with others. To respect higher levels of expertise than they have, and to really consider their staff members without being threatened. The benefit of this style becomes really apparent when you contrast this with the staff sergeant, 'do-it-my-way, do-it-now, end-of-conversation' style we used to have."

A soft style helps you read others' resistance; in contrast, hardness is less sensitive. The person who can sense another's tension and resistance is in a position to use these, judolike, toward positive ends.

Softness has its healing aspect, too. Some vital points used to maim or kill can also heal when palpated in a soft, controlled manner. For example, a tae kwon do method for stopping nose bleeds involves firm, gentle pressure at the base of the skull, a place where potentially deadly blows may be delivered. It's a question of control. These vital "healing" spots are points of power. Too much force harms; too little does nothing. Gentle, controlled force animates. The same is true in managing. To bring people to life, learn to apply the right amount of force in the vital areas.

LEADING THROUGH INVITATION

Martial artists and master leaders don't create unnecessary resistance. They deal with people as "softly" as possible by inviting or influencing, not controlling, others. Influencing can be done in many ways. In *Precepts of the Martial Artist*, Walter Muryasz writes about moving an attacker where you want him by leading his attention. "The true lead draws the opponent into the space where you want him. To give him what he wants also draws him into that space, but only if you are aware of what he wants. It is the mind you are leading, its intent, conditioning, and perceptions."

Interestingly, *leading* here means "drawing" or "directing," not pushing or pulling. Muryasz is inviting others to move in a certain direction by understanding and using their natural inclinations.

In organizations, the best leading also takes place through invitation. Controlling less allows people room for doing more. "Many organizations' staff are overmanaged. Hire people who are bright. Let them know what you expect, then give them freedom to move. Even young people can blossom and don't need as much direction as a lot of administrators think they need," advises Ross Merrick, Executive Director of the National Association for Sport and Physical Education.

Avoid needless control. Be practical. Make only those rules that are absolutely needed. Are dress codes for backroom staff necessary? What about rules prohibiting personal pictures on desks? Are you managing for productivity and profit or for power? Lao-tzu gave a relevant leadership suggestion in the *Tao Te Ching:* "If you allow the person to act, then he develops his abilities."

The manager is in the center of his business unit; all eyes are on him. When he moves, he invites others to follow. He draws them after him; he takes the lead by doing. He doesn't tell them what to do; he invites them by doing it the desired way himself. His intention and commitment are "hard"; his style is "soft."

Instead of searching for devious ways to get people to do what you want, he asks them. This sometimes converts the most virulent adversary into an ally. For example, he calmly and sincerely approaches a dissident board member prior to an important meeting and says, "I really need your help on this for us to prosper."

There's another reason to manage staff softly as well as firmly. For any organization, high employee morale is vital for smooth, efficient operation. This is especially true in information and service organizations where the product is no more than the efforts of its employees. Staff who are dissatisfied cannot deliver as high-quality service to clients and customers as those who have high morale. "If you don't have happy people, you don't get the work done," contends an expert manager of a service organization.

Invitational power can also be used to hold together a rapidly growing company whose staff threatens to splinter into special interest groups. Invite them to recommit themselves to organizational mission, values, and goals.

Using Secondary Pressure

Like any subtle strategy, invitational power is difficult to master. But its subtlety is its strength. John Clodig teaches black-belt students a concept called "secondary pressure," which means not putting your strength at the point of attack. Mr. Clodig shows that using direct force is inefficient against a strong, prepared attacker. If he grabs your wrist, don't attempt to overpower him with arm strength. This only works when you can clearly overcome your opponent. Even then, sophisticated attackers can counter any reaction they can feel. Instead, focus your strength away from the point of attack, where they can't feel it. Move first from your shoulders or hips, not from the point where you are held. This is similar to the "not being trapped" exercise described in the first chapter.

How can you apply secondary pressure in leadership? Have you ever wished you could help your boss change, but he rejects anything critical you have to say? You know he will resist direct suggestions. So put your pressure where he can't feel it. Find nonthreatening ways of approaching him. Leave an article on your desk—or anywhere he is likely to see it—that offers some solutions to his problem; discuss offering staff a training session you know would also benefit him; or, if appropriate, talk to a trusted peer of your boss, or to his friend or spouse.

Clearly, these can be dangerous strategies. Be sure of your own motivations. If you're really trying to harm him or just release anger, he will likely sense this and direct force back toward you (and probably much harder).

Lasting Motivation Is Self-Motivation

Ultimately, you can't motivate others externally and have it last. Yet some people keep fighting this losing battle. They hire a "motivational speaker" who brings in lots of energy, but no concrete skills. They pass out inspiring books and constantly exhort staff to "win one for the Gipper." These strategies, while useful in their place, will not motivate anyone in the long run. At best, all that happens is that staff become "hooked" on motivational excitement, but the effects are always short-lived.

Ruth Engle, a consumer loan center supervisor in a bank, is painfully aware that her employer mistreats its workers. To offset this, she periodically uses creative tricks to keep morale high. Sometimes she holds drawings where staff can win a day with an hour off. She also encourages potluck lunches and initiates staff holiday celebrations. These strategies somewhat soften the impact of heavy-handed upper management, but they don't change the reality. Employees feel good about their supervisor for trying, but they are still angry at their employer. This is reflected in their service to customers.

Don't try to motivate staff. It's like filling a cup with a hole in it. You have to keep pouring the motivation in because it leaks out almost as quickly. This is very tiring and inefficient. Besides, what happens when you are not around to fill the cup? Instead, plug the leak. Help employees motivate themselves.

In the martial arts, the most efficient way to move people is first to make contact with them; then join with their direction of movement; and finally steer them to the desired course.

In an organizational context, making contact does not require being another's friend; in fact, there can be disadvantages to this. First, get close to them by sitting down and talking in a nonthreatening location. Match their pace and tone of voice (unless they are really upset). Above all, really listen. Listening is not a passive skill; it is an active art that few people have mastered. Stay black-belt calm. Listen by really focusing on them and letting go of your own concerns for that moment. If you listen to your staff, they'll know you are concerned about them and will work doubly hard for you.

Second, match their emotional direction to understand how they see things. This doesn't mean you should be as angry or negative as they are, just see things from their perspective. Don't offer advice too quickly or judge their situation with thoughts like "if it were me, I wouldn't have let myself be placed in that position to begin with."

Third, while maintaining contact with them, move yourself. Gradually raise your own energy level and attitude. Slowly suggest ways you can remedy the situation. Most of the time, they will come along with you, feeling immediately more hopeful and calm. But how can you make this positive tone last? It has to be grounded in reality. Words are not enough. The original problem has to be overcome and their work really has to improve.

The literal meaning of *samurai* is "one who serves." The duty of the samurai was, at any moment, to give their all to the leader to whom they were pledged. The warrior dedicates his service to his lord or master; the accomplished manager focuses on serving his employees.

Follow the wisdom of Lao-tzu: "To lead the people, walk behind them." Knowing his own productivity is really the output of his department or organization, a black-belt executive leads by making it easier for others to do their job.

When there is a staff problem, the black-belt leader does *not* immediately draw a sword to sever the employee from the ranks. Instead, he sees the problem as his own. What has he done to allow this? What can he do differently to help this employee perform? This approach especially applies when the performance of a previously able worker begins to dip below acceptability. Of course, there are times when the employee seems determined to self-destruct. But if the employee is valued, the wise manager will try everything in his considerable arsenal to get this person back on track.

There are many methods for teaching martial arts techniques. Sometimes the traditional approaches—demonstrating the technique or analyzing the component movements—don't work. One effective technique used to help people who aren't getting it, and who often feel foolish or frustrated by this, is to move alongside them. To teach them how to parry a punch, literally stand behind them, pick up their hand, and deflect the incoming blow. Do this several times. At first, ask them to let you move their limbs, then direct them to concentrate on feeling your path of movement. Finally have them parry under their own power with you watching. It's amazing how fast even nonathletic students can pick up new techniques this way.

As leader, work closely alongside those with problems until they are back on an even keel. Once they're doing well, gradually pick up the work pace. In effect you are teaching them how to walk by letting them lean on you for the first steps. Once they get the feeling of walking, they will depend on you less. They can, and eventually will, motivate themselves to act effectively.

Motivating the Unmotivated: The Apathetic and the Dissident

The experienced martial artist would rather face a strongly rushing assailant than one who enters slowly. This form of attack may be less psychologically threatening (less speed is involved), but it is more difficult to counter. The physics of movement apply: "A body at rest tends to remain at rest; a body in motion tends to remain in motion." The more static the attack, the more balanced the opponent. In contrast, a highly energized assault tends to be less balanced and thus more easily diverted.

In the same way, an apathetic employee is more difficult to motivate than one who is vocally dissident. If people are unmotivated, the reason for their resistance may be because they already feel pushed. As an initial strategy in dealing with this, back off so you don't further harden any existing resistance. Then search for areas where they are motivated. For example, they may be enthusiastic hikers, and when you ask them what they get out of it, they tell you that they love the feeling of being alone and free. Then try to create a way to harness this existing motivation at work. Ask if they would prefer a project on which they can work autonomously. Once you've got them moving, it's just a matter of steering them in the right direction, into alignment with the organization.

In contrast, the dissident worker is much more aggressive about expressing dissatisfaction. But it is possible to turn his charge to your advantage. Don't think about fighting his natural tendencies; instead try channeling them in a useful direction.

This kind of employee is already motivated, just not aligned with organizational goals. Meet with him and hear him out. Ask if he would be interested in helping make things better by being a part of the solution. Enlist his perceptiveness and energy toward organizational goals and you may develop an excellent employee. One organization, frustrated with low productivity and morale, decided to promote only vocally disaffected employees to supervisory positions. With careful training and supervision, productivity and morale soon skyrocketed.

As the employee relations manager of Potlatch Corporation's southern division, Jerry Ginter knows the power of softness and hardness in communicating. Using his genuine concern, sense of humor, and honest, sometimes pointed feedback, Jerry has been successful at melting the resistance of and generating enthusiasm from employees that other leaders had given up on.

Customizing Supervision

You can't teach all martial arts students the same way. Beginners learn by imitating. They are shown in stages exactly where to place their feet, and how to kick. In contrast, intermediate students don't need this simplistic instruction. They are shown how to make their movements smooth and well timed. Advanced students are learning how to develop their own techniques. They go beyond imitation to think through underlying principles they can adapt and use creatively. Walter Muryasz said that when students get their black belt, "their practice is their own; they are independent learners," able to progress without explicit supervision.

A national judo champion attended several jujitsu classes. He expected it to be easy, thinking that he'd be able to learn new movements the first time through. But it wasn't so. He put so much pressure on himself, he couldn't learn. When he saw martial arts novices surpassing him in skill, he gave up in frustration. He couldn't mentally take off his black belt and become the white belt that he truly was in this different form.

Similarly, a manager definitely should not ignore her staff members' individual levels of expertise. Trusting a new person to make crucial decisions is not trust at all, it's naïveté. Instead, a manager needs to perceive the employee's actual level of competency, then help him grow to the next stage. If the task is new to him, he's a white belt. He may progress through the ranks quickly, becoming a purple-belt intermediate, then a black-belt expert. But the fastest way for him to get there is by being supervised according to his present level of expertise.

Not only do people learn this way; the job gets done well. Musashi was a proponent of this principle in 1645. In *The Book of Five Rings*, he wrote,

> The Way of the foreman carpenter is the same as the Way of the commander of a warrior house. The foreman carpenter must know

natural rules. . . . He allots his men work according to their ability. Those of poor ability lay the floor joists, and those of lesser ability carve wedges and do such miscellaneous work. If the foreman knows and deploys his men well, the finished work will be good. The foreman should take into account the abilities and limitations of his men, circulating among them and asking nothing unreasonable. He should know their morale and spirit, and encourage them when necessary. This is the same as the principle of strategy.

Just as most martial masters are dedicated to teaching, black-belt leaders enjoy helping others grow. Ron Swingen believes his role as a manager is to help employees learn that their power is inside themselves. He emphasizes training and cross-training people, and rotating them where appropriate. He helps them by customizing his supervision to their level of skill.

As Andrew Grove points out in *High Output Management,* whenever someone undertakes a new task he has a low level of maturity. It makes no difference if he was highly accomplished in his old job. The expert programmer promoted to supervisor, the engineer assigned to train others, or the salesman asked to add a new product to his product line are all beginners at that time.

Here is a key to successful leadership. Match your style to each employee's task maturity level. If he's new at the task, a white belt with a low task maturity, treat him accordingly. Be directive and structured. Tell him specifically what to do, when and how to do it. If she wears the colored belt of medium task maturity, employ her skills while helping her gain a black belt. This is the time to emphasize two-way communication. Make strategy together. Support him when he either fails or does especially well.

With mature black-belt staff, you can be minimally involved as a supervisor. Establishing and monitoring objectives should be sufficient. But remember, like that judo expert, when a black belt changes arts or tasks he becomes a beginner once again, at least for a time.

In the martial arts one need only look at a student's belt color to get a general idea of how experienced and accomplished he is. But how can you gauge subordinates "belt rank" at work? First you need to notice the quality of their work; also watch how they get things done—frantically, at the last moment, or calmly paced? Also watch how they move—in large, small, or "no" circles. Do they feel confident enough to listen well, ask questions, and request needed assistance?

Timing for Learning

One strength of martial arts training is that it teaches people how to learn. The student discovers that learning requires commitment to a lifelong process of trial and error. There is never a point of "having totally arrived." In fact, certain throws are informally labeled a "twenty-five-year technique," another a "lifetime technique." By keeping in mind that some skills can take a long time to acquire, you will be more realistic when helping others—and yourself—develop their skills.

There is a popular expression, "If you give a person a fish, he will eat for a meal. If you teach him how to fish, he will eat for a lifetime." The point is that continually bailing others out of their problems keeps them dependent and doesn't help them learn. But this idea can be taken too far. In such instances it's like taking seed corn to starving people, intending to teach them to farm. They will eat the seeds, not because they are backward, but because they are hungry. Feed them first, then when the gnawing in their bellies has quieted, teach them how to get their own food.

Similarly, some managers lose their perspective and go overboard with training. They treat everything as a chance to train staff. It's not a bad philosophy overall, but one that's sure to frustrate others at certain times. If someone comes to you with a problem *he* considers important, show him you take it seriously. "Fill his stomach" by helping solve the problem. Then, and only then, look for ways to make the situation into a learning exercise and longer-term solution.

ADJUSTING THE WORK CLIMATE

Musashi's nine guidelines listed in chapter 1 highlight the importance of "trifles." Martial artists modify their movements and strategies for different opponents and varying conditions. The adjustments are minute and may seem trifling, but they are absolutely essential. Techniques that are fine on an open street may be disastrous in a phone booth. What works against a tall, powerful opponent may not work with a small, fast adversary. With subtle adjustments, you can improve productivity and morale by tailoring the workplace to fit the employee.

With the right tools and workplace design techniques, it is possible to eliminate most environmental problems. Workplace design techniques involve ergonomics, the science of energy and of work, the principle of which is to improve the fit between workers and their environment. Many people associate ergonomics with specially designed chairs for computerized offices, but ergonomics has far wider application than just in expensive furniture.

Consider the whole environment. Make sure work stations are the right height for comfortable assembly or computing. Clearly, too much straining creates useless tension, will lower employees' productivity, and can cause disabling injuries.

Frequently used materials should be easily accessible. Furniture should comfortably fit the human body. The employees can use bent-handled tools to reduce wrist strain (preventing a condition known as carpal tunnel syndrome) and more efficiently transfer their power to their tasks. If you buy specially designed chairs or tools, be sure to train employees in their use. Otherwise you may be wasting your money; without the proper instruction, employees can still slump in an expensive chair.

Using Body Mechanics to Ease Work

You can train employees to use their bodies more efficiently. Motion analysis, pioneered by Frank Gilbreth at the beginning of the twentieth century, uses principles of body mechanics identical to those of the martial arts.

These principles can help your staff move more efficiently. The martial artist knows that thoughts, emotions, and bodily feeling are connected. In the workplace effective physical motivation can lead to increased emotional commitment and mental dedication. Training can energize what I call the "Organizational Critical Triangle":

- *Productivity* increases with less wasted motion, reduced fatigue, and better-controlled nonverbal communication.

- *Safety* is enhanced as balance and coordination improve.

- Morale improves as stress diminishes. There is more energy available from greater movement efficiency and less pain from poor body mechanics.

Training should always be upbeat, exciting, and practical. Motivate people by offering them the benefits of this training. Don't force it on them by saying, "This will improve your productivity and safety." Instead, offer it: "How would you like to learn some methods you can practice on the job that will improve your performance in any sport or hobby and also help you feel less tired at the end of the day?"

A good way to increase staff self-motivation is to teach them methods that increase their sense of self-control and power. If you show them the following techniques (as well as the methods of physical leverage in chapter three), their internal power should rise—and so will your credibility.

- Warm up to your tasks. Develop a one-minute warm-up that prepares the specific muscles to be used.

- Work with your elbows in front of your ribs.

- Cool down at the end of the day to reduce tension.

These principles will make you feel and seem stronger, more confident, and relaxed.

Job Redesign

Some "body types" seem more suited to certain martial arts. Judo, with its get-under-opponents'-center-of-gravity throws and leg sweeps, seems designed for those with shorter legs. Tae kwon do—in which most techniques are kicks—seems to favor those with long, supple legs. But stockier people can become excellent tae kwon do practitioners, and taller artists can become strong *judo-ka*. But they may have to redesign some of the techniques they study to suit their types.

To improve the fit between employees and their jobs, consider job redesign. It can be difficult to find good people, and tougher still to keep them. Often it is worth the expense to redesign a job to make a good fit.

If you have a valued employee who has outgrown her duties, or just doesn't fit her department, try adjusting her duties to her skills, or switching her to another division. Remember to involve her—and both her old and new supervisors—in planning this change. Typically, employees' morale and performance will improve with such a move.

The positive effects from doing this are often more far-reaching than the benefit of helping a single employee. Other staff members who are aware of this redesign process will usually feel better about management as a result of your efforts.

You can also train promising people for new positions. In the martial arts, just about everyone can become a black belt with the right attitude. The same is true in the workplace—if you find the right place for them.

Raising Low Morale

It is often the simple things that are effective. Everyday motions can become self-defense techniques, and leaders can employ simple actions to boost morale, thereby improving production, quality, creativity, and safety.

Julie Hale, a city-government worker, noticed the people in her financial services department were becoming too stressed, so she instituted a "take a lap" program. Whenever she sees a staff member taking things too seriously or becoming too angry, Julie pulls her aside and smilingly says, "Enough is enough. Why don't you just take a lap?" She expects this staff member to take a break (up to fifteen minutes), work things out, and come back feeling better. This works, probably because of the way Julie does it. She catches the problem before it becomes massive and uses humor and her "no-nonsense-you-can-do-it" attitude to support the person. After a time her staff started telling peers in need to "take a lap." Department morale, and productivity, is extremely high, even though Julie's organization is in the midst of profound changes.

If you sense staff morale is low and you ask staff members to voice their concerns, you have entered the realm of raw power. First, be prepared to be initially inundated with negative responses. These will always surface first. Second, control your reactions and hear your employees out, even if you begin to feel personally threatened. One of the worst things you can do is shut off expressions of anger or dissatisfaction after you have opened the way for expressing them.

After hearing people out it's crucial that you do something. Any time you ask your staff to share their concerns, they assume you are making a tacit contract to do what you can to improve the situation. So, listen and thank them for their frankness and their interest in making the organization stronger and a better place to work. Then explain what you can and can't reasonably do to make things better. Give them specifics, what you'll attempt and when you'll get back to them. Then follow through. This is a high-leverage time. You will lose tremendous credibility if you don't take them seriously or if you let their concerns fall through the cracks. But if you follow through as promised, and improve a few critical things, you can encourage tremendous loyalty.

The Loyalty Balance

In the *Tao Te Ching*, Lao-tzu writes, "Fail to honor people; they fail to honor you." It seems every leader wants loyalty. But many try to secure it the wrong way. Loyalty is a two-way street. Be loyal to your employees and they will be loyal to you. In an employment interview, asking prospective employees for a two-year commitment doesn't make sense— and prospective hires will know it—unless you, as an employer, are willing to give them the same promise. Try honestly to improve others' work situations and they will be more willing to go the extra mile on your projects.

Loyalty in an organization can be seriously undermined by gossip. The way to control gossip is to direct it, as a martial artist defends himself against a knife. Don't block it—it's too easy to make an error and get cut. And trying to shut off rumors usually has the opposite effect. Instead, think of the knife as your own weapon: direct it away from you and toward the attacker.

Bring things into the open. Secrecy not only excites more speculation, it also requires lots of energy to maintain. Ask people what they've heard. Tell them what you know: "We're watching this quarter's sales. And we don't know now if we will have any more layoffs. We'll tell you as soon as we know." The truth frequently makes rumors less enticing.

STRENGTHENING THE TEAM

It's important for the martial artist to tap his talents effectively when working with others, as well as when working alone. It has been said that "the code of conduct of the sixteenth-century samurai is summed up by the phrase 'for the team.'" But it is difficult for many people to think in this way. Western training and culture go against this. Growing up, we are told, "You're unique and can be anything you want," not "You are part of a society and need to work with others." Many people deplore the idea of "groupthink," losing individuality, and merely going along with the crowd. So we have a workforce of free-agent individuals, many of whom have difficulty working on projects with others, dread meetings, and quarrel when diverted from their personal goals. (Of course, on the other side, this system encourages *individual* creativity.)

But in this complex and changing world, no one person has all the information or answers. We need to pool our efforts to create what is beyond any individual's scope. Black-belt leaders make it easier for their staff to work as a team.

Meetings are a good starting place to examine teamwork. First, it is important to acknowledge why people resist meetings:

- Meetings use more collective time to perform a simple task than any individual would use.

- Participation in groups can be frustrating for those who don't get what they want.

- People may be forced to associate with colleagues who they would rather avoid.

- Group work dissipates the glory any individual would have received for individually doing a good job.

- Committees can encourage controversy and/or conflict.

- Groups can make the simple, complex. Hence the expression "a camel is a horse designed by committee."

- Committees are frequently used to postpone work or to avoid facing a controversial problem.

- Meetings can put individuals on the spot by pressuring them to state opinions publicly.

- Groups can lessen personal accountability for work.

- Group assignments can foster unequal workloads that are a

fertile ground for resentment and lowered morale.

- Meetings are often just plain boring, especially for those who already know the material being covered, or for those who operate at a faster pace than others.

No wonder many people have negative feelings about committees or other work groups. And frequently, staff expect future groups to be similarly ineffective or boring. But this doesn't have to be. On the other side of the argument, "teamthink" can be extremely effective. It can:

- Increase creativity. While follow-the-leader "groupthink" leads to narrow-mindedness and tunnel vision, a team approach synergizes thought. Participants stimulate one another, so that the whole becomes far greater than the sum of the parts.

- Reduce resistance to change by encouraging those who implement a program to feel allegiance to it. A good way to invite commitment to any project is to ask for involvement in its planning.

- Spread workload around so that more gets done.

- Improve planning. A critical group, with numerous viewpoints, is less likely to miss an important contingency than is a person working alone.

- Foster more satisfying work relationships as people get to work in a positive, productive manner with peers.

How can you sharpen work group effectiveness?

- Provide training in group dynamics to make any team more efficient.

- Rotate leadership so everyone has the fun—and frustration—of keeping the meeting on track.

- Encourage members to do their homework in advance by completing subcommittee assignments, reading meeting minutes, and thinking through the objectives of the next meeting. Meeting time can then be dedicated to exploring ideas and making decisions, instead of rehashing old business or arguing about easily verifiable information. Nothing is more frustrating than an ineffective meeting, and it leaves a sour taste about team projects in employees' minds.

- Start off all meetings by reminding participants of the meeting's purpose. Review the goals and objectives of your team. Read the organization's mission statement. Have a prepared agenda.

- Call off unnecessary meetings. Ask yourself whether a memo can accomplish the same purpose.

- Shorten all meetings. A good rule of thumb is to limit informational meetings to forty-five minutes and decision-making meetings to ninety minutes.

Making meetings more efficient and enjoyable will change the bad image some people may have of work groups. Staff will look forward to well-run meetings that increase their creativity, productivity, and social interaction.

By understanding why people resist and how to enlist the mechanics of softness and hardness, you can build stronger, more dedicated staff. You will also strengthen your leadership power and control.

Motivating through Softness and Hardness: Techniques for Action

- Notice your reactions to being pushed or forced. Can you observe these feelings without reacting?

- Reinterpret the meaning of "soft." Think of the synonyms flexible, malleable, adaptable, supple, yielding, lenient, limber, and resilient.

- Critically assess your past motivational style and that of your organization. What has worked and why? What hasn't worked? How much of this motivation is based on "supercharging" or on making subordinates uncomfortable?

- Look for new ways of inviting, rather than controlling, others. Think of controls that are unnecessary and could be given up without adverse effect on productivity.

- Use secondary pressure to reach an "unreachable" person. Notice when indirect strategies will take you closer to your goals.

- Encourage employees to become self-motivated rather than trying to motivate them externally.

- Practice making real contact with others. Look for the subtle feeling that you are "in contact."

- Practice seeing things as others see them.

- Look for cost-effective adjustments you can make to the workplace; solicit employees' ideas on this.

- Practice motion efficiency.

- Develop a customized supervision plan for each of the people you supervise. Start by asking yourself, "What is each one's belt color (level of task maturity)?"

- Train all staff in group leadership and meeting skills.

- Give them a fish, *then* teach them how to fish.

- Give as much loyalty to your staff as you ask from them.

- Ask yourself, "How else can I strengthen my staff?"

6

HARNESSING CONFLICT

Men are your castles
Men are your walls
Sympathy is your ally
Enmity your foe.
Takeda Shingen, sixteenth-century warrior

There is no opponent or enemy in true budo. True budo is at one with
the universe which means being united with the center of the universe.
True budo is a labor of love. It involves giving life to all that exists
and not killing or opposing one another.
Morehei Ueshiba, Aikido

Who overcomes by force, hath overcome but half his foe.
John Milton

In Japanese, *budo,* The Way of the martial arts, literally means "to control the conflict." In his *Ideals of the Samurai: Writings of Japanese Warriors,* William Scott Wilson quotes the Chinese source Tso Chuan: "*Bu* means stopping the spear. *Bu* prohibits violence and subdues weapons. . . . It puts people at peace, and harmonizes the masses." As might be expected, over the centuries the martial arts have developed powerful strategies and techniques for managing conflict.

In feudal Japan, the sword was commonly said to be the "soul of the samurai." Two sword makers, Masamune and Muramasa, were both known for making excellent blades, strong and sharp and not easily broken. But Muramasa was known to be a lover of war. It was said those who owned his blades went mad with violence. Legend has it that one could tell the difference between Masamune and Muramasa swords by placing the blades in a stream. Leaves would bypass the former, but would be attracted to and cleaved in two by the latter. Although both were excellent pieces of workmanship Masamune blades became highly prized while Muramasa's were shunned.

Traditional martial artists were proponents of peace, and the most valued warriors were those who could maintain a calm, peaceful outlook, even during a conflagration. Hojo Soun is quoted in *Ideals of the Samurai* as supporting this position: "There is a saying that goes 'Even though one associates with many people, he should never cause discord.' In all things one should support others." Martial artists viewed conflict as a natural part of life, but they also developed a wide range of methods of control to make conflict work for them.

Like martial artists, leaders get ample exposure to conflict. Most executives I have surveyed believe there is more conflict now than there was twenty years ago. Increases in stress, the rate of change, and competition for market share and resources have increased conflicts. A recent American Management Association study revealed that corporate executives and managers spend from eighteen to fifty percent of their time dealing with conflict, depending on their position level and the type of organization for which they work.

The ability to manage conflict has become increasingly important. Poorly managed conflict diverts energy from productivity, obstructs cooperative action, and fosters a climate of suspicion and mistrust. But conflict doesn't have to be your enemy. By applying martial arts methods, you can become a more skilled and confident manager of conflict, and learn how to use its inherent energy to your advantage.

THE CONFLICT PRINCIPLE

There are always people ready to push on us, whether they are customers demanding special treatment, subordinates acting sullenly obstinate when we delegate tasks to them, bosses setting unreasonable expectations without providing adequate support, highway tailgaters demanding we get out of their path, or children probing for our weak spots and insecurities. With any of these examples, the result is usually conflict, even if the symptoms are subtle, because when people feel pushed, they push back. Or they dig in their heels. They give in to authority only grudgingly, hide behind their job description, do things as slowly as possible, or even miss work.

Nonverbal communication is a major source of "pushing." Communication experts say over 90 percent of all communication is nonverbal, embedded in the way something is said: tone and volume of voice, speed of speech, and body movement. Nonverbal "pushes" can include abruptly assigning someone a task without even first saying hello or making eye contact, throwing papers at someone ("Please get this done as soon as possible!"), not respecting someone's distance, conversing too closely for comfort, or hovering over an employee's shoulder.

Most conflict management strategies for the workplace focus on verbal communication; that is, we should say this, repeat that, or negotiate so. Although verbal communication techniques can be effective in conflicts that involve facts and methods, the most difficult conflicts are emotional, involving goals and values, because they don't lend themselves to intellectual and purely verbal solutions. In nonverbal communication people read actions, not words.

In *The Art of Japanese Management*, Robert Pascale presents a study that reveals what most people know by common sense: when there is stress in an organization, people cease believing what is said and give more credence to how messages are given—as the saying goes, actions speak louder than words. These skills also apply to personal and family relationships, not just professional ones.

ORGANIZATIONAL HARMONY AND CONFLICT

Martial artists ultimately strive for harmony. Real harmony is vibrant! It is a vital state. Nature continually demonstrates that great stability exists only in the midst of movement, as in the eye of the hurricane or the center of a gyroscope. Stay in the center of the circle of attack— that's what many martial arts instructors teach. Move so your opponent circles around you. Let things swirl outwardly; keep your core calm.

A harmonious workplace is marked by high efficiency, strong morale, and creative use of conflict, and by a staff that feels interdependent: "If you do well, we all do well. If the company goes belly-up, we all suffer." Harmony is not characterized by symptoms of stagnancy, boredom, or low productivity, or by the signs of fear—sycophantic agreement (yes-men). In organizations with such symptoms, harmony exists only on the surface. The organizational reality underneath seethes with a low level of vitality, individual depression, and anger.

In a harmonious organization, competition, both internal and in the marketplace, is not perceived as a lurking menace, but as a force that strengthens the company. In an excellent book about learning, *The Inner Game of Tennis,* Tim Gallwey observes that good competition challenges people to stretch beyond their present limits. The result, he suggests, will be higher performance.

Unfortunately, many organizations try to preserve an illusion of placidity and control. Grumbling and dissatisfaction are pushed below the surface and erode organizational strength from within. A climate of fear is created—fear of ruthless internal competition, of overcontrol by management, and of retribution. In such environments employees learn what to avoid and how to appear busy. They spend more energy covering themselves than doing their job or trying new approaches to their work.

In the harmonious organization, on the other hand, disagreement does not have to lead to discord. When people feel confident and safe in expressing their opinions and when the focus is on team achievement rather than on self-serving actions, dissension can actually increase productivity. For example, the power of brainstorming springs from an emphasis on group achievement and from ground rules that protect people from personal criticism. Without conflict, there is no creativity; controlled conflict drives new ideas and approaches. Good conflicts are also learning experiences.

There are specific practices that can develop more true harmony in an organization. Rules—which usually cause resistance—are kept to a minimum, so as to concentrate on crucial matters such as pursuit of the mission, organizational survival, or worker safety. Policy and procedure manuals are thin, and are based on common sense. (People rarely read or use them for day-to-day functioning anyway.) The best-accepted policies are those developed with employee and managerial input. Once procedures are formulated, it's best that everyone concerned receives training.

Employees also are treated as adults. People resent being patronized or treated like children. Conflicts are recognized early, when they are still small, and dealt with before they grow bigger. Feedback is regularly solicited and unhappy workers are encouraged to reveal the causes of their dissatisfaction. Managers sincerely respond to employee concerns.

All organizational staff members are expected to have conflict management skills. Staff is trained to intervene appropriately when peers need help. The harmony that results from these practices assures that fewer harmful conflicts occur. When conflict does flare up, they are more susceptible to resolution before they reach a level of resentment and anger from which it is difficult to recover.

CONTROLLING CONFLICT
BY CONTROLLING YOURSELF

The strongest martial artists go out of their way to avoid physical confrontation; they have nothing to prove. Author Terry Dobson tells a story about when he was an intermediate martial arts student. He wanted to prove his strength to the world. One day while riding a train he saw a drunk accost a group of people. Just as Terry got ready to do physical battle, a martial arts master quietly intervened. He quietly spoke to the drunk, who, ashamed of his actions, fell to his knees and cried. The threat was over; no blows were needed. Terry says he learned more about the martial arts, and himself, from this one incident than from years of training-hall practice.

All kinds of people practice the martial arts, and there are those who do so because they like to fight. Usually, as they mature in their practice, this fighting nature withers.

Martial artists experience the emotions of conflict. Being attacked, even in sparring, can elicit fear, anger, aggression, and frustration. In anyone, these emotions can provoke overreaction. Controlling conflict begins with controlling ourselves.

Master Shiba Yoshimasa's famous advice for developing martial arts students is quoted in *Ideals of the Samurai*:

There is nothing more base than for a man to lose his temper too often. No matter how angry one becomes, his first thought should be to pacify his mind and come to a clear understanding of the situation at hand. Then, if he is in the right, to become angry is correct.

Becoming angry simply on account of one's own bias is unreasonable, and one will not be held in respect. Thus, though one may become more and more angry, there will be no result. It is reason alone by which people feel humbled and for which they feel respect.

How do martial arts experts successfully control their emotions when under attack? Master Don Angier advises his students in yanagi-ryu not to get emotionally involved when attacked. This is easy to say, he tells them, but achieving such detachment requires much work.

Martial artist and leader both should be able to recognize the dynamics of conflict, to see their own attitudes and feelings honestly, and to develop skills to influence conflict situations. They learn that conflict is not the enemy; in fact, it can be skillfully directed toward the greater good. Terry Dobson tells his students that when he is attacked, it is a "gift of energy wrapped in violence. I simply accept the energy without the package."

Successfully managing the energy of conflict requires taking control of fear. This is a real problem for many of the managers I've worked with. People are often hampered by fears of rejection, losing status, or appearing ignorant. They may also be afraid of retribution by their peers or superiors, of what someone will do to them when their backs are turned. Still others fear losing control or appearing to be afraid; they often compensate for their fear with overaggressiveness. ("How dare they object? I'll show them!") Though they are continually demonstrating their "courage," fear controls them.

Some managers have trouble managing conflict because they fear new problems, that if they bring up an issue it will snowball into something unmanageable. Some fear that speaking honestly will cost them their jobs. Many managers don't believe they actually can control themselves, worrying that if push comes to shove, they'll just explode. Still others are concerned their supervisors will overreact.

A small number of people fear physical retaliation and, unfortunately, they have some reason for fear. Statistics reveal that physical attacks directed at coworkers or supervisors are on the rise, with employees in frequent contact with the public being especially at risk. Even when actual physical attacks don't occur, the resulting undercurrent of intimidation drains energy from strong performance. How can a fearful manager enact unpopular measures? Whatever the fear involved, it can harm job performance and prevent a manager from dealing decisively with conflict.

Fear aside, any rigid style of communication may disable a leader from successfully working with conflict. Martial artists know that a person's strength will also be his weakness. A strong kicker may rely too much on his foot strength; a good thrower may always try to close distance, even when it's not appropriate. Any one style has its limitations.

In the same vein, a manager who has a set interpersonal style (for example, he always tries to smooth out any signs of conflict) will only be effective within a narrow range of conflicts. The desire to smooth conflicts and not face them head on can play into the hands of someone who refuses to be quietly mollified and threatens to make a scene. A one-style manager may be stymied if the situation calls for a different approach.

Making Conflict an Ally

Martial artists employ the physical laws of energy and mass to maximize the power in strikes and throws. Conflict is a form of energy, which, as Einstein's Law of Conservation of Energy shows, cannot be created or destroyed. But it can be channeled toward productivity or other corporate goals. Organizational dynamics expert Gordon Lippitt agrees: "Conflict releases energy at every level of human affairs, energy that can produce positive, constructive results. . . . The goal is not to eliminate conflict, but to use it, to turn the released energy to good advantage."

Because part of being a leader entails being a problem solver, conflicts in an organization fall squarely on the leader's shoulders. The leadership role is basically an aggressive one. The job is to help others (employees) *change*, become more efficient, work better together, and align themselves with organizational goals. Expecting change can be a potential source of conflict.

Through strong conflict management, leaders influence where and how organizational energy is directed. For instance, conflict can be exciting enough to wake up a slumbering department or organization. And conflict can be the parent of creativity. When people are satisfied with the status quo, and everything runs smoothly, there often is little creativity. Conflicting values, opinions, and ideas spur the development and trial of new, more efficient methods.

Just as sparring partners feel the harmony of comradeship after a good workout, an organization that has a healthy approach to conflict can achieve true harmony. Once people express their objections and hash out a difficult problem, the groundwork has been laid for calm problem solving.

Well-managed conflict also

- brings alternate sides of issues to the surface

- clarifies an issue by letting people air and work out their objections

- increases participation and involvement

- improves the quality of problem solving

- makes communication easier

- strengthens relationships

- enlivens and renews an organization

- is a powerful training aid, providing an example to employees of how unexpected problems with coworkers can be realistically handled

- helps an organization clean house of excess emotional baggage

- fosters organizational, professional, and personal growth

Conflict is truly not your enemy. By learning to see its dynamics as a martial artist does, you will learn to harness it to positive ends.

Conflict Is Blind

Unfortunately, conflict often blinds the combatants. Walter Muryasz asks a partner to push her fist strongly against his. Mr. Muryasz then places his other fist on top of her hand and takes away his original hand.

Almost always his partner immediately pushes against the second hand. Whereas she was first pushing forward, she is now pushing up *without being aware of the switch.* When people are in a forceful frame of mind, they seek conflict everywhere. They push and look for a push back.

Mr. Muryasz has mastered this principle to throw opponents. He maneuvers to push against them so that they will exert their force toward a direction of unbalance—they are, in effect, heavily leaning on him; at that point, Mr. Muryasz merely removes his support and they fall.

So people will follow perceived or real resistance, wherever it leads. Once involved in conflict most people cannot see what they're doing. They become ineffective when dealing with colleagues or making important decisions. Emotions cloud reason. Even brilliant managers may do something that is potentially unfixable.

Conflict also is blind in another way. When people are in a conflicted frame of mind, they generally are unable to see that they are contributing to the problem. Ask any two warring parties what has happened and you'll hear each say he believes the other is mostly to blame: "I wasn't doing anything; he came up to me and went crazy." Most important, neither side sees that he may have escalated the conflict by pushing back *just a little bit harder.*

Of course, all of us try to push back where and when it is safe. If it is too risky to respond directly when pushed upon, there are numerous ways to push back indirectly:

- working only when we believe we are being monitored
- passing the conflict on to others by mistreating our subordinates, peers, vendors, and customers
- criticizing our bosses and the organization
- leaving for other employment
- stealing from the organization
- sabotaging

If you find yourself slipping into anger, calm yourself. Watching for the symptoms of hidden conflict can prevent it from blindsiding you. Following are the seven warning signals of negative conflicts:

1. changes in relationships from helpful/supportive to hindering/resistive

2. emotional wounds that don't heal

3. unusual emotional outbursts or preoccupations (dwelling on past incidents) that continue

4. persistent resistance to change

5. a climate of anger or fear

6. aggression or looking for fights

7. difficulty making decisions or getting work done

More than one of these signs is usually present before there is a serious conflict problem, but even a single symptom is worth investigation, simply because conflicts are generally easier to solve when dealt with early.

Although conflict is an emotional issue, almost anyone, no matter the age, size, sex, or position, can learn to manage conflict successfully—not just to squelch it, but to take the best possible advantage of it. First we need to acknowledge that conflict is normal—it does not have to cause overwhelming shame or fear. The three-step approach to managing conflict is this:

1. recognize the kind and level of conflict

2. decide what action to take

3. when taking action, use martial arts–based conflict management techniques and strategies

These last two steps are closely related, so they'll be considered in the same section.

RECOGNIZING THE CONFLICT

Martial artists see conflict as an energetic process—nothing more than a cycle of building, releasing, and lowering of energy that is potentially useful to them. They must recognize and assess the conflict because it determines how they will react.

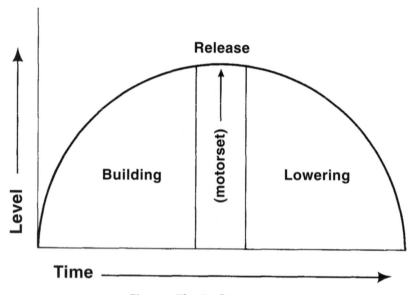

Figure 1. The Conflict Continuum

Conflict means "to strike together," hence it happens between two or more people. If we don't push back, there is no real conflict. Push back, consciously or inadvertently, and energy is delivered. Voices rise or speed up, actions become more aggressive or accelerated, shoulders rise, blood rushes to the face, eye contact becomes more intense, and responses are overly forceful.

When people are highly charged, near the top of their conflict curve, they can't be reasonable, so don't expect it of them. Solutions aren't appreciated, even those that might solve the problem. So this isn't the time to be logical with them. Not only is it difficult to get those in conflict to consider that there is a potential solution, there also can be resistance and overidentification on their part with issues: "Are you suggesting there's something wrong with my project?", as well as a lack of appropriate caution, and jockeying for power. Should you jump in (and who hasn't), you will likely hear: "Yes, but . . . ," or "I tried that . . . ," or "You don't understand. . . ." You'll see that their energy level doesn't decrease; it may even rise. You're actually reinforcing the conflict.

At some point, which varies according to the situation, the energy in the conflict peaks, and then releases. Releases may be varying sorts— screaming, crying, stomping away, slamming doors, throwing things, or

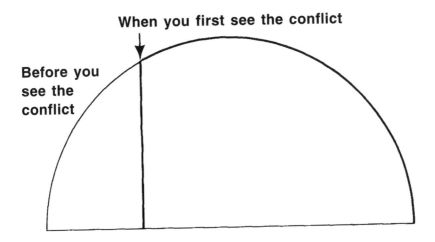

Figure 2. Your Initial View of the Conflict

even physical attacks. Then, after the release, there is a phase when the energy level lowers, the calm after the storm. Because they have let go of emotions and energy that were clouding their vision, people at this point are usually more open-minded and approachable, unless something was said or done that had lasting repercussions and that they wind up dwelling on.

Just before someone releases energy there is usually a point where nothing happens, a point of free fall. It's like the moment at the height of a jump when you are momentarily suspended, neither rising nor falling. This is a critical moment. At the peak of the conflict curve, someone can move either toward explosion or toward calmness. Walter Muryasz calls this point "motorset." Muscles are braced for action and yet held in check, as if they were simultaneously stopped and waiting for a starter's command to "Go!" Motorset is the moment of thick tension when "you can hear a pin drop," the suspenseful second when everything is on the verge of releasing.

In motorset the mind has given the body contingency instructions: "If this happens, you will immediately react." Mr. Muryasz says motorset is fairly common, even in everyday situations. Have you ever waited for a stoplight to turn green? The green arrow comes on and you involuntarily start to go? If so, you have experienced motorset. Your mind has commanded your body, "Go on the green." Even though you

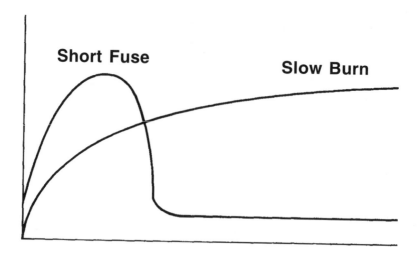

Figure 3. Different Conflict Styles

received the "wrong" stimulus—an arrow instead of a light changing—you still reacted.

It's important to be able to recognize when people are at motorset. If you do not want them to explode, don't do anything. Even a conciliatory gesture can push them over the edge. If you wish to help them become calmer, take control by doing nothing to them. Relax yourself, breathe, and control your own attitude. Motorset is a state of high tension that takes a large expenditure of energy to maintain. Shortly, if not pushed over the edge, a person's motorset energy will relax, bypassing the most dangerous moment.

Recognizing when a person is at motorset isn't always easy. When you encounter an angry person, his level of anger may not have mounted before your eyes. The conflict may have had a long history, so that by the time he reaches you, he was already close to motorset. Make it a practice to approach upset people carefully and look for signs of motorset. When you discover their position on the conflict continuum, you will be able to deal with them more effectively.

Individuals react to conflict differently and reach motorset at their own rate. Working closely with someone enables you to note their conflict style. Recognizing their individual speed of building a conflict curve will allow you to intervene adeptly to make conflict work for you. Some people are "slow burners"; generally, their energy rises and releases slowly, but they can tend to hold onto grudges for longer periods. In contrast, others have a "short fuse" and are more explosive. Their energy builds and releases quickly. They often are able to "forgive and forget" once their anger is released. Some people are a combination of the two.

Although you may know the people involved, read the conflict situation like a martial artist. Look beyond facial expressions—most people are somewhat adept at putting on masks—and concentrate on their entire body. Watch their hands.

Knowing *when* to say something can make the difference between heightened conflict (and wasted time) and profitable problem solving. Like a martial artist, wait for the *suki*, the opening. This opening comes as the conflict curve drops, past the point of motorset. Things are more calm and reasonable—this is the right moment to intervene. So when an upset person is no longer speaking and has wound down, the energy level is lower, and he or she will be more calm and receptive. This is the time to give your advice or make your suggestion.

CHOOSING AND ACTING ON A STRATEGY

Dealing with Threat and Intimidation: Throwing Fuel on the Fire

In the martial arts one learns that conflict has many guises, from angry glances to maneuvering for position to outright fighting. At work, conflict may be expressed as intimidation, threats, confrontation, back-stabbing, shunning, and harassment (including sexual).

Among the most direct and personally distressing forms of conflict are intimidation or threats, the weapons of a bully. Bullies are people who continually push others with the hope of drawing a response, a push-back. Intimidation and threats are like an extended motorset. The bully maintains a conflict curve close to the point of release, the tension and energy held at a constant, high level without being released. The message is "I am right on the edge. If you do (or don't do) this or that, I will explode/quit/fire you/never speak with you again/take retribution." Most bullies are quite perceptive. When bullies sense you pushing back, they know they've gotten to you. You cannot pretend to ignore or humor an intimidator when you're distressed, because the nonverbal

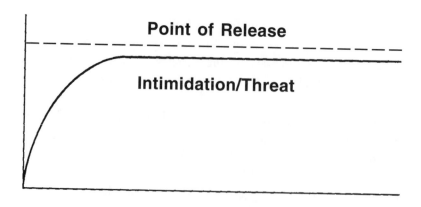

Figure 4. Intimidation is conflict energy sustained just below the point of release.

signals are obvious to someone who is looking for them.

Sustaining intimidation requires a great expenditure of energy. Leaking out discomfort while trying to ignore the bully only strengthens him. To reduce intimidation, don't play into it. Make the bully carry the entire weight of the conflict on his or her own. There's a good chance he or she will tire and look for an easier target. Again, being able to not react to intimidation is easier said than done.

Paul Watzlawick offers a useful way to deal with threat and intimidation. In *How Real Is Real: Confusion, Disinformation, and Communication*, he presents the three conditions of successful threat:

1. It must be convincing or believable enough to be taken seriously.

2. It must reach its target—the threatened party.

3. The target must be capable of complying with it.

To neutralize a threat, he suggests, eliminate or disable one of the three conditions. For example, if you're able, you might make an even more serious counterthreat: "If you do that, company regulations require that I fire you; I'll have no choice." Or to prevent the threat from reaching its target, you can put yourself out of the intimidator's reach. Last, you can show that you don't have the power to comply with the demand: "I'm sorry, I would like to help, but that is not within my role. You will have to speak with our Vice-President of Human Resources."

These are useful strategies, but I prefer also to consider the martial

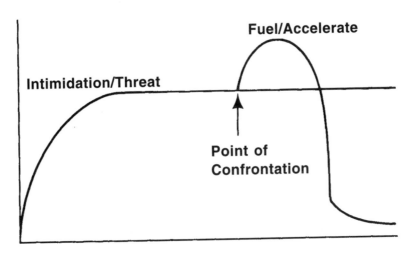

Figure 5. Confronting Intimidation or Conflict

arts approach of changing the conflict curve. In other words, call the bluff. The intimidation plays on the fear caused by anticipation of the unknown (see chapter 2). An unknown threat is usually more frightening than a specific consequence.

Calling the bluff and bringing it out into the open where you can deal with it is much less frightening than imagining catastrophe.

Some fires smolder invisibly, ever ready to flare up. Fire protection professionals may throw fuel on such a fire to make it flare up. When it is visible, the fire can be put out. Or starting their own "backfire" can control the blaze by eliminating fuel that's needed to spread. The strategy of *consciously* pushing with a strategic purpose is called "fueling" or "accelerating."

If you can't easily avoid an intimidator, and team performance is adversely affected, pick your time and place and confront the intimidator. By choosing the setting, you have made the first step toward controlling the conflict. In selecting the spot, ask yourself, do you want it to be more comfortable for him or for you? Is it better to have a group of supporters or neutral parties around, making it harder for him to deny what many others have seen, or is it better to be alone, so no one else sees what may transpire? Is it preferable to meet in your office, in his, or in some quiet restaurant? Sometimes the experienced conflict manager will choose the bully's favorite spot. There he's likely to be less defensive and even slightly disarmed by your selection and timing.

Clearly you will be more effective if you remain calm and relaxed. Practice some of the attitude and calming techniques in the first section of this book. In the fourteenth century, famed samurai Shiba Yoshimasa wrote (as quoted in Wilson's *Ideals of the Samurai*), "The man whose profession is arms should calm his mind and look into the depths of others. Doing so is the best of the martial arts."

It's understandable if you feel angry toward your opponent. But you can be angry *and* calm. When people are angry and out of control, they have little credibility, even when they are speaking the truth. If you don't fight your emotions, you will be more relaxed and communicate with more clarity and power.

Be prepared for an emotional outburst from your opponent. Remember that there's a lot of energy wrapped up in intimidation, and your strategy here is to add fuel to the fire to bring the situation to a head (and eventually resolve it). Confront the person until he cannot deny what is happening—don't let him escape. Lancing this boil can speed the ultimate healing time, saving longer-term discomfort.

Sometimes, an antagonist will bad-mouth you to others, yet to your face refuses to acknowledge there is any problem. Fueling can bring behind-the-back talk to the surface. When people avoid resolving an ongoing conflict, they usually wind up sustaining a cold war. A manager can carefully fan the embers to force recognition of the conflict and to encourage its resolution. Bringing the conflict into the open is not enough—you still have to resolve the underlying problem ("You have always seemed to give preferential treatment to others"). So, after the release process begins, follow through until the conflict curve lowers and the situation becomes safer.

If we choose a fueling strategy, always bear in mind that accelerating conflict is dangerous. If we're not careful, fueling glowing sparks can result in our being burned by a raging fire. Most of all, be careful not to lose control and throw fuel on the fire without careful planning. Fueling is not a good thing to attempt when we're in an out-of-control rage.

But in spite of the risks, there are times when no other strategy will work and the risk is worth the probable gain. It's certainly worth trying when we feel disabled by intimidation or working in fear. In any case, it is important to remember that fueling is only the *first* step; once problems are brought out into the open, the work of problem solving and negotiating begins.

Defusing: Throwing Water on the Fire

More often than not, it is better to reduce the conflict and safely channel the force away before it escalates dangerously. This is like throwing water on the fire, a process I call "defusing." Because defusing can require more time than other strategies it usually makes most sense when one or more of the following circumstances is in effect:

- conflict affects continuing relationships or longer-term harmony
- it is more important to win the war than the battle
- customers are adversely involved (even indirectly)
- time is available (that is, there's no emergency)

If we decide to defuse a conflict, it's best to act at an early stage, at which time less effort will be required. At a higher energy level, fear and anger can freeze people into ridiculous, self-defeating stances, and the situation is more explosive. At such levels, it's necessary not to do anything that could be interpreted as personally threatening if we want to help the other person calm down.

In the martial arts, it's easier to defend yourself than to protect a third party. When the assault is not directed at us, it's more difficult to lead the attacker (as a bullfighter does with his cape) because he's not as easily influenced by our movements. And once we enter the fray, running away is no longer a good option; now we have to think of protecting not only ourselves, but at least one and perhaps both combatants.

The problems of third-party mediation are many: it is like a physical assault, more difficult to control than conflict aimed directly at us. How can we help others deal with their own conflicts without taking their problems on ourselves? When is it right to intervene and when is it better to stay out? Generally, it's best not to get involved unless one or more of the following criteria is in play:

- the conflicting parties have historically been unable to reach an accord

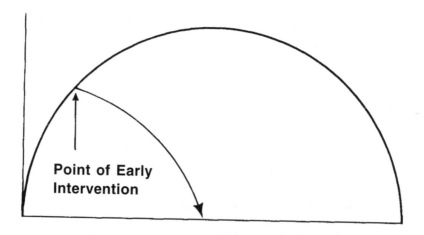

**Point of Early
Intervention**

Figure 6. Defusing or "Throwing Water" on Conflict

- the conflict is adversely affecting others

- the parties are at an impasse

- they both request your intervention

Organizational dynamics expert Gordon Lippitt suggests an interesting approach: "Look at the issues involved coldly and at the people involved warmly." This is akin to the martial artist's goal of staying unruffled during a fight while cleaving to the spirit of protection.

Always keep your own long-term goals in mind. Are you trying to help these two to work harmoniously? Or do you perhaps want each to separately do his job? Or are you just hoping to keep them off your back? Design your mediation to achieve your goals.

Listening is one good way to safely channel away the force of conflict—really listening, not just going through the motions of repeating what the other person says, or of saying "uh-huh" every thirty seconds.

How can you judge the effectiveness of your conflict strategy? Watch the level of energy. In defusing, the energy should decrease—voices grow quieter, tensions decrease. If you're not seeing the results you want, try something different. It makes no sense to persist blindly with a strategy that doesn't help, like the beginning jujitsu student doggedly trying to apply a wristhold to an extremely flexible attacker. While there really is no way to know beforehand what will work, with experience you will tend to select more effective techniques. The following third-party mediation strategies may work.

Use a "separate/together sandwich." Interview each party individually and take notes on what they say. Be especially watchful for any acknowledgment of partial responsibility, as opposed to a purely "it's her fault" stance. Usually by the time the conflict reaches the manager for mediation, both parties are highly defensive and afraid they will be found in the wrong and lose status, advancement opportunities, or even their position. In these individual meetings, help calm them down and reduce defensiveness. Next, meet with them together. Control the tone of the meeting. Show them that you don't want to assess blame, but to get things working well again.

If you choose to have a joint meeting, you can establish some rules as a famous master once did. In *Ideals of the Samurai: Writings of Japanese Warriors*, William Scott Wilson writes, "Both Kuroda Nagamasa [a seventeenth-century lord] and his father Josui were well known for their regard of others, and Nagamasa even set aside one night a month when he would sit with a number of his trusted retainers and allow all to talk freely with the mutual promise that none would become angry over what was said, or gossip about it later. These were called the 'Meetings Without Anger.'"

In a meeting with two opposing parties, it is best to accentuate their similarities: "I am pleased both of you are concerned with important details and that you want the division to seek out new directions." Consider assigning the two parties to a short-term project together. Suggest peaceful coexistence. Sometimes only a nonthreatening invitation is necessary to break a stalemate. Ask for their help: "This conflict is dividing our department. Frankly, things are in a crunch. I need both of you to help." Adjust your style to the situation. You may choose to be authoritarian, a technique that is useful when there is little time to resolve the issues and a quick solution is needed, when the conflict is a long-standing one that both parties express little hope of solving on their own, or when the conflict has been sharp or bitter *from the beginning*.

A less authoritarian style works best when both parties have cooled down and each has strong enough communication skills to work it out. Bear in mind their expectations of you as a mediator. At the beginning of a mediation, try to match their expectations of you. Don't start by being democratic if they're expecting you to smash through their problems with an iron fist. You can ease off or change your style later. Ultimately, however, the more they see the solution as their own, rather than imposed by you, the better and the more lasting the resolution.

The greater your credibility as a mediator, the more successful the intervention is likely to be. When you're highly skilled at managing conflict, people will note this and perceive you in a way that will make your job as mediator even easier in the future.

Enlist other agents. There may be others in the organization—peers of the conflicting parties or human resource specialists—who also can serve as mediators.

Train the antagonists in conflict management and mediation techniques. Now that you've given them a fish, teach them to fish. After the conflict has been successfully resolved, make use of it. Soon afterward, discuss with these employees what they learned from conflict and what lasting advantages they see resulting from it: "That worked out nicely. How would you like to be able to head off these problems in the future?" or "You worked that through very well, albeit with some help. Would you be interested in learning how to help others, as I did with you?" You are modeling effective actions that others can use to improve their conflict management skills without depending on you. Deputizing them this way is a high-leverage activity; it influences others over an extended time. In the future, they can become a force for improved conflict utilization within their own work areas.

Remember that mediation is not the only third-party strategy. You can also choose to separate the parties, support the underdog, or fire either or both. Generally, however, these strategies contribute to an appearance, not the reality, of harmony.

Avoiding or Displacing: Escaping the Fire

Sometimes, even for a skilled warrior, retreat makes sense. In an often-related story, Miyamoto Musashi, while aboard a ferry, was challenged by a young warrior eager to gain reputation Seeing that the youth would not be mollified, Musashi reluctantly agreed. But he pointed out that fighting on the boat might result in injury to innocent people. So he suggested that the two of them take the ferry's small lifeboat to a nearby island. The youth eagerly agreed. Musashi beckoned the young warrior to enter the rowboat first, implying that he would follow. But once his young challenger was aboard, Musashi cast off the boat's line. Without oars, the youth could only float helplessly away as Musashi calmly looked on.

Avoiding or displacing is a conflict strategy that moves the conflict energy safely away, either by moving you from it, or by moving it from you. This is a common strategy, probably because many people are uncomfortable or unskilled in conflict situations; also, avoiding is relatively easy to do. Common examples of displacing are:

- *firing* a problem staff member

- *humoring* or *ignoring* a chronically negative person (who, everyone agrees, "should have been terminated long ago and can't be fired now")

- *separating* feuding people ("Why don't we change their shifts, or even move them to different areas of the building?")

- *withdrawing* from conflict ("I see that's a problem, but I really have to go now.")

- *passing a conflict on* ("Someone else can better help you with this.")

The problem with avoiding is that it doesn't lower the conflict energy, or solve the problem. It merely moves it out of sight, and out of mind. As an example, schools use displacement extensively when they suspend, expel, or remove students to detention. But the anger, hurt, or frustration don't magically go away. Still harboring anger or resentment, expelled students may explode in other ways, committing crimes such as vandalism against the school or attacks on school staff. Admittedly, educators have a difficult job with complex problems, but displacement is not a good answer for discipline problems. Even when a student is "successfully" removed, the conflicts are only transferred from the school into society at large.

Have you ever seen two children fighting? Commonly, adults separate the two and ask them to make up. Sure enough, the children go through the motions of shaking hands. But the conflict is not resolved. Usually, one of two things happens. The children finish it themselves later, or there is a cold war. In contrast, two children who work out their conflict to completion without adult intervention can often resolve their differences and become excellent friends.

Displacement is best thought of as a temporary measure that makes most sense when there are other emergencies that must be dealt with without delay; when you wish to control the time and place of a confrontation; when you are afraid the situation, if faced, might get dangerously out of hand (of course, as your conflict management skills grow, your fear of these scenarios will lessen accordingly); when the long-term relationship with the conflicting party is unimportant; when it is advisable, for safety reasons, to humor a deranged person; or when nothing else has worked.

Displacement can provide the time to restore needed balance. Customer service representatives I've worked with report they sometimes butt heads with an angry customer. Nothing they do seems to work; the customer won't calm down or be appeased. Finally, in frustration, the customer service representatives refer the difficult customer to their supervisors, usually with a warning ("I've got a really difficult one this time"). The supervisor picks up the phone and, wonder of wonders, the customer is extremely polite. What happened?

Granted, the customer was difficult to start with, but the real problem probably developed when he and the customer service rep pushed on each other. Each was unwilling to yield, and perhaps neither wanted to be a pushover or each feared losing face. As a result, both became off balance and rigid by emotionally bracing against the other. Passing this customer on to the supervisor provides a cooling-off period during which the customer can regain his balance. Often people in this situation are ashamed of their previously unreasonable stance or grateful for the end of the battle. So they go out of their way to be understanding, even to the point of apologizing to the supervisor!

You can use a cooling-off period any time you and your "opponent" are at an impasse, or when you are afraid that either of you is losing control and will say or do something rash. If this happens in person, look him square in the eye, say you'll be right back, but you were just on your way to the bathroom. What can he say? Go to the bathroom and assume control of yourself. Use any technique that works quickly for you. Then you will be able to return on a calmer note and be better able to solve the problem.

Briefly displacing conflict during a phone call can also work well. Telephone communication has inherent limitations. There are fewer nonverbal cues to read, so body language communication doesn't work. Because of this, it is more difficult to make and maintain good contact with the caller, and therefore harder to resolve conflicts.

But the martial arts approach is to focus on the favorable aspects of any situation you're in. The advantage of phone calls is that you are invisible. If you are head-to-head with someone on the phone, consider a telephone time-out. You can do this several ways.

- Ask if you can put them on hold so that you can call up further information on your computer. Use the time to regain self-control. For these purposes, it doesn't really matter whether you have a computer or not.

- Tell them you must get further information from someone else and that you will call back within ten minutes.

- Hang up *on yourself,* then call them right back and apologize. This will often break a communication logjam. (This isn't a good strategy if you work for a telephone company.)

Remember, the point of a telephone time-out, or of any cooling-off period, is to use the separation to regain your balance and composure. Unfortunately, we hear of labor dispute cooling-off periods that turn out to be anything but that. During these periods of separation, conflict instead builds as parties mentally replay discussions and incite themselves. Don't waste your time pumping up your anxiety; instead, lower your own energy level. Then you can make contact again with more control.

Displacement is often misused. Yes, dealing with conflict can be uncomfortable, but avoiding or fleeing from conflict creates situations that in the long run are even more uncomfortable or dangerous. Remember that when you avoid conflict, the problem is not solved, only moved out of sight and hearing. That's well and good if you decide not to deal with that dissatisfied person now. But if you want their loyalty and best efforts in the long term, be sure to schedule a time reasonably soon when you can resolve the problem. Putting people off indefinitely only generates lasting ill will.

Displacement can backfire if you use it with a highly charged person. A very irritated customer may become even more upset if you put her off or pass her along to someone else. Have you ever called a business with a complaint, only to get transferred around? Most people become even more perturbed by this and their energy level will rise; if they are past the edge of their conflict curve they may hang up angrily or verbally explode at a hapless operator. The ones that don't release their frustration may harbor ill will toward that business for a long time. Remember this, if you do find it necessary to pass an angry person to another staff member: first help lower her energy level by listening—don't transfer her while she is seething, reassure her that you are taking personal responsibility for helping her ("I will make sure this gets straightened out"), stay in contact for a short time after you make the transfer (phone or in person) until you are sure she feels she is getting adequate assistance, offer your name and number as a backup, and follow up with her at a later date ("I wanted to make sure everything got resolved"). You can modify this approach to be effective with those you supervise, as well as customers.

CREATIVE CONFLICT

Any strategy works in some situations; none of them work in all. A versatile conflict manager is able to handle almost any kind of conflict—with short-fusers, slow-burners, or intimidators, whether the conflict is just beginning or almost peaked. Yet people tend to be more comfortable with one strategy than others. In the martial arts context of honest thinking, it's important to know what is your most preferred approach—fueling/confrontation, defusing, or avoidance/displacement?

Go beyond your self-set limits; don't trap yourself into one style. When circumstances are relatively safe, try other approaches. It's dangerous to attempt a new approach in a volatile situation. The best way to learn something new is under low-stress conditions. The martial artist learns a new defense under controlled rules in practice sessions with a trusted partner, not in a life-and-death battle. With this in mind, develop strength in defusing by selecting conflicts that are relatively safe—with close friends or less intimidating peers. Practicing this way allows you to refine the technique, to develop your own modifications, and to increase your confidence.

As previously indicated, expert martial artists develop techniques they haven't previously seen—creativity emerges from their conflict. In the same way, in dynamic organizations conflict also can fuel creativity. In the energy-building phase, ideas are generated. People disagree, perhaps strongly, but without their egos being lastingly threatened.

Momentum builds to the point of agreement. Things reach a fever pitch as people ask, "What are we going to do? How?" Finally consensus emerges as discussion turns into a plan of action. When talk and planning evolve into action, it can be a tense time of eliciting commitment and choosing direction. Tension levels lower after agreement, and the energy is channeled into the real work.

Creative, dynamic organizations do see ups and downs, tension and conflict. Where there are people, there will be disagreements, insecurities, and different approaches. But black-belt leaders focus on converting this energy toward the positive, to strengthen the organization and the people who are a part of it.

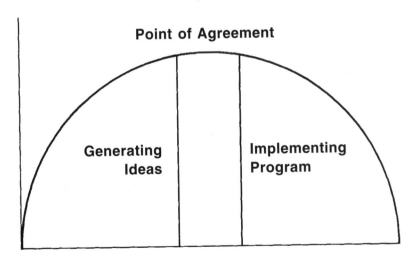

Figure 7. Conflict in Creativity

DEFENDING AGAINST ROLE ATTACKS
AND PERSONAL ATTACKS

It's not unusual for martial artists to be challenged by people wanting to test their fighting skills. One martial arts instructor was having a drink with an advanced student after class in a tavern. His equipment bag was partially open, revealing his black belt. A stranger approached the instructor and asked in a belligerent and slurred voice, "Are you a black belt?" "Yes," the *sensei* reluctantly answered; he watched the questioner. Within a few minutes the stranger screamed and rushed the instructor, who simply swiveled on the stool out of the line of attack. The man ran into the bar counter and knocked himself unconscious. The instructor caught him and gently lowered him to the ground. "Let's get out of here," he said to his student. And they left.

There was no real conflict between the instructor and the attacker—it takes two or more parties to make a conflict. It was merely a test of a martial arts black belt, an example of a role attack. It wasn't a personal attack. The martial artist and high-level leaders should distinguish between these two basic forms. Differentiating between the two will enable you to respond more effectively to both.

Role attacks focus solely on a person's position. While individual employees react differently to their manager—some are approval-seeking, some are supportive, and others rebellious—this is generally not a personal response to the manager. (Although personal factors of course do enter into these relationships.)

A worker may confront a manager by saying, "What is the matter with you people in management? None of you know what is going on; no one does any planning! You messed up my vacation schedule again and I'm not going to stand for it!" This is not a *personal* attack, so don't take it as such. The "you people" and "none of you" categorize the manager as part of the management of that company.

Basically, in role conflict one party attacks another on the basis of a class, or a stereotype. This can be directed toward any number of things:

- job role ("You've done it again. Shot from the hip. That's a typical Marketing move.")

- job level (management vs. line staff, midmanagement vs. upper management)

- job category (white collar vs. blue collar or office staff vs. field personnel)

- sex ("You're just like the other women executives.")

- location ("You people in the head office never understand our needs. You're up in the clouds.")

- race, religion, or national origin

- age ("Things are different now. What's the matter with your generation? Why can't you change with the times?")

- many others ("You single parents spend more time on the phone than doing the job. That's why I can't get through when I need assistance." "That's a typical response for your organization!" "You bureaucrats are preventing me from getting my work done on time.")

Role attacks are worth hearing; they can show up interdepartmental frustrations and anti-organizational attitudes that may need changing. Listen for the message, but don't view them as personally threatening.

In contrast, personal attacks clearly stand out as direct, negative shots at an individual: "You've had it in for me ever since I was transferred here. What's your problem?" But even when an attack is meant to be personal, you don't have to respond to it as such. It's up to you whether you do. Remember, even when you're under attack, there is no conflict without your resistance. You can be in control.

The Technique of Untargeting

One of the first self-defense movements budding martial artists learn is to *get off the line.* That is, they move out of the path of the attack by ducking, sidestepping, swerving, or doing anything else that gets them out of the line of attack. Fancy kicks, punches, and throws can wait, because if a good blow from an opponent lands on you first, you may not get another opportunity to use your own techniques.

Likewise, when a verbal, emotional attack is unleashed at you and you don't wish to get hit, move out of the line of fire. To control a role attack, don't respond in your role! When you hear, "What is the matter with you people in management?" don't say, "How dare you speak to me that way? I'm your boss and don't you ever forget it if you want to continue working here." This kind of retaliation only accelerates the conflict from which neither of you may be able to disengage before serious consequences occur.

Instead, respond *personally.* "Joe, I know how you feel. I'd get pretty upset too if my vacation seemed up in the air. Give me some more details. Let's see if we can straighten this out. By the way, where are you planning to go?" A response to role attack ("What the hell do you managers know about sales anyway?") might be, "Sharon, I'm sorry about this problem" or "Not much beyond my summer selling job in college, Sharon. But I've been assigned to see this one through."

Notice the use of the first name, which can diffuse a tense situation. But because nonverbal communication carries the meat of the message, words often are less important than the delivery in this situation. The key is to make your tone of voice informal; this is what makes a response personal. Although, keep in mind, there are situations in which it may not be appropriate to call someone by first name. You have to be the judge of that.

Conversely, when you're on the receiving end of a personal attack, make sure to respond in your role. If an employee says, "You self-important s.o.b. You've had it in for me since I got here," you might reply, "Mr. Erickson, I am sorry that you are unhappy. You understand there are certain procedures we must follow. But, of course, we will do our best to work through your concerns. Now what is the specific problem?" Notice the use of the more formal address; more importantly, the tone is more distant, more in *role.*

Basically, this untargeting technique means not pushing back when a conflict is offered. It's easy to write about, but it's hard to do because it requires self-control. Most people's first impulse is to respond in kind. But a personal response to a personal attack actually enlarges you as the target. It's as though an arrow were flying your way and instead of ducking you puffed up your chest and said, "OK, hit me!"

As a response, untargeting can disarm even the strongest attack. Answer in a totally unexpected manner and use the power of distraction. The attacker is focused assaulting the front—your role—but you counter from the side, as an individual, surprising the attacker and leading him off balance.

Another disarming technique is distraction. Scott Rohr, former tae kwon do world champion, has developed the art of setting up a devastating kicking sequence by first pointing with his fingertips. Even when an opponent knows what Scott is trying to do, it is difficult to prevent a slight flutter in concentration; this momentary opening is usually all Scott needs to land his first kick.

It's not always easy to determine whether an attacker is role directed or personally directed, particularly when there is minimal communication, as when an employee who seems disgruntled is unwilling to discuss his problem or a supervisor only receives negative feedback secondhand. But if you can tell whether an attack is mostly role or personal, use untargeting. Note that this strategy, like most conflict management techniques, does not solve the underlying problem. But it does help lower the conflict curve, prevent escalation, and put you and the attacker in a position to calmly problem solve together and strengthen your working relationship.

NONVERBAL TECHNIQUES FOR CONTROLLING CONFLICT

Remember, the greatest warrior conquers himself first. There are many techniques for controlling conflict, but in all cases, it is essential to keep in mind that the focus has to be on controlling yourself, not others. If you attempt to use the following techniques to control another, they will be far less effective and can even backfire. Your intention is crucial; others can read it. Also, these techniques are individual. What works for one person (or against one adversary) may not for another. Things are never the same. A method that defuses conflict between Joanne and Peter today may not work tomorrow during another similar conflict between the very same two people.

These methods are predominantly nonverbal. There are twelve main factors in any conflict situation. Control them and you can direct the conflict.

Mental Techniques

1. **Attitude.** Martial artists work continuously on their attitude. What is your conflict attitude? Do you have a "victim" attitude? ("Oh no, I'm

in for it now!") Or do you have a "punishing" attitude? ("How dare you challenge me? You'll pay for this!") Do you see conflict as destructive, as something that should always be smoothed over?

Some of the attitude control methods in the first section can help you develop a strong conflict-utilization attitude. You can learn to see that conflict can be natural and healthy, and that you can direct it to desired goals.

2. Timing. Can you sense when others are receptive? How well do you stay in contact during conversation? Do you typically jump ahead or lag behind others? Good timing involves seeing and using openings, and waiting for the space before intervening. Waiting is an art in itself. Discipline yourself to wait like a cat stalking a mouse, relaxed, yet fully alert, ready to act when the opportunity presents itself.

Martial arts expert Walter Muryasz says people rarely stay in contact with others for more than a few moments when carrying on a social conversation, discussing a business deal, or executing a self-defense movement. They are impatient to get their point across and their job done. But openings usually appear and close quickly. By the time they are noticed and action is attempted, the opening has disappeared. So the moment of receptivity is gone, the opportunity has evaporated, and the person is on guard once more.

In contrast, good timing, Muryasz emphasizes, entails staying in close contact with the other person—"hugging the surface." If you're searching for a door opening in the dark, run your hands along the door surface, rather than patting for it. When a gap opens, you won't have to search for it, because you'll slip into it.

3. Presence. Have you ever met a martial arts master? They seem to be big, larger than their actual physical size. They have a strong presence—there's a feeling of great energy about them.

Presence comes from single-mindedness. It's the ability to be "present" with others. To increase your presence, practice focusing single-mindedly when you listen or speak with others. Discipline yourself not to become distracted by what has just occurred ("What did she mean by that?"), by what is going to happen ("Where is he going? Is he going to ask me to resign?"), or by thoughts about other places ("I wish I were in my garden right now"). If your mind races or dwells during conflicts, bring it back to the present so you don't miss anything important.

Techniques of the Senses

Ninja warriors were known for their ability to move easily in the dark and seem invisible to others. Attune yourself to ninja level by using the following techniques of the senses during conflict.

4. Hearing. How well do you listen? Can you hear without overreacting to loaded words? ("You called me a what? How dare you!")

Use the copper wire technique. Copper is an excellent conductor that allows electricity to pass through it without being harmed itself. In contrast, a resistor is something that actively blocks the flow of electricity; it gets hot when current is passed through it. So when emotional current is coming your way, don't resist. If you do, you, too, will get hot.

Make sure both feet are flat on the ground. Imagine there is a copper wire running through the middle of your body from your head, down your torso, and splitting off into two branches through your legs, your feet, and into the ground. Allow the opponent's emotional current to pass through you, and be grounded out. Don't resist it and let it heat you up.

Listen fully to what the other person says. Allow your own reactions—emotions, thoughts, or physical feelings—to pass through the copper wire into the ground. People have reported this technique is especially easy to use over the phone where they can close their eyes to visualize the copper wire. This technique will help you to remain calm and be more perceptive.

In a tense situation remain in control like a martial expert. Don't be goaded into a fight that does not serve you. To prevent your overreacting to loaded words during a heated conversation, control your attention as though it were a stereo: turn up the music, turn down the words. You won't miss anything important when you downplay the words and tune up an opponent's tone of voice and body language. You'll hear everything, but the words will be in the background. Since you're now less likely to take offense, it will be easier to help your opponent lower his energy level. Then, firmly in control, you can move on to productive problem solving.

5. Eyes. Many martial arts instructors advise students to fight with "soft eyes." They teach how not to become so focused on one thing, one part of the body, or one person that you miss seeing other dangers. Open your vision. Focus softly and let your peripheral vision widen.

Strong leaders can do the same thing during conflict. Practice widening and narrowing your attention span. Consciously shift your focus so you see both facial and body cues, even taking in onlookers' reactions, when these may be important. Use soft eyes and see the entire scene.

Don't get trapped into only seeing an opponent's eyes. A staring contest, or staredown, becomes a push-push conflict. Neither side wants to look away, as this would be an admission of weakness or defeat. But sustaining this kind of eye conflict can be uncomfortable, and may even escalate the discord. Try this simple martial arts technique as an alternative to giving in or playing "stare wars."

When the stare-off becomes uncomfortable, slightly shift your focus to a point between your opponent's eyes. Now look at him with soft eyes, seeing his entire facial expression. This movement is so small that he won't be able to tell you're not looking him squarely in the eyes. But despite its subtlety, such a slight shift will relieve the tension and prevent you from feeling overpowered. You'll both have an opportunity to back off and regain your mental balance.

6. Voice. Martial artists use their voices extensively. There is even one martial art, kiaijitsu, that focuses on sophisticated methods of shouting as its main weapon. Experts in this art are said to be able to disable opponents with just their voice as a weapon.

Such remarkable voice power is beyond the layperson, but a trained, well-timed voice can strike fear into an opponent, distract him, or focus one's own strength. For example, hypnotists use a soothing voice to instill calmness. Large-animal trainers also use their voices to take control and forestall attacks. Opera singers can shatter a glass with a single, sustained note.

Practice modulating your voice. Basically, the voice is a wind instrument whose sound comes from breathing through the larynx and a formed mouth. Breathing exercises can aid voice control until you develop the ability to raise or lower vocal pitch and volume at will.

People who tend to displace—to avoid or suppress conflict—often have voices that operate mostly on the soft side. If you are like this, I suggest you practice turning up your vocal volume at times.

Those who are prone to fueling conflict by accelerating or confronting the situation may wish to work on lowering and slowing their voice when they become angry. Any time you are alone and out of earshot, you can practice changing voice pitch, speed, and volume. Driving alone with the car windows rolled up is one time to practice.

7. **Touch.** Except for the expert in kiaijitsu (see number 6), martial artists work primarily through touch. In the throwing arts (jujitsu, judo, etc.), which control another's balance, it's vital to develop a sensitive and strong touch. Similarly, practitioners of wing chun, who rely on first reading and then redirecting an opponent's direction and strength of attack, devote a significant portion of training time to fine-tuning their tactile perception through the practice of chi sao (sticking hands). They enlist contact for control.

Similar principles apply at work, assuming they do not feed possible perceptions of harassment or intimidation. How comfortable are you with touch? Do you know when it is appropriate to touch someone else?

If touch is to be an effective means of dealing with a conflict, it helps to know how to read another's "touchability." The research of Dr. John Kappas in his *Professional Hypnotism Manual* is interesting in this regard. He says that generally you can tell in advance whether or not someone is comfortable being touched. People who accept touching tend to touch other people themselves and to use broad gestures when they talk. They also tend to wear loose-fitting clothing. On the other hand, those who dislike being touched tend to speak with limited hand gestures, not touch others, and wear more tailored clothing. Making physical contact with a "no-touch" person can escalate a conflict. In contrast, a calm, relaxed touch between those who are comfortable with it can calm emerging antagonism.

Also know where to touch. This depends on who the other person is and his or her cultural orientation—a spouse, best friend, casual coworker, or first-time customer. It is best not to use touching to defuse conflict if it might be interpreted as a sexual advance.

Generally, it's also wise to avoid touching a coworker's face, head, arms, or back of hands. This can be seen as patronizing or overly intimate. In Western culture, the shoulders are usually the safest place to touch. If you're operating in a different culture, it is important to learn how touching might be interpreted there.

Know how to touch. It's better not to approach a person quickly or directly from the front. This may seem as if you're rushing the person and can induce a protective reaction. It's preferable to move closer slowly and from the side. In addition, pushing down too hard on someone conveys that you're trying to dominate. At the other extreme, touching too softly may communicate weakness or unsureness.

Touch is a useful conflict-defusing technique only when both you and the other person are comfortable with it. You don't necessarily have to know in advance whether this will work. Just pay attention. If you begin to touch someone, and he starts to tense, back off. If you still insist on touching, he'll see it as an attack.

Movement Techniques

During conflict, moving like a martial artist can keep you in control, as well as safer.

8. Posture. In chapter 3, we examined ways posture can affect your emotional state. Your posture also influences others' perceptions of you during conflict.

I have shown photos of people in various postures to thousands of seminar participants throughout the world. Amazingly, they report similar conclusions: People who are slumped (C-shaped posture) are seen as weak, disinterested, unapproachable, or bored. People who assume a rigid, I-shaped posture are described as aggressive, tense, or rigid. When someone maintains a natural, S-shaped posture, he is seen as relaxed, confident, equal, and approachable.

By consciously assuming the appropriate posture, you can enhance communication and your control of conflict. And don't slip into a posture that contradicts what you are trying to do. Saying "OK, I'll give in and do it your way" while assuming an I-shaped posture is not effective because it sends out a mixed message. This will either confuse the other person or lower your credibility. Others tend to believe your nonverbal communication and disregard your words, so it is critical that these both agree.

In the right situation each posture has advantages. For example, a C-shaped posture is best when

- someone is intimidated by you and you want to offset your threatening appearance

- you are trying to placate someone's anger and want to emphasize that you are giving in to his demands

Assume an I-shaped posture when

- you wish to show you are unyielding on this point, that "the line is drawn here"

- you're attempting to overpower someone

And a natural S-shaped posture is best when

- you wish to communicate on an equal level

- you want to feel—and be—relaxed and confident

9. Balance. Martial artists know that the more balanced they are, the more relaxed and stronger they'll be. Black belts have long known that our state of balance communicates our level of vulnerability to others.

Communications professor Betty Grayson wanted to determine whether nonverbal communication affected "attackability." She showed ten-second silent videotapes of different people walking to a prison audience of convicted murderers, muggers, and rapists. The audience rated each person's "assault potential" on a scale of one (most assaultable, a very easy rip-off) to ten (would avoid them, too big a situation, too heavy). The filmed subjects were males and females of all ages.

After the criminals had rated the victims, she took the clips of the most attackable people (rated one through three) and the least attackable (rated eight through ten) to someone trained in labanalysis, a form of body movement notation. Professor Grayson asked this expert whether there were any differences between the two groups and whether the members of each group had anything in common, and the labanalyst said that the most and least attackable people showed markedly different body movements.

According to an article in the *Washington Post,* Grayson reported that

> five movement characteristics were common to all the selected victims. First was the way they lifted their feet. Instead of walking from heel to toe, they picked up their whole foot and put it down—like a Spanish dancer. They all used exaggerated strides, either too long or too short. And they moved laterally. Instead of swinging their right arm with their left leg, they moved the same arm as leg. Then there was the way the top of their body moved in conjunction with the bottom of their body. It was as though their torso moved at cross-purposes, with the right shoulder moving in conjunction with their left hip. And they

walked so that their arm and leg movements appeared to come from outside their body instead of from within. Although women in the "45 and older" group were nearly twice as likely [as other people] to be judged easy victims, an equal number of men and women in the "35 and under" group were picked as easy targets.

I suspect "45 and older" women were deemed most attackable because of culture, not sex. Perhaps these women grew up during a period when it was less acceptable for females to appear physically robust.

Usually, when someone is intimidated, his balance drifts back over his heels, making him an emotional and physical "pushover." Control your balance. Enhance how strong you feel. Don't lean away or be off balance during conflicts.

10. Distance. Positioning is critical in any conflict or competition. One way to control position is to choose the correct distance; this allows you to use leverage most effectively. In face-to-face communication, it's important to make good contact. Too much physical distance in conflict dilutes emotional contact; too little space can be threatening. Again, the appropriate nonverbal working distance between people is determined by relationships. In some cultures, it's considered rude and emotionally cold not to be able to smell the other's body odors; in others, more distance is considered proper. We generally tolerate friends and family standing closer to us than strangers.

Some people are space invaders. They attempt to intimidate by getting too close. But you don't have to allow yourself to be taken off balance this way.

You can keep them at arm's length. When they begin to move in, pat them on the shoulder. *Pat down, not away.* This will tend to plant them in place. If you push them *away,* you invite escalation.

When the space invader moves in, turn to the side. People will tolerate someone standing closer to them side-by-side than squarely in front. Turn your head and speak to them shoulder to shoulder. This will help you feel less attacked and more in control.

11. Speed. On the mat or in a fight, speed is important. If you move too slowly, you can lose an advantage. But faster isn't always better. Sometimes, performing a martial arts technique too quickly can wake up an opponent. It's often better to wait until they are really off balance before making your move.

Consciously control your speed. When the conflict is close to the top of its curve, rapid motion can trigger a strong defensive reaction. Practice slowing down and speeding up your intensity of motion and voice, at will. Besides helping you control conflict, being able to change your pace will also help command attention during presentations.

12. Breathing. Breathing indicates the state of excitement. So, learn to control your breathing. Don't hold your breath during conflict. Remember, you want your brain fully oxygenated and alert. Read others' breathing in order to perceive their level of anger.

By reading these nonverbal factors, you can recognize the rising and falling of conflict energy in yourself and in others. By controlling these factors from within, you can influence the course of the conflict.

In the martial arts everything is interrelated. When and how you move influences your opponent's response, which, in turn, affects you. Communication is never linear. All of the above nonverbal factors are interrelated; changing any factor affects the others.

Controlling your breath immediately affects your voice. Slight changes in posture will correspondingly adjust your balance. And a small attitude shift can influence your ability to maintain eye contact. So it's not necessary to try to control all of these factors. This would take too much effort.

Moving the hub of the axle most efficiently moves a wheel. Understanding this, martial artists seek to control the center of a conflict. The center of any conflict is your internal conflict management system. Your relationship with yourself is its foundation. It is the center from which conflict-handling ability ripples outward.

Compare two days, one when you are feeling internally peaceful and another when you woke up on the wrong side of the bed. On both days, a car cuts you off and nearly causes an accident, or someone sneers at your favorite project. You react very differently on the two days. On your better days, you are not as easily upset.

Using the Techniques for Immediate and Long-Term Improvement

Note the two or three factors in conflict control that you presently feel comfortable with. These are already a part of your bag of tricks. You may now be able to sustain eye contact or you may have excellent timing. Also note your present limitations, those factors you currently have difficulty with or are uncomfortable using. In any given conflict there's no way to predict what will work best. Try something—if one factor doesn't help, try another in which you feel proficient.

To make immediate changes in your ability to control conflict, focus on your strengths and steer clear of your weaknesses. If you know your voice cracks nervously during confrontations, defuse the conflict through your excellent listening skills. Immediate gains will come by using the techniques at which you are already skilled. Save experimentation for practice sessions or other low-threat situations.

To make long-range changes in your ability to control conflict, transform your limitations into strengths or at the least neutralize them as weaknesses. If you tend to jump into discussions too often, work on your timing. This approach takes longer than focusing on current strengths, but it is an excellent way of strengthening your conflict management range. Moreover, your overall self-control will strengthen.

Use these methods at home as well as at work, with family and friends as well as with coworkers. Conflicts are common during these changing times. But you can harness conflict's energy to strengthen yourself, others, and your organization.

The Martial Art of Conflict: Techniques for Action

- Observe how you become emotionally involved in conflict. Know your fears. Watch your reactions. Don't try to stop your emotions, let them pass by like scenes in a motion picture. Remind yourself that anticipation creates fear. Does your voice become squeaky or scratchy when you're nervous? Is it artificially husky when you are trying to be assertive?

- Assess your usual style of dealing with conflict. In which situations is this style most and least effective? Experiment with different approaches.

- Change negative attitudes about conflict to positive; think of using conflict as an ally. How has it already helped your organization and you? Whenever there is a conflict, think how you can channel the resulting energy toward organizational ends.

- Notice company controls. How thick is your policies and

procedures manual? Delete rules that are unnecessary or create too much resistance.

- Monitor the conflict climate. How do staff in your organization escalate conflict by pushing back?

- Catch yourself in a blindly forceful mode.

- Watch how conflict builds over time. Which employees are slow-burners and which have short fuses?

- Practice your timing. Restrain your intervention until there is a receptive moment.

- Learn to recognize motorset in everyday activities.

- Observe a bully and objectively observe how he sets up intimidation.

- Consciously decide whether it's best to fuel, avoid, or defuse each conflict. With time, these decisions will become more and more instinctive.

- Practice differentiating between personal and role attacks. Shift into your role when personally confronted and shift into a personal response when attacked in role.

- Remind yourself that you are not the target. When you are in the path of a car, handcart, or person coming your way, practice "stepping off the line." Apply this technique to verbal conflict situations.

- Observe where distraction and humor can momentarily divert a building conflict.

- What is your conflict management history? Honestly assess your own conflict attitudes and how they help and limit you.

- Practice looking for openings. There's no need to force them. When you calmly watch, they will jump out at you.

- Take account of your two or three nonverbal conflict strengths, as well as your two or three greatest weaknesses. Make more use of your present strengths. In less threatening situations, practice your weaker skills.

III

MASTERING CHANGE

Change is the order of heaven and earth. . . . To remember troubled
days in days of peace and to constantly train one's body
and mind form guiding spirit and character.
Gichin Funakoshi, Karate-do: My Way of Life

Within constant motion and change there is tranquility,
and within tranquility there is motion and change.
Prof. Henry Seishiro Okazaki, "The Esoteric Principles of Judo"

In nature, things move violently to their place
and calmly in their place.
Sir Francis Bacon

7

RESPONDING TO CHANGE

In this uncertain world, ours should be the path of discipline.
Shiba Yoshimasa, Chikubasho

Men knowing the Way of life
Respect their foes,
They face the simple fact before it becomes involved.
Solve the small problem before it becomes big.
The most involved fact in the world
Could have been faced when it was simple,
The biggest problem in the world
Could have been solved when it was small.
The simple fact that he finds no problem big
Is a sane man's prime achievement.
If you say yes too quickly
You may have to say no,
If you think things are done too easily
You may find them hard to do:
If you face trouble sanely
It cannot trouble you.

Lao-tzu, Tao Te Ching

SELF-DEFENSE AND CHANGE

Life never stands still; situations are never the same. In *The Tao of Jeet Kune Do,* Bruce Lee wrote, "The stillness in stillness is not the real stillness; only when there is stillness in movement does the universal rhythm manifest itself. To change with change is the changeless state." Changes can be like a sudden attack, springing in an instant, or like a slow wave or a steadily marching army. However it approaches, change is inevitable. Stability only comes from being able to float safely on each wave of change.

When tae kwon do students begin their training, they kick the air hundreds, even thousands of times, for balance, flexibility, and body alignment. But kicking like this is easy and doesn't approximate real life. So the students spar to get practice defending against constantly changing attacks. In a sense, the martial artist puts in years of training for an attack he hopes will never occur, developing the habit of being watchfully alert and ready for anything.

Nevertheless assaults may still occur. Late one night, after flying home from a business trip, I stopped to pick up mail at my postal box. As I turned the corner to the post office I saw two men laughing and cursing each other as they passed a bottle between them. Minding my own business, I walked around them. Just then, out of the corner of my eye, I saw one of them kick out at me. Without thinking, I sidestepped and moved in on him, with my hands up and ready. He fell back against the building wall. "Really sorry, just kidding," he stammered. No harm was done. They hadn't touched me nor I them, so I went about my business. All of this happened in the space of a few seconds, which was too fast to think. Unfortunately, the reaction set in a few minutes later. I was so revved up with adrenaline that I had to run around the block a few times just to discharge my excess energy and calm down. This served to remind me that I shouldn't be too proud of myself. I still had a long way to go.

Responding to change involves both preparation for the sudden attack and awareness of the more gradual patterns of growth and decline. By charting results, watching how they grow, we can prevent disasters that might have been. Perceiving and avoiding small problems, paying attention even to the "trifles" (see chapter 1), can avert the larger, life-threatening ones. As a manager, for example, when you are aware that growing worker dissatisfaction is building, you can act (document the dissatisfaction to establish the need for new policies, and adjust those practices contributing to low morale) to forestall a major problem.

In the classic *The Art of War,* Sun-tzu wrote, "It is functional military law that one does not rely on the enemy not coming, but relies on the fact that he himself is waiting; one does not rely on the enemy not attacking, but relies on the fact that he himself is unassailable."

In real life when plans are made in a void, they are easily foiled by changing situations, countered by new ground rules, or frustrated by sudden changes in the market. Competitors rarely hold to our initial assessments of them.

Why is managing change so difficult? Life often feels like a multiple attack, issues and problems never coming as you expect. It's like driving on a multilane highway where other drivers don't follow the rules of the road. Their speed varies and many act unpredictably, even to the point of jeopardizing their lives and yours. The only way to protect yourself and get to where you want to go is to be ready for anything, just like the martial artist. Be prepared for swervings or stops in any direction. When these do occur, use free technique *(jiuwaza);* create a defense; don't wed yourself to set forms. Sounds both hazy and complex? This is why managing change is an advanced skill, challenging even high-ranking black belts.

Clearly, master leaders, like martial artists, are open and ready to adapt to anything that comes their way—your main product is blamed for a fatality; changing demographics reduce the demand for your most profitable services.

Shifting technology, regulations, markets, and staff reactions affect most organizations. The accelerating pace of work can make it difficult to know how to react or make effective decisions. Especially during these swirling, competitive times, mastering change can make the difference between business strength and bare survival or worse. Because black-belt leaders eschew seeing themselves as victims, they develop strategies for reacting to uncontrollable change. Self-defense is easier when you can see the threat at an early stage. So they start by amplifying *aware* concentration.

There is a well-known Japanese folktale about a great swordmaster who demonstrated to a visitor the teaching he had given his three sons.

He wedged a heavy vase on the corner of a sliding door so that it would fall on whomever entered the room. Then he called for his oldest son. Before opening the door, the son sensed the danger. He slid open the door, caught the falling vase, then entered and replaced it over the door. The swordsmaster introduced his son to the visitor, "This is my oldest. He has learned well. One day, he will master kenjitsu [swordsmanship]."

The father called for his second son, who entered without hesitating and only caught the vase just before it struck his head. "This is my middle son. He is improving, but still has much to learn." Then the youngest son was summoned. He entered hurriedly and was struck a heavy blow by the vase. But before it could hit the floor, a quick stroke of the boy's sword cut the vase in two. "This is my youngest. He still has a long way to go."

In times of change, narrow concentration won't do. Most people are surrounded by concerns, challenges, and problems. There is rarely only one thing going on at a time. So if you brace hard against one problem, seeking to block out others, you risk being blindsided and overwhelmed. Rather, develop a 360-degree readiness, without anticipating an attack from any one direction.

An impatient young man asked a great swordsman to take him on as a student. Seeing latent talent and clear desire, the martial artist agreed. He instructed the eager young man to start his learning by cleaning the house and stables. The young man worked at this admirably, but as days became months, he grew more frustrated. One day he approached the master. "Sir, you agreed to take me as a martial arts student. Yet all I have done so far these months is simple chores."

The swordsman assured the student that if he would continue with his duties, his practice would begin in earnest. From that day on, the student was never safe. During the young man's work, the master would suddenly leap out and beat him soundly with a *shinai* (bamboo sword). The student was determined to continue and over time learned to anticipate the master's attacks. While the attacks didn't abate, he was able to avoid an ever greater percentage of beatings.

Many months later, the student happened upon the master making soup. "Now is my chance to get even," thought the young man. As the swordsman was stirring the pot with one hand and holding the lid with the other, the student soundlessly crept close, and suddenly aimed a ferocious blow at the master's head with a broom handle. Without interrupting his stirring, the swordsman calmly raised the lid and blocked the blow.

The moral of this famous martial arts tale is that you can concentrate fully on the task at hand without leaving yourself vulnerable to the unexpected. In *The Tao of Jeet Kune Do*, Bruce Lee explains, "A concentrated mind is not an attentive mind, but a mind that is in the state of awareness can concentrate." Awareness is never exclusive; it includes everything. One way to practice this state of awareness is by strengthening your peripheral vision. When you are reading, let your senses expand to take in the desk and room. Be aware of this peripheral information in the background while you read. Simultaneously seeing both foreground and background will take practice, but you can develop this awareness (hint—use soft eyes, as explained in chapter 7).

Do you remember the last time you were startled? Martial artists believe that being startled is a sign of too narrow concentration. Have you ever noticed the reaction of someone after you turned a corner and unexpectedly came face-to-face with him? He freezes. When a person "jumps out of his skin," he's too tense and vulnerable because he's unable to react quickly to changing circumstances. You can control the startle reflex by reminding yourself to drop your shoulders down and relax. This body-leverage strategy will help you react quickly and with balance to unexpected events. You'll still experience a rush of feeling when you're surprised, but you will be better able to react and move.

To respond successfully to change, black-belt leaders are aware of the changes that affect daily work. These include growing financial uncertainty, shifting values and expectations, increased competition on all levels, litigation, rapid advances in technology, a movement of personnel to the service sector, a new mix of people in the workplace, different governmental regulations, and reductions in management levels. There are many social changes that also affect the workplace. Volumes have been written about these and other factors.

"Change is always stressful," notes IBM medical consultant Dr. Alan McLean. "It always involves losing something." Even relatively minor changes can be uncomfortable—the street on which you drive home closed for repaving or your favorite TV show moved to a new night. But there are many more important, uncontrollable changes, such as when your company merges with another, the market shifts strongly, or your new boss has a markedly different style from your old one. As a result many people initially feel overwhelmed, helpless, out of control. Finding yourself in one of these situations is like being a martial artist who, while minding his own business, is attacked by several assailants. What can we do when we feel attacked from all sides?

STAYING CALM UNDER PRESSURE

Judo master Henry Seishiro Okazaki noted, "Only by cultivating a receptive state of mind, without preconceived ideas or thoughts, can one master the secret art of reacting spontaneously and naturally without hesitation and without purposeless resistance."

Controlling yourself is the key to reacting successfully to change. Once again, this is something that's easier said than done. Think of clicking yourself into a calm mode (practice will make you more facile at this). By being flexible, alert, and watchful, you will be more able to swim in an ocean of uncontrollable change. Calmness does not mean never being ruffled; it's natural for strong winds to agitate the sea. But the deeper the water, the calmer it remains. Stay down within yourself; concentrate on relaxing your hara, your center of gravity.

For a period of several years, Kodak fell upon painful times of cost-cutting and layoffs. This kind of environment would have upended many people. Not Al Weber. A manager of central maintenance at Kodak's worldwide headquarters in Rochester, New York, Al is a bastion of calmness, strength, and dedication. During these difficult times, his calm demeanor had a ripple effect, helping others to focus on personal self-control and on the job at hand—that of improving and elevating Kodak's position.

Find calmness within movement. In *The Zen Way to the Martial Arts*, Taisen Deshimaru writes, "Tranquility in movement is the secret of *kendo*, the way of the sword." He continues, "Look at a top: at first, when it's spinning slowly, it wobbles, it moves; then, when it has gathered momentum, it becomes stable and no longer moves. And at the end, like an old man, it starts to totter again, and at last it topples over."

Pressuring yourself to hold still during times of great change is like "forcing" yourself to relax—it doesn't work. Use movement to help create your stability. Be a warrior, not a worrier: active outside, but calm within.

It's difficult to relax under pressure, but extremely helpful. Bruce Lee wrote, "Not being tense but ready, not thinking yet not dreaming, not being set but flexible—it is being wholly and quietly alive, aware and alert, ready for whatever may come." Visualize yourself being alert and relaxed. Don't allow fear to control you. Remember your strengths and remind yourself of other changes you have previously weathered. This is the time to practice some of the attitude control exercises in the first section.

Retain your equanimity. During a fracas, remind yourself that all things pass, and react in the best possible way. In *Wisdom from the Ninja Village of the Cold Moon*, Stephen Hayes explains, "The ninja gains his perspective by expanding his perceptions to see that everything is change and reality is at best temporary."

In your professional life you will surely face some uncomfortable situations. When the merger is announced, or you've received word that your budget will be cut by 30 percent, stay calm inside yourself. Let discomfort reside on the surface. Be patient with yourself when learning new procedures. Once again you're a white belt; focus on what you have to do to become a black belt.

Neal Mckenzie is a manager and engineer with Northrop, an electronics firm. In his spare time, Neal is a black-belt martial arts instructor. He's used martial arts principles to remain resilient in dealing with constant changes in his professional field. Neal was trained at Stanford University in vacuum tube technology. Since then there have been at least two revolutions in the field—transistors and microchips. In many professions, Neal's gray hair would be a sign of respected experience. But not in the fast-changing world of electronic engineering, where graying signifies obsolescence. But Neal is respected by his staff because he has stayed current with the principles and practices of his profession and handles his workload very well.

BEFRIENDING CHANGE

Make change work for you. Say you're surrounded by many attackers or threatening changes, but with the right attitude and correct movement, you can actually turn multiple attackers to your advantage. Move in the best way and they'll get in each other's way, making it harder to reach you. Perhaps you can use one as a shield against the others. Or confuse them and dictate the timing of the defense.

The Chinese symbol for great change is composed of two characters, one meaning "danger" and the other "opportunity." Any change really has both positive and negative elements. Happenings that appear to be the most dire always contain positive elements. In every recession, for example, many people lose money, but there are always some who do very well by focusing on the opportunities created.

Anytime an evidently negative change comes, look for the hidden benefits. Budget cuts mean a chance to manage more creatively, to use more leverage (finding ways to do more with less), or to learn new skills. One manufacturing division manager, seeing the writing on the organizational wall, accepted early retirement to pursue an old dream of taking an equity position in a high-tech environment. A colleague went into business for himself. Neither manager wasted energy bemoaning the changes that came; instead they rode the currents toward new and advantageous positions.

On the other side, remember there will always be negative effects from seemingly idyllic changes. Winning the lottery may strike you as totally wonderful, but there will be more taxes to pay, financial decisions to make, a loss of privacy, and a deluge of new "friends." If you balance your perspective, you will be able to embrace the opportunities that lie in seemingly negative changes and avoid potential dangers in windfalls.

Some change is just part of a wider landscape. "There has been a lot of organizational change at Shearson," says Karen Nish, "but that's appropriate; there's been a lot of change in the [stock] market."

Most of all, remember that you're not helpless. There are many things you can do in advance to prepare yourself for periods of great change. Put support systems in place when things are going smoothly; this way they'll be ready when the gale winds hit. Your personal commitment statement can provide a strong guide when change threatens to unhinge you. Family relationships can also help anchor you while you ride out changes at work that threaten to capsize you. Contrastingly, work can provide a short-term safe harbor in the face of family storms.

Cultivate the supportive relationships of trusted colleagues and friends. Regularly have lunch or coffee with peers, and seek them out during times of difficult change. Discuss both your frustrations and plans for action with them. They can offer many kinds of support. First, you can go to a friend, close the door, and let your hair down, knowing what you say will not be repeated. Second, a confidant often can suggest strategy options you may not see, simply because stress creates tunnel vision and you might miss what is clear to others. The third kind of support—the rarest and most valuable—comes when another person, upon hearing your repeated complaints, kicks you into action. ("I've heard you sing this song many times. You sound like a broken record. When are you going to get up and do something about it?")

You can also find support in professional associations. Others who have gone through similar circumstances can provide perspective and model solutions to your problems.

Your favorite leisure or recreational activities can help. But even these activities take discipline! Under duress, the last thing you may think of is leisure time. But recreation can provide the perspective and stress release you need to make strong, long-term decisions.

CONTROLLING YOUR POSITION: BE WATER, NOT ROCK; BE ROCK, NOT WATER

The martial artist knows that in self-defense, there is time to penetrate and time to yield. Two useful sayings are "Be rock, not water" and "Be water, not rock." When things are in an uproar around you and your staff is stressed and consumed with fear, "Be rock, not water." Stand firm and hold your position. Be a pillar of stability; reaffirm that everything will work out. In the midst of one major departmental change, the staff found itself well below its work quota; predictably, they began to blame the change plan. The manager became a rock. Holding firm, he reminded them that the plan had worked until then, that it was good and would work again. Their confidence came back as the wave of fear passed. He then helped them figure out how to restore lost productivity to its expected level.

But when confronted with resistance to change, when fear turns staff or customers into stone, "Be water, not rock." In *Diary of the Way*, Andrew Lum is quoted as saying, "With flexibility you can change to any position. Like water, we must be able to change to all forms. If a room is filled with water and there is a small hole in the floor, one inch by one inch, all the water will escape. But suppose there is a rock two inches by one inch. It cannot escape; it is trapped. If you are like water you can escape through even the smallest of openings."

You don't have to allow resistance to stop you—you can flow around it. Is it difficult to calm others' fear of layoffs from pending automation? Flow around the fear. Acknowledge their resistance and go ahead with your plans. Don't let unfounded fear block the new system.

There are times to become Rock, situations to become Water. The black-belt art is in knowing which approach to choose and when.

BE READY AND ABLE TO MOVE

The Chinese masters taught students never to distribute their weight equally between the feet because when so "double-weighted," they could not move quickly in the event of a sudden attack. Any good karate-ka (a practitioner of karate) knows that attempting to kick with the weight still on his striking leg will cost him his balance. He must first transfer his weight to his supporting foot.

"In general, the body weight should not be divided fifty percent on each foot," tai chi ch'uan master Andrew Lum writes in *Diary of the Way*. "When the weight is divided unevenly you are most flexible. There is one free foot with which to move in any direction."

Too much stability makes it difficult to move, and bracing is dangerous. Of course, taken to the other extreme, putting all the weight on one foot also deprives you of some balance. The masters recommend having an 80/20 distribution of weight. During times of change, if you are leaning the wrong way, you will be highly vulnerable. Look for and leave yourself room to move to a new position.

In much the same way, black-belt leaders don't double-weight. They value being ready to move and don't spread their operating base too wide. They aren't overly committed to stability. They maintain contact with the minority points of view. This helps them stay ready to shift their stance when the situation warrants.

In a broader sense the same applies to organizations. For example, developing too much manufacturing capacity can be dangerous; this may prevent you from being willing or able to adapt to changing consumer demands.

This is one of the reasons it's a wise idea to keep policies lean and few. Too many make you heavy and unable to move quickly. To transfer weight (shift your direction), you'll have to make intermediate moves and reassess all policies before you recast them. Only then will you be able to move. So keep focused on mobility and don't anchor your organization to policies that emphasize what *not* to do.

Control your sphere of influence. Remind yourself to focus on what you can control (yourself) and directly influence (your own organizational unit). If you overextend yourself and try to do everything you see needed in the corporation, you'll only lose your balance. Do your own job and help those you work with directly to do theirs.

Many leaders report feeling overwhelmed and unable to keep up with changes in their field because there is so much data available these days. By becoming an efficient information processor, you will be better able to anticipate and to react to industry-wide changes. Listen and read carefully to sift out the vital information you need. Learn which information sources to scan and which may be put aside without loss. Make productive use of your time by using high-leverage technology that lightens your load—microcomputers or microcassette recorders when traveling, hand-held digital assistants, or mobile phones.

This way when changes come—as they will—you will be prepared. Rather than fighting them, you will direct their movement to your benefit. By searching for opportunities, you will be positioned to make an ally of any change that threatens, and you will be calm and victorious.

Reacting to Change: Techniques for Action

- Remind yourself that everything changes and nothing is static. There is really no such thing as maintaining market share; you must re-win it each quarter.

- Use your self-discipline, especially when adverse change strikes. Don't let yourself bow to desperation. Do what is necessary to make yourself as unassailable as possible.

- Assess the broad changes affecting your organization, but don't miss the subtle ones. Cast your information nets wide so you see change when it is still in the offing.

- Make a habit of keeping your shoulders down. Notice your reactions when you do become surprised.

- Practice mental readiness in your favorite sport or when driving. Relax and watch. Don't allow others' unexpected moves to throw you.

- Work on concentrating with awareness while reading, doing paperwork, or speaking with someone. A good time to enlist this skill is during a group presentation, when you're answering an individual's question. Focus on the questioner, but be able to peripherally see the entire group's reaction.

- When you get beaten, learn from it. Don't make the same mistakes over and over again. If you're going to make mistakes, make different ones.

- Remember to manage the stress in any change.

- Practice the art of waiting without tension, like a cat before a mouse hole.

- Assess when to "be rock, not water," and to hold your position; when to "be water, not rock," and to flow around fear or resistance.

- Remember it's all right to be comfortable being uncomfortable.

- Look for advantages even during the most dangerous periods of change.

- Develop supports you can use in the face of change.

- Be ready and able to move quickly, don't be double-weighted. Watch out for areas where you are braced or too emotionally invested.

8

THE ART OF STRATEGY: PLANNING FOR CHANGE

The strategist makes small things into big things.
Miyamoto Musashi, The Book of Five Rings

If one plans to abide in a place for one year, he should plant the five grains. If his plan is for ten years, he should plant trees. If one's plans are for his whole life, there is nothing like sustaining his retainers.
Sixteenth-century Japanese proverb

Only by moving with focus can one have stability. Only by being stable can one have peace. Only by having peace can one be secure. Only in security can one deliberate. And only with deliberation will one be able to attain.
Anonymous

Ulitmately, the martial artist's most powerful weapon is her mind. This "secret" weapon is the source of strategy: the ability to plan for, see, and make use of opportunities. Whoever masters the skills of strategy has the power to survive and act effectively, in both adverse and bountiful times.

In both the martial arts and leadership strategy is the art of making choices that move you toward goals and strengthen your position without leaving you overly vulnerable. Each martial arts style is a strategy designed to protect the practitioner in specific situations by making the most of his position. For example, each *kung fu* style is designed to set up a uniquely strong defense; the "white crane style," with its broad "wing" parries, is excellent for long-range fighting; and the famous "drunken style" is designed to lull an opponent into feeling overconfident in the face of a seemingly out-of-control defender——that is until a surprise flurry of apparently haphazard moves defeats the attacker. Still other martial arts focus on best defenses when you are attacked in a kneeling or reclining position.

Any leadership style is a strategy appropriate for certain situations and less useful in others. And every option has its price. The martial artist learns that the more stable a stance he assumes (lying down, for example), the less mobile he will be. Generally, the price of a greater ability to move is a reduction in balance. The wise strategist keeps in mind that situations change: a previously strong approach may become weak under different circumstances. When you deliver power—punch, kick, push—it is best to be solidly planted; if you receive power—get kicked or punched—it makes sense to be loosely connected with the ground so as to absorb the force by "floating away."

To become both fluid and well balanced, the martial artist looks for and uses counterbalancing forces. You may have seen a karate expert throwing a forward punch with his right hand, while simultaneously drawing back his left. This combined movement both provides him with a powerful thrust and prevents his becoming overextended and off balance.

Organizationally, a plan that retains a large degree of freedom of movement may leave you less stable and more vulnerable. A wise strategist sees the potential negative outcomes in any proposed change and plans to minimize them, balancing the costs of a change against its returns—for example, the effort required to institute new procedures against the time to be recouped when the new ways eventually take hold. Most planners consider these factors, but in my experience too many inaccurately assess the underlying cost of any change: reduced trust and increased suspicion, possible resistance, and lower productivity. If you don't consider staff resistance to change, you will have no plan to minimize it.

Timing and position are two critical strategic elements in the martial arts. In *Strategy in Unarmed Combat*, Paul Maslak writes of the martial arts strategist, "Even before the first kick is blocked, he has planned how to use his physical advantages most effectively against the opponent's disadvantages." That is, he has planned the process of action, reaction, and further action.

In combat, the ideal position protects you, allows you to use your force most efficiently, and lets you react easily when things change. In reality, the ideal position changes from moment to moment, as conditions shift. Clouds pass over the sun, the lay of the land changes, or the opponent varies his attitude and line of attack.

In managing, your decision about the ideal position to take will also be determined by market and financial conditions, competitors' approach, employee morale, and other factors. Just as martial artists search for an edge, creative leaders try to spot potential for positive change, even when everyone else believes the situation is fixed. Larry Vance, an owner-manager of a small restaurant chain, has found his edge in training. Most of his competitors believe staff training is wasted on employees in a high turnover industry. But Larry realizes the way he treats staff will be passed on to customers as better-quality service, so he aims to make work inspiring and enjoyable. By providing his employees with strong training in line with a clear mission, he reaps the benefits of return customers and lowered turnover costs.

Your position will determine how and what you see. The closer you stand to something, the more detail you will be able to see in it. This is probably why the grass seems greener in the neighbor's yard, or why other organizations seem to have fewer problems than we do. From afar it is difficult to see all but broad patterns—divots, weeds, and other flaws are more easily perceived only as you get closer to the field.

So when you wish to assess specific problems of performance or morale, get closer to the field. Don't hole up in an office and allow yourself to be surprised. Move out and see the lay of the land. Spend time with staff from different levels, departments, and branches. Allocate enough time to make real contact with select staff, so that you're not merely flitting through to make an impression.

Sometimes you can gain perspective by stepping back to get a detached overview of your organization. Vehicles for getting this kind of perspective include retreats, conferences, appropriate reading, working off-site, consulting with outsiders (consultants or peers), benchmarking, and comparing current conditions and performance to that of other years or to parallel organizations.

PLANNING FOR ACTION

Planning change means watching and adjusting your attack, looking for the opening, and sensing the prevailing rhythm so that you emerge victorious—or in the case of leadership, that you accomplish your goals. In the sixteenth century, renowned warrior Takeda Shingen wrote about this very thing. In *Ideals of the Samurai,* he is quoted as saying, "A man with deep far-sightedness will survey both the beginning and the end of a situation and continually consider its every facet as important."

Executives must manage change powerfully. Undeniably change puts a crimp in the smooth fabric of our routines; it's almost instinctive to stick with the status quo. But we can't do that because the world continues to change; in fact, it takes an injection of energy just to remain at status quo. In many instances, leaders have to plan as much to retain current market share as to achieve further growth.

Strategize to defeat your real opponents. In an expert leader's case, these foes may be fear, resistance to change, self-centeredness, or negative expectations of staff capability. Your adversaries in this case are not dangerous people, but detrimental attitudes and practices. Find your opponents' strengths and weaknesses and plan your attack accordingly.

Planning is the first strategic step in taking action. It's not a substitute for action or movement, but a preparation for it. As Will Rogers said, "Planning gets you into things; hard work gets you out of them." People may stand in place if they are too afraid of the risks in trying something new. And so courage is still needed. Perhaps because of their own fears, many managers overplan, trying to account for every possible contingency. "If this situation arises we could do that; then if this happens, we can go with a or b; then again. . . ." Remember that strategizing never removes risk and taking action is always uncertain. But the risk involved in *not* moving or acting may be even greater. Not deciding, not moving are strategies, too, although they are ones that few would-be leaders admit to choosing consciously.

In fact, there is a special danger in simply repeating the proven formulas from past experience instead of deciding to implement change. Martial arts instructor Frank Doran explains why he looks in the mirror every day and mentally washes off his old techniques. If he doesn't wash them off, Mr. Doran says, in twenty years he'll be performing yesterday's techniques. The world will have passed him by. Leaders and organizations face this same danger.

At the workplace, planning for change is basic self-defense. In a rapidly changing world, proactive planning prevents making yesterday's decisions today, and helps assure that the organization is current and able to compete.

If you start by looking at situations with fresh eyes, you will see openings. Walter Muryasz advises martial arts students to use "positive space" in defending against an attacker with a knife. New martial arts students focus too much on the weapon, he claims, so it appears, to the frightened defender, to be much larger than it really is. Mr. Muryasz points out, "The closer you pass by the weapon, the more control you have over it and the person who wields it." Advanced students see the positive space, the place where the weapon is not. With this focus, they can safely defend themselves from a thrusting knife or sword.

Positive spaces are "openings" (see chapter 6), and black-belt leaders also learn to focus on the positive space in the organization, spotting where change is possible or even welcomed. There are times when staff is willing to try almost anything—when a situation has bottomed out, when there is a calm after the storm, or when you are wearing a halo after a recent accomplishment. These are the best times and situations in which to pilot a new program.

Positive space is useless, however, if you don't know where you are going. In any endeavor your strategy always should spring from your mission, values, and goals. Black-belt leader John Fling knows this. As loss control manager of a stevedore company, John operates in an environment where there are complex, historically mistrustful relationships between the labor union and management. He uses position and timing to improve economic strength and reduce employee injuries in a work climate where "swords" are perpetually swinging. Sensitive to a long history of tension, he has instituted gradual and significant changes that helped heal mistrust between all parties, improved employee safety, and strengthened employer profitability.

DEFLECTING RESISTANCE TO CHANGE

The martial artist welcomes change as an ally, seeing it as an opportunity to develop new skills. Change creates room to move. Old obstacles in a problem may shift, providing new chances to work it out.

Much resistance to change is based on attitudes. No matter how remote an upcoming change is, the first thing people think is "How will this affect me?" Typically, people look first at the potentially negative effects on them, and then resist. But it is also possible they will embrace positive elements of change. Understanding both can help you to package the change more attractively to reduce resistance.

Different individuals have varying appetites for change. Some drive home from work the same tried-and-true way; others find taking a different route refreshing. Certain people reposition their furniture every six months (often they are married to others who would rather the arrangement stay just as it is). Some remain in the same job for many years, but an increasing number of people move between companies or within the same organization. Those who are less tolerant of change almost instinctively oppose any threat to the status quo.

Organizations that thrive on creating new products do best when they foster a climate of change. For example, change is the driving force in high-tech industries. "We are in the business of creating reality," as one manager of a multinational high-tech firm said. "The [corporate] culture here is never satisfied."

To promote this sense of urgency-for-change, some corporations have policies to ensure that their employees are neophiliac (literally, change-loving). They hire fresh-out-of-school employees who they consider hungrier for innovation than older candidates. Such companies often have periodic reorganizations, whether necessary or not. In addition to trying to better meet market demands, restructuring keeps employees slightly anxious; the company operates on the belief that employees who are too content become complacent.

One high-tech company ranks performance reviews on a curve. In other words, a certain percentage of employees in every department must be ranked below par. So an engineer who does excellent work for fifty-five hours each week (not uncommon in this industry) is given a substandard evaluation if department peers also work hard, but longer. There is a theory behind these anxiety-producing tactics. Although the corporation doesn't acknowledge it, this system is designed to keep staff perpetually on edge so that they will continue to create.

When one technique always accomplishes the job, there may be little motivation to learn new ones. But in the high-tech field, yesterday's solution can result in rapid extinction today. Just as there is nothing like a sound thrashing to get a martial artist working on new blocks and kicks, some companies believe that fear and anxiety force greater creativity.

The high-tech company leaders may be partially correct. Generally, when things are comfortable and going well, the desire to change is reduced. The problem is that too much of any one thing can backfire. While it may be true that younger workers are fonder of innovation, they may also be less stable, which may be a factor in burn-out or in loss of perspective. Moreover, a strong need for change can turn into career impatience, resulting in spin-off companies or job-hopping.

High stress levels bred by competitive performance reviews may translate into greater work drive, but in some staff it results in performance-lowering worry. At one seminar a staff engineer indicated he felt his company was antifamily: "It's subtle, nothing they ever talk about, but it's there." When he said this, most other people in the room nodded agreement.

As in the martial arts, balance—this time cultural—is the key. It is dangerous for staff to see the company as antifamily. By being overly change-oriented your organization may push out the very talented and creative people who can sustain lasting change. Finding and maintaining the balance is an art.

It's obvious that change is needed when an organization stops creating and becomes stagnant. In *The Tao of Jeet Kune Do*, Bruce Lee quotes Napoleon: "The art of government is not to let men grow stale." Rather, it is "an act of unbalancing." Remember, though, to seek balance in any unbalancing you do. Too much can have negative results. Plan on organizational change, but ask staff for their ideas. Shake them up positively, not just to make them uncomfortable. Reorganization can work well without jeopardizing morale.

You are not planning change to cause pain to people or to show your power to put strain on the organization. You want to influence the balance of the organization for the better and to move it in a desirable direction. For example, the purpose of the advanced martial arts wrist-lock techniques is *not* to cause pain or to twist a joint. By controlling the wrist, pressure is placed on the shoulder through the elbow, which takes the opponent's balance. By taking someone's balance, you control him. Think of planning change as taking and moving the target's (department or individual) balance.

Participation is an important element in the acceptance of change. When employees feel involved in the decision making, they have an investment in the solution. Master Nabeshima Naoshige is quoted in *Ideals of the Samurai* as having said, "Encourage and listen well to the words of our subordinates. It is well known that gold lies hidden underground."

Many management books and seminars reinforce this, but a real shift to greater employee involvement in planning change is happening slowly. An educated and aware staff expects and wants to give input into decisions that affect them. They have a unique and practical perspective that should not be ignored. However, this doesn't mean going overboard and abdicating your responsibility; there are some managers who turn to participative planning as an easy way out—they feel little confidence in their own ability to plan and to make decisions. Management should still make the strategies and seek direction, but with advice from the staff.

When changes are first discussed there may be some expressions of emotional distress. Don't let employees' emotional reactions to change solidify into nonproductive resistance. Harness those reactions to make the organization more efficient and stable. The following is a case in point in which planning for change accomplished the "miraculous."

JOHN CHAPMAN: BLACK-BELT CHANGE AGENT

Have you ever tried to manage people into happily working themselves out of jobs? Or persuaded staff to do what they consider impossible? John Chapman has. Armed with advanced planning techniques, he convinced a staff that had previously distrusted technology to embrace automation.

The Mapping Department of Portland General Electric manually processed increasing tides of information, to maintain a database for other departments' billing, job planning, and service delivery monitoring.

Suburban sprawl continuously changed PGE's service area. And the maps had to be updated. Staff ranks swelled. Eventually, management decided that computerization might stem the increase in staff. Aesthetic illustrations would be replaced by data that could be generated quickly and accurately. But a significant investment in technology didn't produce the expected results. The technology-suspicious artists found it hard to change their values. Mappers resisted the new machines, and the result was a steadily mounting backlog of five years' work.

Chapman was assigned the project of making sure automation took hold with employees. First, he pinpointed why staff resisted the computerization. In their view computers would jeopardize both their jobs and their way of life; peer communication and power patterns would be unbalanced. In addition, previously valued skills such as the ability to create accurate maps by hand had become the responsibility of a machine.

Next, he drafted a change-management plan to eliminate within one calendar year the department's five-year backlog. Afterward, a smaller staff would keep maps current. By the year's end, departmental productivity had risen 300 percent, teamwork and morale had improved even as the staff was reduced by 47 percent. A project previously scheduled to take three years was completed in one, saving PGE $1.1 million. According to Chapman, "artists became information engineers" and the project was "a new learning experience for senior management."

How was this accomplished? Chapman used martial arts principles.

Clearing the field of battle. Knowing it is difficult to fight on two fronts, Chapman arrived at realistic changeover goals that upper-level management could accept and support.

Enlisting allies. He also met with mapping's internal clients to prioritize their information needs. Then he took his plan to existing mapping supervisors to invite their input and enlist their support.

Seeing the real enemies. Chapman realized his real "enemies" were the fear of job loss and change. He promised that no one would be laid off before the scheduled project completion date, even if it were finished early. He told staff that one of his main concerns was helping them protect and further their careers.

With his manager's support, he created the first performance incentive program within PGE. Staff helped determine the performance levels required for bonuses. The total cost of the incentive program was $103,000, compared to the $1.1 million saved.

Harnessing Do. The project was presented as an opportunity for transcending personal limitations. People were reminded to be committed to the idea that the plan would work.

Defusing negative conflict. Prior to project start-up, Chapman hosted a staff meeting to explain fully the objectives of the project and the incentive program. Understanding that direct force creates further resistance, Chapman did not order compliance with project goals. Instead he encouraged staff to respond honestly to the objectives outlined. He calmly responded to openly negative comments; he became "rock, not water."

Managing morale. Understandably, pockets of low morale and performance surfaced during the project. Chapman combated these by reminding staff that they had already accomplished the impossible. One mapper agreed, "My attitude for the first few months was 'there was no way.' Then we'd do it and I'd be excited. As soon as we started making our monthly objectives, morale really picked up."

Increasing team responsibility. Chapman encouraged a samurai "all for the team" ethic. He shifted task responsibility from individual employees to teams. Employees said that team support motivated higher performance. Accordingly, all incentives were paid for group, not personal, performance.

Mr. Chapman also focused on results. He instituted flexible time, with emphasis on completion of tasks rather than hours worked. Many chose to come in early when computers were more accessible and phones weren't ringing.

Focusing on personal development. He helped employees move from a "PGE owes you a job" mentality to a "you are responsible for your own career" mentality. The department, he reaffirmed, would be cutting positions, not people. He helped employees prepare themselves, meeting with each one to develop an individually tailored career marketing plan and résumé.

Fifteen out of thirty-two positions were terminated. Most of these employees found jobs within the utility at better pay; one became a consultant to the mapping industry. Another invented a device to speed up map delivery and quality control, which he intends to market independently.

In retrospect the changeover was a powerful growth experience for most of the mapping staff. One employee reflected, "It was a good experience. Learning how to create our own jobs caused us to grow a lot. Since the project, people are a lot more gung ho." In addition to securing better positions and protecting their jobs, many staff learned how to become more responsible and more in control of themselves, to manage change better, to work together more successfully, and to tap their inner power to go beyond what they thought were their limits. And John Chapman was subsequently promoted to general manager in the company. He currently operates a consulting firm specializing in refining executives' personal leadership skills.

THE UNBALANCED ORGANIZATION: CANDIDATE FOR CHANGE

A focused martial artist is one who strives for continual self-improvement, makes use of natural forces, and is dedicated to a higher purpose (Do). A strong organization is defined by a common purpose, effective internal communication between its parts, and a willingness to cooperate.

When she is progressing and learning, change helps the martial artist to continue to grow. Change can help get her out of a rut when she becomes stagnant or disillusioned.

Similarly, organizational change may be needed in two instances: as a prescription for a troubled organization or as a means of strengthening a basically sound one. It's important to know when the corporation is edging onto less stable ground. There are some specific danger signs of an unbalanced organization.

First, people lose focus. Staff members disregard the mission or become confused about their goals. They become overly concerned with the short-term (for example, quarterly profits) at the expense of longer-term planning. They don't monitor the marketplace. There is too much emphasis on status. People spend much more energy on covering themselves than on seeking creative solutions to problems. The number of safety problems surges upward.

Interdepartmental rivalries get out of hand. People lose the ability to communicate or cooperate. They put each other down or engage in scapegoating, refuse to share vital information, try to make points at other departments' expense, don't talk with those in other departments, or feel more allegiance to their own department or division than to the organization as a whole.

Morale breaks down. People are chronically unhappy. Turnover increases. Employees pine for the "good old days" and rush to leave at the end of their day. Or they only talk about their time off.

Emotional outbursts surface. There may be screaming incidents, door slamming, episodes of throwing things, or even attacks on coworkers.

No one of these signs is necessarily cause for alarm. But when several occur in tandem or one persists, this may indicate the organization has entered the danger zone and that strong remedial action is needed.

THINKING—AND NOT THINKING— STRATEGICALLY

The martial artist believes it is better to deal with reality than fantasy. He knows there will always be up periods as well as down periods. What is your response when you get hit, or when major problems occur unexpectedly? This is not the time for recriminations. When he sees a student berating himself for missing a block, Walter Muryasz teaches, "The attack begins at this point. While you're criticizing yourself for getting punched, your opponent will hit you several more times. Instead, imagine you're practicing a specific defense, one that begins after just being hit once. Martial arts don't make you invincible; you may get hit. Just don't add to your own problems by blanking out. Do the best you can with what is presented to you."

From a standpoint of taking action, a problem really begins when you first notice it. It makes little sense to dwell on the should-have-dones and why-didn'ts. When you're in trouble, blaming and fantasizing only allow matters to continue along a destructive path while you waste time and energy that could be used to steer the organization onto safer ground. So when you hear of an exodus of talented people, ask "What has been going on?" and "What has been tried and what hasn't?" and "What can we do now to stem the tide?" It's unproductive to think, "Why wasn't I informed sooner?" or "Why didn't you do something about this?"

Chinese martial master Lun Yu is quoted in *Ideals of the Samurai* as having said: "Making a mistake and not correcting it, this is a real mistake." So after you take care of the immediate threat, go back and correct the underlying organizational problems—which are likely to include inadequate monitoring and poor communication flow.

Planning can help you to more clearly discern your immediate needs. Those concerns of a few months ahead are less distinct, the requirements of the distant future even less clear. When you make long-term plans don't carve them in stone. Because conditions will change, and your plans should shift accordingly. Periodically review and readjust long-range plans. Ask yourself if market conditions have changed. Are you still on target? Should goals be adjusted?

On the other hand, some managers don't set goals because they think, Why bother? Everything's in a state of flux. Beside sounding like an excuse, this attitude can be haphazard; you may find that you're not moving toward your organizational mission.

Without goals, managers feel more reactive, and, consequently, "manage by crisis." They are like those fighters who are always on the defensive, blocking this thrust and parrying that one. Typically, without any offense (your plan), a blow eventually lands and the harried defender is knocked out. Of course, while you are planning you still have to meet present needs—keep your unit functioning smoothly and serving your customers. In real life, planning takes time, but it pays back dividends. Some tips that might help you:

- Make sure you're not rushing yourself. Musashi noted, "Immature strategy is the cause of grief." Remember to take time in your planning—solicit a range of initial input, make calm decisions, and get feedback on your strategy.

- Use Bruce Lee's advice: "Set patterns, incapable of adaptability, of pliability, only offer a better cage. Truth is outside of all patterns." Think creatively, with the past as an indicator, not as a predictor. Some of the most expensive planning mistakes managers make come from the notion that what happened before will happen again. Past experience is not wholly reliable in a changing world.

- Create planning rituals, similar to martial arts' forms. Hold a planning day or meeting with a suitable name ("Mission in the Future Day," "Smart Strategies," etc.). Meet at the same locale at the same approximate time each year. Involve all necessary staff in some portion of the planning process, even if just to gather ideas.

- Like Johnson and Johnson, use your corporate commitment statement in planning. Review it and use it to set goals and to help staff become rededicated.

- Bigger isn't always better. Enlarging a business, like inflating a balloon, can also stretch organizational flaws. *Before* expansion—branching out, franchising, etc.—is the time to solve small but important corporate problems and set necessary precedents. Smaller organizations are usually easier to control; and communication flows more easily and directly.

DEVELOPING RHYTHM

"The Way of strategy is the Way of nature," Musashi said. "When you appreciate the power of nature, knowing the rhythm of any situation, you will be able to do anything you wish."

Rhythm is crucial in the martial arts. Michel Random wrote, in *The Martial Arts,* "Every movement is a rhythm, just as in painting, music or poetry. If one is aware of the rhythm, it is possible to sense what is in the rhythm and what is not. This new sense would be like a spontaneous master if only one were to heed it. A correct rhythm expresses proportion, balance, universal order. Rhythms reveal whether they are in conjunction or in opposition to each other. Work on rhythms is already a rule of life and in itself an understanding of harmony and discord."

Paul Maslak put it another way: "You yield to your opponent's slightest pressure and stick to him at his slightest retreat. The rhythm of your movements is kept in constant time with your opponent's. You are like water, rushing into his every weakness and ebbing from his every strength, until he has drowned himself in his own actions."

Look for favorable organizational rhythms when planning—when competitors are weaker (at a time when they're regrouping), when staff members appear more receptive to change (a big contract has raised morale), or when there is an opening (capital becomes freer). Sense when people would prefer a period of faster or slower change.

Roger Graybeal heads a statewide chapter of the Automobile Association of America and has applied his martial arts training to developing leadership rhythm. His predecessor was a highly controlling manager who exerted authority over his midlevel managers' smallest decisions. Consequently, these managers became conditioned to check in before they took any action. But Roger knows that in these times no one person can make all the decisions in an organization. To get the most out of people you must give them the freedom to act. His planned solution involved retraining his staff in initiative. But how can you develop a new rhythm like this in a hesitant yet otherwise capable management team?

His staff was ready for change, so Roger made the most of this receptivity. Although interested in swift reform, Roger exercised patience and a fine sense of timing to control the pace of change. First, he set the stage so that managers and employees would look forward to the coming changes. Then he employed a gradual, penetrating approach: "This will take some time, but within two years, we will create a newly vitalized organization." Benefits were improved; salaries were raised; there were more promotional opportunities. Although the staff had some anxiety about the changes, morale rose. Still, Roger is watching and adjusting his strategy to guide his association into an efficient, profitable, service organization.

BALANCING FORCES IN PLANNING

To the martial artist, life is a matter of movement and energy. This view of the world applies to business as well. According to Kurt Lewin, a social scientist, people and organizations exist in a magnetic-like force field. Forces act on them in each moment. Nothing ever stays the same. When things do seem to be constant, there is actually a state of dynamic equilibrium. For example, look at the production level of any assembly team whose output does not remain constant, but fluctuates within narrow limits. Lewin would say this pattern persists because there is a balance between the forces that encourage higher productivity and those that lower it.

Advance planning allows you to adjust the balance of forces with relatively little effort. It also can lead to substantial and lasting changes.

How to Do a Force Field Analysis

1. Decide upon a pattern you wish to change, for example, the low productivity level of clerical staff. Draw a line representing this current level.

2. Draw an arrow pushing up against the line for each "driving force" that tends to increase clerical productivity. Examples include physical factors (soft lighting, ergonomic chairs, comfortable temperature), supervisory influences (close monitoring of work, communication meetings), organizational factors (relatively high pay, incentives for performance). Draw each arrow so its length reflects the relative strength of each force.

3. Similarly, draw an arrow pushing down against the line for each productivity-reducing restraining force. These, too, include physical factors (inadequate working space, distracting noise), supervisory influences (overmonitoring, too much time spent in meetings), and organizational factors (inadequate or poorly conducted training, little say in decision making, long work periods without breaks).

Note that the same force can be deemed both negative and positive, propelling productivity forward at a certain point and hampering it at another. Take, for instance, a concerned supervisor whose employees work hard for her, but whose tendency to do too much for those very employees prevents them from learning from their mistakes, thus putting a lid on potential increases in productivity. Noise level can be a force for both increasing excitement and distracting from work. Perception and experience will help you allocate forces according to their real influence on productivity.

There are two approaches to raising the "line of productivity" where the driving and restraining forces meet. Either push harder from underneath by adding more driving forces, or reduce forces that block movement to a higher level.

Changes that occur from adding forces don't produce lasting results. As discussed in chapter 5, "pushing" adds force to the system, making it more stressful and less stable. Resultantly, when you change by adding more driving forces (for example, more monitoring of clerical work), studies show that productivity may go up for a time, but it soon drops to an even lower level.

Black-belt leaders prefer the second approach to raising productivity, which involves isolating and reducing forces that block people from doing the job. For example, you may decide to reduce distracting noise in the workplace, hold shorter meetings, and shorten work periods without breaks. As force is removed, a more stable, less stressful system is created, and at an increased production level. Studies have shown that this approach brings lasting improvements with less resistance.

Some creative thinking may be needed to discover ways to reduce the strength of a force. If you decide excessive noise is a restraining force, you might provide each worker with ear plugs, install sound absorbing walls, or move the entire department to a quieter area.

Experienced martial artists prefer to parry, not block the force of an incoming blow. Stopping a punch cold can injure the blocking arm because a lot of force is absorbed in a small area. More important, the energy behind a strong attack cannot be checked outright; directly blocking a punch actually triggers the opponent's other hand to strike, or foot to spin kick. It's better to safely play out the force, extending it to where it is of no danger to you.

With this in mind, plan to adjust and reduce blocking forces at work, rather than stopping them cold. Are you concerned about a strong cafeteria rumor mill? Trying to block it will induce a secondhand attack of increased gossip and rumors. You can reduce the strength of the cafeteria grapevine by giving out more information and by openly responding to serious concerns.

When applied insightfully, force field analysis is a proven, high-leverage technique for planning change. With a multitude of forces influencing the level of productivity, how do you know which ones to weaken? Where do you focus to institute change?

Make sure to include all relevant forces in your planning model so your analysis accurately reflects the workplace. When you have recognized these, look to change restraining forces that are:

1. *Most influential.* It's like taking on the leader in a group attack: defeat him and others may fall into line. Interview and observe your employees. What most gets in their way? What do they continually complain about?

2. *Easiest to control.* In other multiple attack situations, it's preferable to go after the weakest attacker, using him as a shield against the others. You may not have the power as a blocking force to reduce low-pay rages. If this is the case, focus elsewhere, putting your efforts where they most realistically can make a difference. Experience will point the way.

SMALL CHANGES CAN MAKE BIG DIFFERENCES

If you try to hold down the wrist of a stronger person, he will probably still be able to raise his arm with ease. If you use two hands to press down, you may not succeed; even if you can, you'll probably not be able to keep his arm down for very long before you tire. But, if you think like a martial artist and use leverage, you will approach this challenge differently. Now you will hold down his fingertips. By directing your force just six extra inches away from the wrist, you can immediately increase your control, effortlessly preventing the strongest person from lifting his arm.

Impatience and lack of discipline often undermine the changes people plan. Whether in mastering the martial arts, accruing wealth, getting into shape, or losing weight, many attempt to succeed overnight. Doing too much too quickly usually leaves people injured or uncomfortable, and not much better off.

With this in mind, warrior Nabeshima Naoshige wrote, "Coming up in the world should be done in the same way as ascending a stairway." Making incremental changes is a lot like climbing stairs. Eventually you progress rapidly, but, in the beginning of a change, make sure to hit every step. If the changes in a business or group are made step-by-step, they will *seem* "slow enough" and *feel* less shocking to staff.

In contrast, changes done by leaps are more stressful, harder to sustain, and make you more vulnerable. In planning, after all, there's no guarantee your strategy will be correct. At least if you're proceeding in increments, you can assess your results and adjust as needed. Employ leverage by planning small changes that make large differences. Search for low-stress steps that move you toward your goal.

There are plenty of examples of this from everyday life. To get in shape you can start by exercising for five minutes, three times each week. Who can't spare five minutes? But if you set your sights at a half hour daily, it becomes easier to find reasons to avoid working out. With the more modest goal, you're using the feeling of personal responsibility to work for you, not against you. Those who try to get in shape in one weekend often only succeed in getting injured.

To lose weight, think of doing it gradually. Taking off half a pound each week will result in twenty-six pounds that stay off. And, all things remaining equal, you can reduce by this amount relatively easily. There are approximately 3,500 calories in a pound of fat; lower your food intake by 1,750 calories by forgoing extra portions of dessert three times each week. The key is to make small changes consistently.

In business, supermarkets generally run on a 1 to 3 percent net profit margin. They're profitable by continuously making that small percentage over many sales.

Similarly, the black-belt leader plans to leverage small changes into large organizational gains. Incremental, unthreatening, step-by-step changes are less likely to be resisted.

Smaller changes can also be more motivating. As John Chapman contends, "It has to be perceived by individual employees that goals are within their reach." Large projects are usually marked by easily recognizable interim periods that can serve as attainable milestones. These are appropriate times to assess problems, make steering decisions about what to modify, and celebrate progress toward the overall goal. By employing an incremental approach to change you can even strengthen an approval-seeking employee by giving him small tasks that increasingly exercise his independence.

Strategy is an advanced art, one that black-belt leaders train a long time to master. Like all martial abilities, good strategy comes from self-control. In *The Zen Way to the Martial Arts*, Taisen Deshimaru wrote,

> In a martial arts tournament, it is impossible to maintain the same intensity of concentration indefinitely. At some point the attention wavers and we show a fault, a *suki*, an opportunity which the opponents [are] able to seize.

This question of opportunity arises in every contest, however, not just in the martial arts—in argument, business, etc. Don't show your weak points, either in the martial arts or in everyday life. Life can be a fight! When this is the case, plan, then act to make change happen, and you will win your most important contests.

The Martial Art of Strategy—Planning to Achieve Change: Techniques for Action

- In planning strategy, be able to answer employees' question of "How will it affect me?"

- How strong is your current position? Assess your standing in terms of market conditions, competitors, employee morale. What would you like to see changed? What are your staff's present abilities and attitudes toward change?

- See the positive space in any planning situation. In the unit for which you're responsible, where is there the most room to maneuver?

- Remember that strategy can show amazing results.

- Watch your planning "balance." Do enough, but not too much, contingency planning.

- Assess your own style. Let go of what you do just out of habit. Create space for improvement.

- Look at participation as a gauge of staff acceptance of change. Think of ways to involve staff in the planning.

- If you "get hit" during a change, don't stop for recriminations. Keep going. You'll have time to lick your wounds later. Think of ways to prevent similar blows.

- In any situation, see the counterbalancing forces—stability and movement; risk and return.

- Think of planning as an ongoing process, not a one-time event. First you plan, then act, monitor, adjust, and replan.

- Sense the rhythms of change in your organization. Does it have spurts of movement followed by months-long lulls? Or are steady, gradual improvements more common? Decide whether to attempt to work within or to change these cycles.

- Assess forces at play by the use of force field analysis.

- For stable change, reduce restraining forces.

- Direct, don't attempt to stop, strong blocking forces.

- Make a change implementation plan and break down the steps into small, easily attainable milestones.

9

BECOMING AN AGENT OF CHANGE

It can be said that the martial artist is in harmony when he has
learned to adapt and flow with change, which is the nature
of the Universe. He is at one with all when this adaptation
and flow are an unconscious part of himself—when it can
be said of him that he is change itself.
Walter Muryasz, Precepts of the Martial Artist

To know and to act are precisely the same.
Samurai maxim

THE BLACK-BELT AGENT OF CHANGE

Martial arts experts are agents of change. Through understanding how to change themselves, they change others. This takes having an understanding of relative position. The opponent reacts to my action, and almost simultaneously, I react to hers. As I move to the left, she twists left. The black belt leads in this dance of change.

Hapkido, jujitsu, chi na, wing chun, and a few others are among the most difficult of martial arts to learn. They teach how to control another person's balance. This requires sensitivity to slight shifts of balance, and making small changes in relative position, angle, or pressure. Push on a person in one position, at a certain angle, and she may be rock solid, but shift an inch to the side, and now just a few pounds of pressure can easily dislodge her.

Think like a judo expert to become an agent of change. An "agent for change" is someone who causes or helps institute positive change. It is their understanding of the conditions of and susceptibility to movement that makes this possible. Many try it, but few are skilled enough to be successful at it. Remember the inertia principle: a body at rest tends to remain at rest; a body in motion tends to remain in motion. On water, a push easily moves a boat; even a much greater force won't budge it on dry land. Helping others make desired changes is truly a black-belt leader's highest skill.

Many managers live by the Rule of Effort: The harder I try, the more I will accomplish. Perhaps this is true, but sometimes people get in their own way by trying too hard to make something happen, as this classic martial arts story shows.

> A young man approached the house of a great swordsmaster and asked, "Sir, I yearn to be a great swordsman. How long would it take me if I practiced every day?"
>
> The master looked him over and replied, "Ten years."
>
> "Sir, what if I practiced at night also?"
>
> "Twenty years," answered the master.
>
> "And if I lived with the sword, slept with it, dedicated my very existence to it?"
>
> "Thirty years," smiled the master and turned away.

Instead of forcing change by overexertion, use martial arts principles that make changing easier. For instance, some martial artists create a "soft spot" in their opponent's concentration by the distraction of screaming. Distraction works in other areas, too. For instance, have you ever tried to change lanes on a highway and had another driver speed up to prevent you from moving in front of him? But if you look toward a different lane, and let him see you do this, he will usually back off; now, he no longer will feel you're a threat to cut him off. When the space opens, quickly and smoothly change lanes.

Martial artists and master leaders focus on restoring balance. Changing, like walking, is a process of risk and recovery. Knowing that change always involves stress and brings some degree of resistance, how do you help individuals survive it, work more productively and efficiently as a team, and adapt to or even welcome new systems?

Mentor Graphics' senior manager Ron Swingen says, "Managers of change—that's what we are for each other. And the only way for people to learn and create is in an environment where mistakes are not punished. There are actions that might produce catastrophic results, and we've got to put safeguards into place, like 'check with me before you act.'"

Shearson's Karen Nish says, "I never forget that dealing with change means dealing with people. Helping them manage change strengthens our business."

John Chapman contends, "Employees can improve their productivity by over fifty percent if [they] are better managed."

SETTING THE CLIMATE OF CHANGE

The martial tradition recognizes that underlying intent is crucial. The Japanese speak of "the sword that kills" and "the sword that preserves life." Both swords are sharp and both are used in battle. But the "sword that kills" is wielded by someone prone to violence, one who plots revenge or fights solely for personal gain. In contrast, the more enviable "sword that preserves life" belongs to one who, during a fight, uses only as much force as is necessary and no more, defending himself calmly, without anger, without thought of retribution.

Remember the importance of intention should the time come for you to plan layoffs or to fire someone. Work at controlling yourself. Drop feuds—having organizational enemies requires too much energy. Let go of anger and don't expose yourself too foolishly. And when you must sever a relationship, choose the "sword that preserves life." Make your cuts with calmness and caring.

Black-belt leaders emphasize creating the right climate, a nonthreatening and productive one where resistance to change is reduced. Leaders who are skilled agents of change trust colleagues and employees by giving them relevant information and by believing they will do well.

And they are trustworthy themselves, maintaining honest relationships, and following through with their promises.

Karen Nish has flown to many cities for Shearson to integrate new brokerage houses into her company. Her strategy? "I live with them for a while, get to know them, and let them get to know me. Then, when the relationship has become less threatening and more personal, I sit and talk with them and explain, 'This is what the division expects.' The biggest thing is getting to know people and getting them to trust you."

TAKING BALANCE

Moving any person can be difficult. If you try to drag someone along by the wrist, she may grimace, take the pain, and shift away, or hit you in spite of the discomfort. If you push a person from the side, she may twist away to evade the force.

When a person is standing in any single position, there are six kuzushi (unbalance) points on the floor, close to his feet. Get him to lean over one of these points and he will lose the ability to deliver significant physical power. This is called "disturbing" someone's balance. Apply downward pressure at this time—as little as fifteen pounds will do on the strongest man—and he will fall. This "breaks" his balance.

The easiest way to accomplish this is to control a person's centerline. A martial artist who understands this Centerline principle will be able to move the largest attacker wherever she wants him.

Think of a person as an upright, almost cylindrical shape. The easiest way to move the "cylinder" is to push through its middle. Because the object is not completely round, its centerline, running from top to bottom of the object, may shift away. You have to follow it and keep pushing down through its middle. A ten-pound push through the center of a linebacker will guide him wherever you want, whereas he can shrug off one hundred pounds of force that is off his centerline.

To move an organization where you want it to go, first determine where its centerline is. It runs through the middle of the organization, through its head (upper management), its heart (middle management), abdomen (line staff), and legs (support staff). Determine who is on the periphery and who is on the centerline. Experience and observation will help you determine where the centerline is in any department. Departments have their own centerline, located in natural leaders and crucial staff through whom work and communication flow. Other staff gravitate toward these people.

Control the centerline and you have the power of position. Concentrate your efforts on those in the centerline; the rest of the organization will come along.

CREATING INDEPENDENT AGENTS OF CHANGE

Martial masters point to the number of their black-belt students with pride. The more highly skilled people a master has developed, the more honor he accrues. By expanding your sphere of influence through training people to be black-belt agents of change, you won't have to foster change all by yourself.

Sometimes the way to support someone is to not be there to support him at all. Don Angier calls this principle "The Void." During the middle of throwing someone there is a time to position yourself in one of his kuzushi spots. When he subsequently leans on you, vanish so that he falls into the space you just occupied.

Similarly in the workplace, there's a time to disappear and let the people who are committed to doing the work be on their own. In certain situations, they're positioned and ready to go, they've succeeded with a similar job before, but they *just don't have the confidence* to complete the project. Rather than letting them remain dependent on you, let them "fall" into a stronger spot.

Offer support by telling them, "I know you can do it." Give them more guidelines if you wish, then step away. If they come to you for help, don't make necessary decisions for them. Place the decision back in their lap. ("What would you do if I weren't here?", "Could you take care of this, and keep me apprised?") You can even plan to be unavailable for a short time.

But soon after, it is important to restore the balance by getting back to them. By reviewing what has happened and what they have learned, you'll help them achieve a new level of capability. Fostering independence is imperative for high-level functioning.

Karen Nish says, "My managers have to be independent. I give them a lot of support, but realistically they have to be able to make decisions on their own. With new managers, I never criticize their decisions unless they're jeopardizing the firm or costing us money. I can give them alternatives and forecast probable consequences, but they've got to develop their own style. I give them all the tools and all the guidance, but I never tell them who to hire or how to deal with changes in their office."

J. R. Smith is a senior manager at Boeing who knows the importance of creating agents of change on a grassroots level. Calmness, focus, and enthusiasm are his hallmarks. As a member of a joint union-management institute, J. R. has led the way in deputizing line employees to train their peers. The International Association of Machinists/Boeing Health and Safety Institute is respected worldwide as a pioneer of involvement, positive morale, and measurable results—even in a cyclical industry.

In a similar vein, Anheuser-Busch's CEO August Busch III has been a visionary in adopting peer training to his industry. A staunch proponent of quality and productivity, Mr. Busch knows that his line employees are ultimately the key to success. By training workers to help lead their colleagues, Anheuser-Busch has realized clear gains in morale and cost control. And by the way, Mr. Busch is an avid martial arts practitioner.

Like martial arts experts, black-belt leaders have to be able to recover after a mistake. IBM founder Tom Watson Sr. did. One of his managers made a critical decision that cost the company a million dollars. The manager offered Watson his resignation. "Let's not hear more of this," Mr. Watson said. "We just spent $1 million training you." Change managers employ mistakes as teaching devices. And if the error is large enough, it will create a lasting memory.

In the martial tradition, teaching is a part of learning. It helps the instructor as much as or more than the student. It's common to see a brown belt or even a lower ranked student lead a portion of class. Students who know teach those who know less. Similarly, Karen Nish has her managers consult with newly acquired branches. She says everyone benefits. "They work really hard, but they enjoy being the outside expert. What they learn in doing this makes them better at their own branches, too."

Of course, you can only teach to the level of your own understanding. Paul McClellan reports that a peer trainer he trained for the Phelps Dodge Corporation laid it out this way, "You can just as easily teach what you can't do as come back from where you've never been."

THE POWER OF CONNECTION

Have you ever observed a martial arts class? Students frequently bow—upon entering and leaving the training hall, to the picture of the master, the instructor, and to each other before practice or sparring.

This *reigi* (courtesy) is more than Oriental politeness. It is practice in staying calm and making contact. To fight well, you must make real contact with the other person. How can you read a changing situation if you are disconnected or preoccupied by your own thoughts?

Making contact is the first step in helping others change. Experience feeling connected to them. See things from their perspective. I have never seen someone change another positively without this empathy.

Master warrior Takeda Nobushige explained, "If one is dealing with a weak and powerless person, he should handle that person as though handling water. When dealing with the powerful and mighty, he should use the same respect as when handling fire."

WHAT MAKES IT HARDER TO CHANGE?

As in the martial arts, successful leaders don't go about their work haphazardly. They see both the smooth parts of their path and the obstacles. In doing so they can successfully traverse more of the former and avoid the latter. And there are some specific obstacles that all leaders should watch out for and avoid.

Too much stress. This makes it hard to tolerate and learn from change.

Lack of support. Not supporting others and outright obstructionism are the tactics of threatened people. Be cautious of people who are jealous or easily threatened in any organization. They may not be thinking in terms of mutual benefit, only about blocking change and maintaining their position.

Have you ever gone to a seminar or read a book and been charged up as a result about changes you wished to make in your organization, only to find others downplaying or criticizing your insights? ("Never work here. Pie in the sky.") Typically they are projecting their own negative attitudes on you.

Poor attitude/self-image. These can make even tearing a paper bag an overwhelming task. The right attitude, on the other hand, can give you the strength to shatter stones. I once taught an underconfident student to take lengthy "projection rolls"—such rolls are an important skill for self-protection on a crowded training mat. He dove over one, then two, then three crouched students. I stopped him, and asked him to repeat this three more times. The first two went quite well. Then, in midair on his last roll, something came over his face. For some reason he lost all confidence, and with it, his control. He fell heavily and poorly, bruising himself. A failure of attitude short-circuited his ability to repeat a recent success. We talked about this incident afterward. It became a strong learning experience for us both.

Right attitudes are just as significant for organizations as for self-development. If your organization has a loser's attitude ("We'll be one of the ones analysts are projecting will go belly-up; we just can't adapt"), work toward helping the staff think of themselves positively, give recognition to excellent adaptations of techniques or processes at work, reformat your commitment so it is clearly future-oriented, and make strategic use of internal public relations such as newsletters and company recreational teams.

Another kind of attitude/image problem many people have is mixed feelings about change. Part of them wants it, but part of them doesn't. Acknowledge and accept these feelings—fighting them only makes them stronger—then provide the information and assurance required to reduce ambiguity and threat.

Lack of awareness of the benefits. Resistance may arise when the staff does not understand what good may come from a change. Why would anyone pay the price of the bruises and the huge commitment of time required by martial arts, unless they saw the benefits of its practice? People usually don't have any problem seeing the costs of change, so it's natural that they'll tend to dislike a change if they don't understand its benefits.

Let them know specifically how they will benefit from the change. And if you can't see any benefits for them, don't expect your staff to buy the change.

Inertia. This is the greatest obstacle to change. Many people would prefer to stay set in their ways. You've got to get them moving in some direction, any direction, as this is the very essence of motivation (see chapter 5).

An unsupportive physical environment. A bad environment discourages most people, but especially the inexperienced. The training hall is designed to help the martial artist grow psychologically and physically, so that when he is skilled enough, he can thrive anywhere. Any place can be his training hall. But in the beginning, environmental support can make a needed difference.

Let's say you wish to break a habit like smoking. If all your friends also smoke, there is a lot of pressure to continue, and going to smoke-filled places—bars, bowling alleys, bridge clubs—can make it even more difficult to quit.

In organizations, inappropriate environments can negate any momentum for change. Environments do affect communication. For instance, moving employees toward a team orientation can be undercut by meeting in a hall where the chairs are fixed in impersonal rows or in a boardroom with long tables. So choose your meeting rooms—and their setup—with care.

Uncertainty. Waiting can erode the protective calmness that is necessary for approaching change effectively. It's a lot easier to defend yourself when you know from when and where the attack will come. I recall being the *uke* (attacker, literally, "one who is thrown") in a well-attended martial arts demonstration. The instructor was showing the finer points of a high-hip throw. He parried my attack, took me over his hip, and *held me there* while he explained technique to the group. I knew that at some point he would complete the throw with some force. Waiting was difficult. I had to will myself to relax and be ready. It was a lot easier to take the same falls when he demonstrated the same technique at full speed.

For many people, not knowing can be more difficult than knowing the worst. I have asked participants in seminars, "Would you rather be told 'Your position will definitely be eliminated at the end of the year' or 'There's a fifty-fifty chance you'll be laid off?'" Most say they'd rather hear the first. The uncertainty makes them feel less in control, even though there is still a chance that they may keep their jobs. ("If I know I'll be leaving, I can plan for it. If I have a chance to stay, I wouldn't know whether to job hunt or not.")

It's possible to reduce fear of the unknown by keeping people abreast of information related to the change. Share your battle plans, at least the broad strategy. The specifics may be inappropriate. Ironically, you can reduce some anxiety by letting staff know when you're uncertain: "We hope not to have further layoffs, but this will depend on how strong the yen is and other factors. We'll let you know as soon as we ourselves know."

When an organization faces technological change, it's especially important that the staff know what's coming and what results are expected. Providing them with strong training can help the new technology appear less intimidating. When members have the time and opportunity to develop skills gradually in a nonthreatening climate, resistance withers.

WHAT MAKES IT EASIER TO CHANGE?

Support by management. This is as important as the support of peers. The samurai knew the power of team support, just as a good leader knows that change in any group should be supported by management or else the group will be the target of mistrust from others within the organization. In other words, be wary of creating a "renegade" department. If the department undergoing change is truly serving the organization's needs, top management should acknowledge its work. This way you benefit from the ripple effect. Ideally change should start with the policy-making body and spread down. In a department, it is the supervisor or manager who best instigates change.

Reinforcement from managers prompts further changes. Whenever possible, support requests for change that come from within the ranks. These overtures place you in a responding position, so employees will feel pushed less and, needless to say, resistance will be reduced. A good suggestion program can generate many ideas for positive changes.

The agent of change knows he can succeed by getting department staff to think as a team. My consulting company, Strategic Safety Associates, provides "Movesmart" programs that apply martial arts methods to help reduce back and hand injuries and slips and falls at work. In our seminars we emphasize "playing team defense." We remind employees that even safety is a team effort: in any sport the best teams win by playing strong team defense; on the job, if you cover for your coworkers and help them stay injury-free, they will do the same for you. People usually respond to this approach enthusiastically.

Supportive physical environments. These enhance the prospects for change. Poll staff on the environmental changes they believe will improve productivity.

Timely positive feedback. Feedback is needed by those experiencing change, especially those with low task maturity. This is one of the main reasons the belt-color system was instituted in the martial arts. In many traditional martial arts, there were originally no belt ranks, but to sustain their students' efforts and confidence, instructors began to award colored belts. As she moves up through the ranks, the beginning martial artist feels reassured she is progressing. Essentially, belt promotions are milestones.

Change takes effort and things usually don't progress linearly: Often it is three steps forward, two steps back. The master or the expert leader shouldn't let staff members who are changing in overall positive ways become discouraged. Instead, he lets them know how well they've done. A staff's self-motivation recharges when they see progress; in fact, success is probably the best attitude setter.

Fear of sticking with the old. Many people begin martial arts study because they're afraid of being attacked. But they usually move beyond this self-defense motivation very quickly.

Smart change agents see their role as making sure their people succeed with change. When a person or an organization realizes the old ways no longer work, they often look for a way out. Don't wait for them to try anything out of desperation. ("We're losing money? Let's cut our sales staff. We're paying out too much to them anyway.") Provide them with ways of changing that have a good chance of succeeding.

HELPING THOSE RESISTANT TO CHANGE

Mature martial artists have to be able to deal with strong-minded students. Not everyone easily surrenders to learning. Those in leadership positions also frequently work with change-resistant people. Individuals have varying tolerance levels for change. But when they feel their organization has asked too much of them, many employees will dig in their heels.

Engineers, for example, tend not to like change, says Ron Swingen. "They are taught laws and models that are supposed to be fixed. As a group, engineers don't like deviations of any sort, in people, systems, or machines. Not only that, they are geared to work on their own. Yet so much of our work is team, project-based. I continually try to help them see change as an ally, not necessarily as an enemy, and to provide models of people who've made successful changes in their personal as well as professional lives."

Any industry that has been relatively static may have more than its share of security-conscious (often the same as change-resistant) staff members. Leaders in such industries face a distinct challenge from people who are resistant to change. Suddenly, these people are told that their old ways of doing things are now inadequate and they must change their ways. A good example is the field of health care. After a long period of stability the industry has been changing rapidly, and many health care professionals are concerned with professional security as well as the quality of patient care. There are many external and regulatory pressures and on top of this, competition has become ferocious. In this climate staff acceptance of change can be crucial to the very survival of their health care organization.

To move a resisting opponent toward change, shift his balance. This is a momentary move; it doesn't mean trying to *keep* a person "on his toes" or uncomfortable. Besides creating ill will, sustaining this would take tremendous effort and control.

Instead, *disturb* the resistant staff member's balance and then, as quickly as is practical, guide him into a position of better balance. Just as there are six kuzushi points around the body, people also have emotional "change points." Resistance is a symptom that one of these points is exposed and can signal fear or the loss of emotional balance. A person usually braces because he is afraid of being pushed over by some threatening force. By stiffening and leaning into it, he hopes to avoid getting hurt (ironically, bracing is the worst thing to do against superior force). On the other side, someone who is sure of her strength and position won't stiffen against an attack. She knows that staying relaxed and fluid will help her protect herself more effectively.

There are also some individuals who are not just inert resisters, but very strong, dangerous obstructers. When attacked by such a strong opponent, be careful not to get hurt. You also want to avoid injury to bystanders or to the attacker himself. (In chapter 6, it was noted that protecting others requires a high level of expertise.)

THREE STEPS FOR CREATING MOVEMENT

Think of judo, in which a person's own resistance can be used to unseat his inertia and get him moving. This approach also applies to individual employees, departments, and entire organizations. For example, you may decide that a person has become ineffective in one important area. She needs to improve quickly, but she has a history of resisting change efforts. What can you do? Disturb her stability by creating movement and channel her toward the desired change.

Think of this as a three-step process. It is as if you have a heavy block of ice stuck in the doorway and you want to move it to a safer place. First, melt the ice. Then channel the water where you wish it to go. Third, refreeze it so it stays in place.

Step 1: Melting/"Unfreezing" Strategies

"Melting" means separating an opponent or resistant person from the strength of an entrenched position that needs changing. Some Chinese martial arts do this by "uprooting," or disconnecting the opponent's feet from the ground.

It may seem easiest to neutralize any attacker—or fire an uncooperative employee—without regard to other consequences. But firing someone is a waste of a potentially valuable resource and should never be the first strategy used. Firing is expensive when you consider the costs of replacement, lowered productivity, unemployment compensation, and even wrongful discharge suits. Also, arbitrarily firing staff will be seen as unreasonable and will result in increased resistance and lower morale among those who remain. Moreover, what do you do when there are several employees resisting change? You can't very well fire them all.

Turn up the heat on resistive staff members to detach them from accustomed, yet unproductive ways. You want to instill doubt about their old approach and help them to consider change. There are some things to keep in mind when doing this.

Failure can be harnessed and put to good use. In *Zen in the Art of Archery*, the author asks why an archery master had watched for so long the student's futile efforts to draw the bow correctly, and had not taught him the necessary breath control technique right away.

A senior student remarked, "Had he begun the lessons with the breathing exercises, he would never have been able to convince you that you owe anything decisive to them. You had to suffer shipwreck through your own efforts before you were ready to seize the lifebelt he threw you." Sometimes things have to get so bad that the person is ready to abandon his old approach. Be prepared to seize the moment when the resistant "target" is frustrated by failure. Rather than crowing, "I told you so," offer a better way.

As in the example above, timing is essential. For instance, one of the best times to promote safe practices is just after a "near miss." Treat the almost-accident as a waking-up experience. Approach the subject with sensitivity. ("We were all sorry to hear of this, but relieved that there were no severe repercussions. Thinking we've dodged a bullet and forgetting about it is not enough. We have to learn from John's experience so this doesn't happen again.")

Sometimes you have to help an employee see that her ways are unsuccessful. Call her in for a talk. Remind yourself beforehand of the purpose of the meeting, and don't let yourself launch a personal attack. The employee will likely rationalize that away. ("I'm fine, we just have a personality conflict," or "She has it in for me.") Mentally set your attitude. Is this the time to be wood or steel?

It is important to clearly show the resistant person how ineffective her approach has been by having specific evidence. ("You missed deadlines on March 23, April 9, and April 15.") You may then want to ask her to comment on the documentation and to suggest improvements. Be prepared for denial and resistance. This is a good time to be steel— flexible, but firm.

Wise leaders have learned that some people—like different metals— have higher melting points. If a resistant staff member still doesn't get the idea that her ways need changing, you may have to turn up the heat further by enlisting your supervisor. When both of you meet with the staff member, she will be less able to dismiss it as a personality conflict.

In some cases you may wish to carefully confront her at a meeting. Be calm in your descriptions and don't make her a martyr. Talk less about her ("You really screwed up again") and more about the approach of actions ("That method has again failed to get the desired results. What can we do?"). It's best if another person is prepared to support your perception of the actions.

Sometimes resistive people support each other and may launch a counter-offensive against positive changes. Such conspiratorial cabals are no more beneficial to their members than they are to their colleagues or to the organization.

It's tempting to squelch such groups with the heavy-handed use of managerial power—discipline, transfers, and firing. But once again a forceful, authoritarian resolution of a problem is more likely to bring the unwanted side effects of increased resistance and lowered morale. In addition, splitting such people up might spread the virus of resistance through the organization.

On the other hand, there should be beneficial ways to disperse their group solidarity. Think of providing an opportunity for each individual to change a personally destructive pattern. Maybe they're burned out or frustrated and need new opportunities. Perhaps their jobs don't mesh very well with their personal lives. Or maybe they need the challenge and stimulation of working with new people. You can find remedies, but whatever you decide on, make sure that you intend that it really help them and that you communicate this.

If you tailor your actions individually, each member of the resistive group will end up with a different work situation. The specific actions might be quite simple. Rearrange their work schedules or lunch times to fit their lives. Reposition work sites or allow individuals to work alone on satisfying projects. Assign them to different work teams where positive attitudes dominate. Or allow them transfers to other high-performance departments where they would prefer to work.

Timely firing has its place. Sometimes you have little choice but to neutralize a determined adversary who won't break off an attack. When you're inviting motivation and change, some people will refuse your invitation. If someone makes it clear he won't go along with a period of necessary change, you may have to fire him, after you've tried everything else. This challenge must be squarely faced. Everyone else, employees and supervisors, is watching. Backing off destroys crucial credibility.

But firing need not disrupt. According to John Chapman, "The rare times I've fired someone, there were clear-cut problems. I had an immediate meeting with staff, explained what I did, and got out their reactions. In the end, many came over to thank me, saying, 'It was about time.' Morale and productivity always jumped after these incidents. In

217

effect, you're supporting the good employees by doing this."

Firing can also benefit the employee who is let go, releasing him from an untenable position, and providing him with an opportunity to find a more suitable work environment.

Of course, as with anything else, make sure you don't overdo it. As a long-term strategy, motivation through firing loses more than it gains.

Select your position wisely. It's better to fight with the sun at your back, and in the uphill rather than the downhill position. Similarly, start the change where some stress and strain exist, where there is already some dissatisfaction and openness to something new. Is there grumbling in one division? That's a perfect opportunity to pilot a system. Has an angry worker come to you to complain? It's the perfect time to reposition him.

Changing organizational levels above and below the "target" level is an example of indirect or secondary pressure (see chapter 5). Want to encourage a supervisor to change? Shift her key subordinates or boss. Send her to a powerful training seminar and follow up afterward. The heat will be on for the supervisor to shift as well.

You might overextend resistance. A punch's power can be neutralized by extending it a few inches beyond its target. In the same way, "giving enough rope" can allow a resistant employee to try things her way. If her approach fails, you can turn up the heat for change.

Provide rewards. Link promotions and incentives to willingness and ability to change. The change-resistant person shouldn't get organizational approval. Just after a missed promotion, the employee may ask why he missed out. This is a golden moment to be honest with him. You may want to be the one to initiate the conversation in a spirit of personal concern.

Step 2: Changing

The student is convinced. He has thoroughly tested his teacher, whose techniques, as effortless as they appear, really do work. Now the beginner is past the skepticism that prevents learning.

The person's resistance has melted. Now you can help him find more effective approaches. Keep in mind his former resistance makes him a vulnerable learner. This period is one of trial and error and is often frustrating. Stay in close contact with the person. This is the right time to provide appropriate training.

Find ways to help him learn new patterns:

- Introduce change as an experimental approach. Just as master martial arts instructors encourage exploration, so do accomplished change agents. This is much less threatening than asking people to commit themselves permanently to a new style; "We'll try it out temporarily to see how it works. Perhaps we can reassess the results in three months?"

  Give employees adequate time to get accustomed to the new ways. At this point a resistance to change may work for you; workers often choose to continue this method because it has become part of their routine.

- Provide models. Employees tend to learn very quickly when they can copy their movements from an expert. For instance, they can observe how peers perform effectively in similar situations. Or they may experiment with several different approaches. Being specific helps. Define what new behaviors and attitudes you are looking for. Assign them a mentor.

- Be a resource. In the martial arts, students learn more from feeling than from hearing or seeing. Yes, tell them what to do. But also show them and let them feel the technique. Use it with them and let them perform it successfully with you. They'll learn most quickly this way.

  Offer techniques such as mental rehearsal to whomever is interested. Provide them with appropriate reading matter that supports their change.

Step 3: Refreezing

When a martial arts student becomes a black belt, she's become an independent learner. After a change, we want to wean the employee from being dependent and increase her independence. After all of her efforts and ours, we don't want her to fall back into old patterns. She should be able to sustain the change on her own. Here are some strategies for anchoring (or refreezing) those who would benefit from change.

- Let them change. Control your own mind; think of them in a new light, not as formerly troublesome employees. Remember how graceful they've become. Don't treat them as the negative, resistant persons they once were.

In most organizations, there are employees who would like to change an existing reputation. Many people have difficulty shedding their previous image because of colleagues who aren't willing or able to give them a chance to be different. People who have exhibited explosive tempers, had a series of accidents, or who have made a chain of repeated mistakes may find it even more difficult to shed their reputation. Speak with the worker's peer group and supervisor. Remind them of the progress he has made.

Sometimes sending the employee away helps—on a leave, short off-site project, or training seminar. It breaks the negative relationship balance between the employee and her peers and provides them both with the opportunity to recast their expectations. Meet with them as soon as they return.

- Support them. Let them know how well they've done. Publicly acknowledge the target employee's accomplishments.

- Recall the important role they play in the organizational mission, and suggest a personal commitment statement.

- Help them manage the stress from change. The personal control techniques in the first section of this book can help.

DEFEND YOURSELF

Change happens gradually, Bruce Lee wrote, "The control of our being is not unlike the combination of a safe. One turn of the knob rarely unlocks the safe; each advance is a step toward one's final achievement."

Let's review some vital points. During a change process there is often some fear and negativity, so keep your antennae tuned. Clear discontent from the air early by bringing it out in the open (at a group or individual meeting)—don't leave it to fester. Change is complex and rarely linear. Persistent patience and a long-term perspective are the leader's best weapons.

Remember that you never really change others. You may invite them to act differently, but they are perfectly free to refuse your invitation.

And you are equally free, after a firm refusal, to replace that person. However, be sure to give your best efforts before you turn to this as a last resort.

Finally, the simplest actions can make large differences. Don't underestimate the power of thanking people. Courtesy and an understanding of inner motivation can induce great change.

Becoming an Agent of Change: Techniques for Action

- See where and how staff resist your role as a change agent.

- Watch your intent. Before taking any strong action, ask yourself: Am I wielding the sword that kills or the sword that preserves life?

- Look for opportunities to foster support and trust in your organization.

- Where are the kuzushi (imbalance) points in your organization?

- Discern when to "disturb" and when to "break" someone's balance. Change means shifting balance. Disturb resistant employees' balance and move them into a stronger position.

- Who is on the centerline in your organization? How does this change over time and with different issues?

- Look to develop others as change agents. If you approach them properly, you can enlist expert staff, vocal complainers, employee-leaders, or others you wish to help grow.

- Restore the balance after any change.

- Use appropriate reigi (courtesy) to make a strong connection. Observe whether strong connection was ever made in poorly managed changes. Connection reduces resistance.

- Recognize what makes it harder and easier for your staff to change.

- Select environments that reduce threat and support change.

- Reduce fear of the unknown. Share as much of your battle plans as you reasonably can.

• Use "belt ceremonies" or milestones during a change. Keep in mind the general principle of recognizing people for their accomplishments in public. But if criticism or discipline is needed, do that in private.

• Get the most from any failure by using it as a vehicle for change. How can you see resistance melted, change modeled, and strong adaptations "refrozen"?

Conclusion

THE NEXT STEP: THE WARRIOR'S APPROACH

Real life managerial expertise won't come just from reading this or any other book.

There is a story of aikido founder Morihei Ueshiba, who happened upon his student (now a master) Mitsugi Saotome, reading Musashi's *A Book of Five Rings*. Ueshiba remonstrated with him: "Listen closely to me, Saotome. Reading books will never polish your character, nor will they give you wisdom. Wisdom can only come through experience."

Realization—the "Aha! I've got it!"—is both art and science. It is emotional and physical as well as intellectual. An ancient samurai expression was "To know and to act are precisely the same." Wisdom comes through doing. Action heightens clear thinking and is the proof of understanding.

Black belts are action oriented. Bruce Lee said it clearly: "Action is our relationship to everything." But calm action only emerges out of a relaxed spirit, a controlled attitude, and relentless preparation. Frantic, ill-conceived action is often worse than none at all.

Focus on changing yourself first. When you want to create change, become a working gear—others you touch will also begin to move.

How long do you have to train? In *The Zen Way to the Martial Arts*, Taisen Deshimaru emphasizes, "You have to practice until you die." Real life is not like school. You don't finish the term, graduate, and end your study. Black-belt leadership means continuous honing of your skills.

Beginning students often think they comprehend a technique, yet

223

they can't make it work. Their actions show that they don't really understand. Similarly, at work, people often say, "Yes, I see," and continue to perform in ineffective ways. They have not fully understood, either.

It is said that in jujitsu it would require ten years of practice in order to win victory over one's self and twenty years to win victory over others.

Black-belt leaders don't rest on their laurels; they continue to improve. Describing his year-long mapping project, John Chapman said, "When I sensed things were going well, I realized that it was time to listen more."

Maintaining a realistic perspective will protect you from unrealistic expectations. Yes, you can develop many powers, but think realistically. Be wary of being seduced by tall tales and simplistic answers. People are complex and the mastery of any art is broad and deep. Deshimaru wrote, "Do not be narrow-minded, always looking for rules and recipes. Every situation requires its own reaction."

Shodan, first degree black belt, literally means "first step" in Japanese. The meaning is clear. Learning the basics makes you a good beginner, not an expert.

Sometimes growing knowledge is accompanied by an inflating ego. New black belts, puffed up with pride, are usually asked to work out with their instructors, who may soundly defeat them to pound out false pride.

You have learned, yes, but there is much ahead. Don't get lost. Work hard. And congratulations.

Worth is shown only in action. Notice what you do, what you really practice, and the precedents you set for yourself and others. Seek ongoing activities that develop your powers. Remember who you really are, what you have already accomplished, and what you are capable of. Then you can dedicate yourself to forging a high-performance, high-morale organization.

So if we are always to be learning as leaders, what is the best attitude to take and what should our expectations be? Swordsmaster Tesshu is quoted in his biography *The Sword of No-Sword* by John Stevens: "In order not to develop improper habits, strive with your entire being. Forcefully and without restraint, swing the sword over and over. Extend yourself to the fullest, and concentrate on executing the techniques naturally. Eventually, real strength will be fostered; all stiffness will vanish and the techniques can be performed in a free-flowing manner. The opponent's movement can be detected before he strikes—one intuitively knows where to cut and any attack can be repelled. Have no confused thoughts or doubts, do not distort the techniques: without delay, train harder and harder!"

You can unlock the secrets of living and working with greater power, control, and creativity. Being calm under pressure, engendering high performance, feeling your rightful place in the world—these powers can increasingly be yours. You can realize this. Real and substantial change is happening right now with people and organizations throughout the world.

As wing chun master Chow Hung-Yuen reminds us, "You only have to learn the techniques—it's not magic. It doesn't matter how good you are. What matters is how good you can become."

Remember that your true power comes from within.

See, reflect, practice, and adjust. You will inevitably become a black belt in the art of leadership and the art of life.

APPENDIX

LEADERSHIP BELT LEVELS

White Belt
Minimal experience (mostly from books or studies)
Solely imitates others
Doesn't know what he/she doesn't know

Yellow Belt
Knows some basics /"technician"
Primarily imitates others (without knowing if they are good models)
Seeks approval and recognition
Minimal judgment
Limited knowledge of how to create change
Fear-level high, often focuses on self-protection
Begins to know what he/she doesn't know

Brown Belt
Thinks a lot, feels much less
Emphasis on pre-set technique
Inconsistent, tends to play it safe
Can be effective, but in a narrow range
Proud/seeks credit
Effective at motivating others

Black Belt

Independent learner—learns from everything
Takes reasonable risks
Both analytical *and* intuitive
More controlled, focused, maintains better contact
Achieves more consistent results
Better knows own strengths and weaknesses
More internally-driven, able to act "invisibly"
Stronger internal personal/professional code of honor and ethics
Increased focus on principles, rather than just on techniques
Helps others motivate themselves

BLACK-BELT LEADERSHIP PHILOSOPHY

- Have high expectations. Real and substantial change is possible and is happening in organizations throughout the world, right now.

- We are ultimately in control of ourselves. Blaming others for our problems is neither honest nor effective, and it is a waste of energy. Each of us is the director of our own life.

- We all have tremendous potential for power and control. Anyone can immediately learn practical methods for unleashing that control, as well as strategies for developing greater control and strength over time. Age, size, physical condition, education level, etc., are not excuses or blockages to lasting change.

- Leadership is much more than what people might think. It's not just about heading off negative occurrences—it's about helping people live their lives with energy, health, and excitement and helping them to work as part of a strong team that moves toward accomplishing a common goal that is important to them.

- Leaders do best when they utilize, not fight, natural forces of motivation, competition, skepticism, limits of attention, habit formation, desire for control, and self-protection. The best leaders don't motivate others, they help people motivate themselves.

- What people do at home is as important as what they do at work. The challenge of leadership is to help people create positive personal, physical, and mental habits that they use everywhere.

- Change and stress are not our enemies—they are forces we can learn to master toward achieving our goals. They are also a reality of living. We can't force people to change, we can only invite change and make it easy and attractive for them to try new behaviors.

- Actions speak louder than words. It's not enough just to tell people something—they have to feel it to believe it. The best leaders emphasize helping people learn principles and strategies at the same time as acquiring practical, specific methods and techniques.

- There are many ways to accomplish something effectively and safely, based upon experience, previous experience, individual capabilities, and personal preference. There is no "one right way" to force onto others.

- In this world of multiple demands and limited energy, it's critical to act efficiently. The correct, small changes can make large differences in lasting effectiveness.

GLOSSARY OF
MARTIAL ARTS TERMS

aikido   "The Way of harmonious forces," a twentieth-century Japanese martial art, developed by Morihei Ueshiba; it is a "soft" style, purely defensive, that utilizes minimal force to throw an attacker.

aikijujitsu   "Blending forces [mental and physical, yours and your opponents'] style of jujitsu," a Japanese martial art.

budo   Japanese term for the martial arts.

bushido   Japanese term for the Way of the warrior.

chi   The Chinese term for inner energy, life force.

chikung   A system of breathing, postural, and meditative practices destined to cultivate internal energy (*qi* or *chi*) for health and longevity.

chi na   Chinese grappling system emphasizing finger and arm locks and throws.

chi sao   Literally means "sticking hands." A training method used in wing chun kung fu to develop the sensitivity and ability to control an opponent. Initial focus is on controlling practitioner's own reactions, emphasizing fluid, relaxed power.

Do   Japanese term for Way of life.

double-weighted   Weight evenly divided between both feet, a state that martial artists try to avoid because it reduces the ability to move quickly.

gi   (Pronounced "gee" as in geese.) Martial arts loose-fitting practice uniform, usually white or black.

hapkido	A modern Korean martial art that enlists both the powerful kicking of *hwarang* (Korean warrior) disciplines and joint-locks/throwing techniques.
hara	The body's center of gravity, located within the lower abdomen, and life center (believed to distribute *chi* to the rest of the body).
hsing-I	"The Form of mind boxing," an open-armed, circular-movement Chinese martial art.
jeet kune do	Martial art developed by Bruce Lee, who dubbed it "the formless form," emphasizing timing and position, economical movements, and strong hand defense.
jijiuwaza	Japanese term for free-form defense in martial arts, not having any specific technique.
judo	"The Way of yielding," a Japanese martial art developed in the twentieth century by Professor Jigoro Kano.
jujitsu	The "Science of combat through yielding," a Japanese martial art, forerunner of judo; focus is on leverage, using an opponent's strength against him (to throw him).
ka	Practitioner, player; used as a suffix (as in *judoka*).
karate	"The empty fist" or "open hand," an Okinawan-Japanese martial art, modernized by Gichin Funakoshi.
kata	Stylized martial arts forms in which the practitioner defends against invisible multiple attackers from all directions; also the word for a practice form.
kenpo or *kempo*	Chinese karate emphasizing circular movements.
kendo	The Way of the sword, Japanese martial art.
kenjitsu	The Japanese art of swordsmanship.
ki	Same as *chi* (Japanese term).
ki-ai	Martial arts shout (Japanese term) designed for focusing your *ki* into a strong movement (punch, kick) or for momentarily freezing an opponent.
kiaijitsu	Martial art that employs the voice as a weapon; with this art it is said that masters are able to kill birds with one strong shout.
kiyop	Korean term, same as *ki-ai*.
kung fu	"The supreme technique," a family of Chinese martial arts emphasizing internal development.
kuzushi	Point of unbalance, one of six around the standing body.

kyudo	"The Way of the bow," the modern martial art of archery practices with targets; its forerunner, *kyujitsu*, was used in combat.
misogi breath	Purification technique through breathing.
ninja	One who practices ninjitsu, formerly practiced in secret by families who would perform assassinations by contract.
ninjitsu	Martial art employing stealth.
nunchaku	Japanese weapon made up of two sticks joined by a chain.
obi	Belt, sash; the colored belt that holds closed a martial artist's gi.
pa-kua	"Boxing," Chinese martial art.
parry	Deflect an incoming strike without directly blocking it.
samurai	Japanese warrior, literally, "one who serves."
sensei	Instructor, literally, "one who is born before." (*Sifu* in Chinese.)
Shaolin	Sect of Chinese monks who developed a style of kung fu. *See* si lum.
shidare yanagi-ryu	See *yanagi-ryu.*
shihan	Master.
shinai	Bamboo sword used in martial arts practice.
shodan	First degree black belt, literally, "first step."
shuto	Knifehand strike; "karate chop."
si lum	(Shaolin) Chinese temple family of martial arts characterized by styles based on animal forms (tiger, crane, snake, monkey, grasshopper, etc.).
suki	An opening, a moment of opportunity to act.
tae kwon do	"The foot-fist way," Korean martial art; emphasis is on powerful kicking.
t'ai chi ch'uan	"Supreme ultimate boxing," Chinese martial art, practiced by the slow repetition of forms to develop balance and concentration.
Tao Te Ching	"The Way of Life," book written by Lao-tzu in the fifth century B.C.; focus is on how to live wisely in accordance with natural forces and how to lead others.
untargeting	Positioning yourself so as not to directly receive a verbal attack.
wa	Inner harmony.
waza	Japanese term for "technique."

wing chun   Style of kung fu that focuses on mastering changing forces, employing a relaxed and ever changing structure to economically and seamlessly deflect incoming attacks while simultaneously striking strongly where an opponent is unguarded.

yanagi-ryu   Style of aikijujitsu (full name is *shidare yanagi-ryu:* "weeping willow style," from the observation that in the storm, the oak tree that resists is uprooted, whereas the firmly rooted willow yields to the gale and springs back into place when the storm passes).

BIBLIOGRAPHY

Martial Arts Sources

Chen Wei-Ming, *T'ai Chi Ch'uan Ta Wen: Questions and Answers on T'ai Chi Chu'an*. Trans. Benjamin Pang Jeng Lo and Robert W. Smith. Berkeley, Calif.: North Atlantic Books, 1985.

Chu, Robert, René Ritchie, and Y. Wu. *Wing Chun: The Definitive Guide to Wing Chun's History and Traditions*. Boston: Tuttle Publishing, 1998.

Chung-liang Huang, Al. *Embrace Tiger, Return to Mountain: The Essence of Tai Chi*. Moab, Utah: Real People Press, 1973.

Cosmé, Cassandra and Barry. "Ki Redefined: The Ability to Make a Clear Decision," *Black Belt*, vol. 18 (April, 1980), pp. 26–29.

Deshimaru, Taisen. *The Zen Way to the Martial Arts*. Trans. Nancy Amphoux. New York: E. P. Dutton, 1982.

Diepersloot, Jan. *Warriors of Stillness: Meditative Traditions in the Chinese Martial Arts*, volume 1. Walnut Creek, Calif.: Center for Healing and the Arts, 1995.

Frantzis, B. K. *The Power of Internal Martial Arts: Combat Secrets of Ba Gua, Tai Chi and Hsing-I*. Berkeley, Calif: North Atlantic Books, 1998.

Funakoshi, Gichin. *Karate-do: My Way of Life*. Tokyo: Kodansha International Ltd., 1975.

Hayes, Stephen. *Wisdom from the Ninja Village of the Cold Moon*. Chicago: Contemporary Books, 1984.

Herrigel, Eugen. *Zen in the Art of Archery*. New York: Vintage Books, 1971.

Huard, Pierre, and Ming Wong. *Oriental Methods of Mental and Physical Fitness.* New York: Funk & Wagnalls, 1977.

Hyams, Joe. *Zen in the Martial Arts.* Los Angeles: J. P. Tarcher, Inc., 1979.

Inazo Nitobe. *Bushido: The Warrior's Code.* Burbank, Calif.: Ohara Publications, 1981.

Inosanto, Dan. *The Filipino Martial Arts.* Los Angeles: Know How Publishing Co., 1980.

Kammer, Richard. *Zen and Confucius in the Art of Swordsmanship: The Tengu-Geijutsu-Ton of Chozan Shissai.* London: Routledge & Kegan Paul, London & Henley, 1978.

Kauz, Herman. *The Martial Spirit: An Introduction to the Origin, Philosophy, and Psychology of the Martial Arts.* Woodstock, N. Y.: The Overlook Press, 1977.

Kim, Ashida. *Ninja Mind Control.* New York: Berkley Books, 1987.

———. *Ninja Secrets of Invisibility.* Secaucus, N. J.: Citadel Press, 1983.

Kubota, Tak. *The Art of Karate.* New York: Peebles Press, 1977.

La Tourrette, John. *Mental Training of a Warrior: Advanced Manual of Strategy & Principles for the Non-Classical Martial Artist.* Boise, Idaho: Warrior Publications, 1979.

Lee, Bruce. *The Tao of Jeet Kune Do.* Burbank, Calif.: Ohara Publications, 1975.

Lerner, Ira. *Diary of the Way: Three Paths to Enlightenment.* New York: Ridge Press, 1976.

Liang, T. T. *T'ai Chi Ch'uan for Health and Self-defense.* Boston: Redwing Book Company, 1974.

Maslak, Paul. *Strategy in Unarmed Conflict.* Burbank, Calif.: Unique Publications, 1980.

Mukoh (Tr). *Hagakure: A Code to the Way of the Samurai.* Heian, 1981.

Muryasz, Walter. *Precepts of the Martial Artist.* San Diego: General Integration, 1984.

Musashi, Miyamoto. *A Book of Five Rings.* Trans. Victor Harris. Woodstock, N. Y.: The Overlook Press, 1974.

———. *The Book of Five Rings.* Trans. Nihon Service Corporation. New York: Bantam Books, 1982.

Okazaki, Henry Seishiro. "The Esoteric Principles of Judo," unpublished paper.

Parker, Ed. *Secrets of Chinese Karate.* New York: Funk & Wagnalls, 1963.

Random, Michel. *The Martial Arts.* Trans. Judy Boothroyd. London: Octopus Books Ltd., 1978.

Saotome, Mitsugi. *Aikido and the Harmony of Nature.* France: Sedirep, 1986.

Sawyer, Ralph D., trans. *The Art of the Warrior: Leadership and Strategy from Chinese Military Classics.* Boston and London: Shambhala, 1996.

———. *The Six Secret Teachings on the Way of Strategy.* Boston and London: Shambhala, 1997.

Smith, Robert. *Hsing-I: Chinese Mind-Body Boxing.* Tokyo: Kodansha International Ltd., 1974.

———. *Pa-Kua: Chinese Boxing for Fitness and Self-defense.* San Francisco: Kodansha International Ltd., 1974.

Stevens, John. *The Sword of No-Sword: Life of the Master Warrior Tesshu.* Boston: Shambhala Publications, 1986.

Sun-tzu. *The Art of War.* Trans. Samuel B. Griffith. London: Oxford University Press, 1971.

Suzuki, Daisetz. *Zen and Japanese Culture.* Princeton: Princeton University Press, 1973.

Suzuki, Trent. "Soke Don Angier: A True Samurai," *Inside Karate,* vol. 14, no. 12 (December, 1993), pp. 16–23.

Takuan Soho. *The Unfettered Mind: Writings of the Zen Master to the Sword Master.* Trans. William Scott Wilson. Tokyo and New York: Kodansha International, 1986.

Ueshiba, Kisshomaru. *Aikido.* Tokyo: Hozansha Publishing Co., Ltd., 1974.

Wilson, William Scott, trans. *Hagakure: The Book of the Samurai.* Tokyo: Kodansha, 1978.

———. ed. and trans. *Ideals of the Samurai: Writings of Japanese Warriors.* Burbank, Calif.: Ohara Publications, 1982.

Yang, Jwing-ming. *Qigong for Health and Martial Arts.* Boston: YMAA Publication Center, 1998.

Yip Chun with Danny O'Connor. *Wing Chun Martial Arts: Principles & Techniques.* York Beach, Maine: Samuel Weiser, Inc., 1992.

Management Books

Cooper, Cary, and Judi Marshall. *Understanding Executive Stress.* Princeton: Petrocelli, 1978.

Deal, Terrence E., and Allan A. Kennedy. *Corporate Cultures: The Rites and Rituals of Corporate Life.* Reading, Mass.: Addison-Wesley, 1982.

Fitch, Donald. *Increasing Productivity in the Microcomputer Age.* Reading, Mass.: Addison-Wesley, 1982.

Gibb, Jack. *Trust: A New View of Personal and Organizational Development.* Los Angeles: Guild of Tutors Press, 1978.

Grove, Andrew. *High Output Management.* New York: Random House, 1983.

Gruneberg, Michael. *Understanding Job Satisfaction.* London: The MacMillan Press, 1979.

Herzberg, Frederick. *Work and the Nature of Man.* Cleveland: World Press, 1966.

Hultman, Ken. *The Path of Least Resistance: Preparing Employees for Change.* Austin, Tex.: Learning Concepts, 1979.

Lewin, Kurt. *Field Theory in the Social Sciences.* New York: Harpers, 1953.

Maslow, Abraham. *Motivation and Personality.* New York: Harper & Row, 1954.

Ohmae, Kenichi. *The Mind of the Strategist: Business Planning for Competitive Advantage.* New York: Penguin Books, 1983.

Pascale, Richard T., and Anthony G. Athos. *The Art of Japanese Management: Applications for American Executives.* New York: Bantam Books, 1979.

Peters, Tom, and Robert Waterman. *In Search of Excellence.* New York: Harper & Row, 1982.

Prince, George M. *The Practice of Creativity: A Manual for Dynamic Group Problem Solving.* New York: Collier, 1970.

Townsend, Robert. *Further Up the Organization.* New York: Alfred A. Knopf, 1984.

Miscellaneous Readings

Burroughs, William. "The Discipline of D. E.," in *The Exterminator.* New York: Penguin Books, 1985.

Gallwey, W. Timothy. *The Inner Game of Tennis.* New York: Bantam Books, 1979.

Kappas, John. *Professional Hypnotism Manual,* revised ed. Alhambra, Calif.: Borden, 1978.

Lao-tzu. *Tao Te Ching: The Way of Life.* Trans. Witter Bynner. New York: Perigree Books, 1980.

Von Oech, Roger. *A Whack on the Side of the Head: How to Unlock Your Mind for Innovation.* New York: Warner Books, 1983.

Watzlawick, Paul. *How Real Is Real: Confusion, Disinformation, and Communication.* New York: Random House, 1977.

INDEX

ABOUT THE AUTHOR

Robert Pater is principal in Robert Pater & Associates, an organizational consulting company that applies martial arts strategies to leadership and change. He is also the director of Strategic Safety Associates, a company that employs martial arts principles for safety and organizational injury prevention. Strategic Safety Associates' MoveSMART® system for back and hand injury and slip, trip, and fall prevention has been employed by organizations worldwide, including 3M, Alaska Railroad, Alcoa, American Airlines, AmeriSteel, Amoco, Amtrak, Anheuser-Busch, Bethlehem Steel, Boeing, BNSF, BP Amoco, Canadian National Rail, Conoco, Detroit Edison, Earthgrains, Exxon, General Motors, Harley-Davidson, Intel, International Paper, James River Corp, Johnson and Johnson, Kaiser Aluminum, Kodak, Lenox China, McDonnell Douglas, Nabisco, Pacific Power, Phelps Dodge, SeaWorld, Shell Oil, Smithsonian Institution, Textron, United Airlines, United Parcel Service, U.S. Forest Service, and many others.

Pater has been a black-belt martial arts instructor who has studied shidare yanagi-ryu, aikijujitsu, kenjitsu, and hapkido. He currently practices wing chun kung fu.

He is the author of articles in many management and safety magazines and of the manual, "How to Make High-Impact Presentations," published by the American Society of Safety Engineers.

You may contact Robert Pater at:
P.O. Box 80222
Portland, Oregon USA 97280-0122
503-977-2094
e-mail: rpater@movesmart.com
Website: www.movesmart.com